Christopher Wordsworth

Notes on mediaeval services in England

Christopher Wordsworth

Notes on mediaeval services in England

ISBN/EAN: 9783743335660

Manufactured in Europe, USA, Canada, Australia, Japa

Cover: Foto ©ninafisch / pixelio.de

Manufactured and distributed by brebook publishing software
(www.brebook.com)

Christopher Wordsworth

Notes on mediaeval services in England

NOTES ON MEDIÆVAL SERVICES
IN ENGLAND.

NOTES

ON

MEDIÆVAL SERVICES

IN

ENGLAND,

WITH AN INDEX OF LINCOLN CEREMONIES:

BY

CHR. WORDSWORTH, M.A.,

Rector of St. Peter and St. Paul's, Marlborough, Prebendary of Lincoln,
and co-editor of " Breviarium ad usum Sarum," &c.

———————

LONDON:
THOMAS BAKER, SOHO SQUARE.
1898.

MEDIÆVAL SERVICES

IN ENGLAND.

PAGES.

1 —An Enquiry for the TIME-TABLE or
SERVICE PAPER of Cathedral and
other Churches in olden time   7–102

2.—An Account of some old LINCOLN
CUSTOMS and CEREMONIES, with
notes on the titles of the Altars
and Chapels in the Minster   103–308

3.—An Index to the Kalendar of Lincoln
Use 309–313

A Summary of the Contents of "An Inquiry for the Time-Table or Service-Paper of Cathedral and other Churches in Olden Time."

INTRODUCTORY.

PAGE

Reviving interest in the practical utility of Cathedral fabrics and the true activity of Cathedral bodies exemplified in the remarks of Rev. G. Venables at Norwich   I

His scheme for engaging residentiary and non-residentiary Canons, individually or in groups, for special and particular employment, involves utilising side-chapels   2

Partial disuse—and revived use—of minster fabrics within the author's lifetime   2-5

An enquiry, partly practical, partly upon antiquarian grounds, respecting the Times of Service in earlier ages 5, 6

PART I.—CATHEDRAL SERVICES.

MATTINS. Mattins was sometimes (1) at night: The peals of bells for this service: sometimes (2) at early morning: Morning Prayer Chapels, of Elizabethan times and later, for plain early Mattins: (3) in the evening: Invitation of guests and other tokens of brotherhood. LAUDS...   7-10

Mattins of B. V. Mary. How far were artificial lights in choir allowed? or books of service? *Mattins of the Departed.* "LADY MASS." Bp. Grandisson's weekly masses at Exeter...   12

Lincoln morning peal. CHANTRY MASSES. Ave-bell and Lady-bells. Table of masses current at Lincoln cir. 1505-45 (p. 15). Their number. Morrow masses. Dean of Lincoln's Chaplain's mass (*a*) for souls, and (*b*) for travellers   13-17

PAGE

PRIME. (1) Prime in Choir (p. 17). Choristers in attendance: the choir-boys' customs. (2) Prime in Chapter. The Martiloge, the wax-brede or service-table, and the devotional reading, with other proceedings in the Chapter-house 19, 20

Capitular mass (at Lincoln, Durham, Wells, Ottery St. Mary's, and Exeter) 20–23

Preparations for HIGH MASS: procession with holy water and ornaments 23

Terce, etc. How far were Canons and others obliged to attend Services? 27

High mass. Its ceremonies 28

(Sext and) None, when said (*see* pp. 22, 28, 43-4) ... ...

Ceremonies at high mass (continued) 28

Time of high mass. Concluding devotions 34

The Canons' DINNER 34, 35

Meals and Manners of the Choristers 36

Peals of Bells. Preparation for Evensong 36, 37

AT EVENSONG. The order of censing 37

Evensong of B. V. Mary 40

(Evensong of the Departed) ... ...

COMPLINE. Arrangements for the Boys 42, 43

Order of services in Lent 43, 44

Meaning of "Evening Mass" 45

"*Dirige.*" "Collation" or reading in Lent 47

Black copes. Choral habits. Amesses 48

Lenten evensong before noon 49

Time of Good Friday service at Exeter, and of evensong at Hereford 50, 51

The Curfew 51

Scrutiny by the watchman after curfew: and in winter again after midnight mattins 51, 52

The searcher's supper. The night watchman. Enclosure of precincts. Condition of the close and its inmates. Gambling. Feast of Fools. Abuses and misdemeanours 52, 53

Record was kept of these, where good and orderly behaviour was naturally left unregistered 54, 55

PART II.—PAROCHIAL SERVICES.

Scarcity of information relating to times of service in smaller churches before mid-XVIth century 56

The writer's own recollections in a Berkshire parish where there was no resident squire 56, 57

Times of bell-ringing in various parishes (1) on Sundays, (2) on week-days 57–59

PAGE

Curfew. Ave-bells. Pancake-bell. Bells in Lent. (Lenten Mass and Evensong at Exeter.) Shakespearian reference, p. 61 ; see above (p. 47). The friars' church and parish mass. Piers Plowman 59–62

MATTINS and MASS on Sundays 63

Undern (*Terce*) and Evensong (Vespers) all represented by traditional bells ... ...

Saturday service in the afternoon 63

Denis Granville (at Durham) and Beveridge (in London) revive weekly Eucharist, cir. 1685 64

The standard maintained as to week-day services by Sancroft and Simon Patrick 65

Daily service not maintained everywhere in mediæval times. Communion of lay-folk had become very rare indeed ... 65, 66

Denis Granville's directions to his curates in charge (1669) as to divine service and instruction 66

Directions as to instruction in parish churches given by Bp. Shaxton and Abp. Lee (1538); by Abp. Peckham (1281); by 13th century synods; by Egbert and Bede 68

Times of service at Norwich... 69

Early prayers at Durham (1728) ... ...

Litany at Cambridge and Oxford 69, 70

Paterson's *Pietas Londinensis:* times of service in London (1714); at St. Lawrence Jewry, St. Paul's, and Westminster Abbey ... 70, 71

Canterbury (after 1660) 71

Worcester (cir. 1704) ... ...

Testimony of Hamon L'Estrange (1659) 72

P. Heylyn (1636-7) 72

Ant. Sparrow (1655) 72

Detailed directions in Peterborough diocese by Bp. Towers (1639); in Norwich diocese by Bp. Wren (1636) 72, 73

Cosin's note. Laud's instruction to the Dean of Christ Church, Oxford. Geo. Herbert's practice (cir. 1630) 73

Bp. Parkhurst, for towns in Norwich diocese (1561) 73

Bp. Scambler, for towns in Peterborough diocese (1571) ... 73

Bp. Cosin's Devotions for the Canonical Hours in use at Peterhouse, Cambridge (cir. 1638) 74

Latin prayer-books in the chapel there (1633) 74, 75

Ri. Crashaw and N. Ferrar 75

Latin prayers on Ash Wednesday (and through Lent) at Oxford in Laud's time and earlier... 75

Services at Little Gidding (1625-6), (1) on Sundays, (2) on week-days

Morning Prayer at St. Antholin's, London, 1559 76

PAGE

Arrangement of services proposed in "Reformatio Legum" (cir. 1552) for cathedral and collegiate churches and town parishes; and in the country 76

Scheme for York minster (mattins, high mass, evensong with compline), Abp. Holgate (1547) 77

Draft "*Rationale*" or "Book of Ceremonies," cir. 1540 ... 78

Morning prayer (daily) at St. Edmund's parish church, Salisbury, cir. 1547-1607. Ringing "None" on holy-days there (cir. 1560). Other records relating to bells there 79

The Daily first mass, or "Jesus mass" there in 1500 80

Mass, Mattins, and Evensong on Sundays and Holy-days were of general obligation under Card. Pole (1557) 80

Lauds included with Mattins. Sermon provided, as well as Evensong. 81

Rules for freemasons and others as to standing and kneeling. Sitting at the Epistle. Old bench boards... ... ...

Example of Knights and Kings 81

"Meat and Mass"... 82

The placing of priests and clerks in parochial and conventual choirs 82

On the numbers of the clerical staff attached to churches and chantries in various parishes—in Somerset and Yorkshire—and their obligations respecting days and hours of service and other duties 83–88

Office and Mass of the Dead 88

Questions as to times of day indicated by "prime" and "underne." 89

Notes of time gathered from the "Myrroure of our Lady" (1430-1530 89–91

Rule for parsons to say divine service in the church where they serve on certain days at least (1452) 91

Evidence gathered from the "Vision concerning Piers the Plowman," etc., as to the change of the time which was called "none" at various periods, and the common rule to attend mattins, mass, and evensong on Sundays 91

A mid-day bell on Saturdays and Eves. Its significance ... 92

Communion of lay-folk. Sermon and Bidding Beads. Bidding Prayers for the Departed at chantry masses 93

Obligation of parsons and chantry priests to say certain offices before celebrating their mass 94

Time of mattins at a "hospital" in Nottingham. Mattins of B. V. Mary. Order of service in a "college." Mattins of the day. Prime, and Mass of B. V. Mary. Devotions said by women in churches on week-days 95, 96

PAGE

Postscript :—Order and times of various Services at Lichfield (*circa*
A.D. 1190-1250), pp. 98–102. Some particulars relating to
the rule of St. Gilbert, of Sempringham (cir. A.D. 1140, etc.),
pp. 100, 101, *notes*. Note on Mass-time and the fasts called
'Stations' ... ... 101, *n*
Conclusion of this subject 102

PART III.—LINCOLN CUSTOMS, ETC.

The Author's Note 103–105
His obligations to friends ... ... 104–105 *n.*
ALLELUYA. All Saints. Altare Magnum s. Summum. Amictus.
Almitia, almutium. Amitia. Altars. S. Andrew (his altar).
S. Anne. Apertura. Aumbry (*see* 'Piscina'). Aurora diei.
Averium 105–109
BANCUS. Beam. Bells. Bellringers. Beneficia eccl., Linc. Bene-
factors. Bishop's eye. Bladum. S. Blaise. Board rent.
Books. Borough's Chapel. Boungarth. Brotherhood. ¹Bread.
Broad Tower. Buckingham Chantry. Burnet. Bursa Domini
Episcopi 109–114
CALEFACTORY. Camera communis. Camera Episcopi. Candle-
sticks. "*Cantate hic.*" Capitarium. Cap. Capicium.
Capitulum. Carpentarii. Carucata boum. Cerotecæ (*see*
'Serotecæ'). Chanter's aisle. Childermas. Choristarum
domus. Christmas. Choir habit. S. Christopher's altar.
Churches in Lincoln. Cimiterium. Cissor. Clock. Collacio.
Colours. Confraternity of the Church of Lincoln. Consistory
Court. Constable of the Close. Cope-bell. Coronation of
Mary. Corpus Christi. Crucifix. S. Crucis. Cruets. Curfew.
Curialitates. Custuraria 114–141
DALDERBY'S SHRINE. Day-bell. Dean's aisle. Dean's chapel.
Dean's eye. *Defuncti*. S. Denys. Dove. Duplifestarii ... 141–145
EDWARD THE MARTYR'S ALTAR. Egidius 145
FABRICK. Fertory. Ly Ffolcfeste. Flagellum. Fleming, Ri., bp.
Flute. Forms. "*Frater, ascende superius*" 145–146
LE GALILEE. S. George. Gilds (of St. Anne, Benet, Christopher,
Clement, the Clerks. Cordwainers, Corpus Christi, the Resur-
rection, S. Michael-on-hill, Great Gild of B. V. Mary of
Lincoln, the Fullers, S. George, S. Luke, Shoemakers' Hall,
Tailors, Tylers or Poyntours, Weavers, Company of S. Hugh
and our Lady Bell-ringers). S. Giles' Hospital. "*Gloria,
laus et honor.*" Gradale. Ly Grecefote. Grates. Grosse-
teste, Ro. S. Guthlac's altar 146–156

¹ An unintentional departure from strict alphabetical order.

HEARSE. S. Hugh's bells. S. Hugh's altar. S. Hugh's tomb.
S. Hugh's shrine. Feretory of S. Hugh. S. Hugh's relics.
Little S. Hugh's shrine   156–162
IMAGES. The Irons. S. James' altar. The Jesus Mass. S. John
Baptist's altar. S. John the Evangelist. Judas   162–170
S. KATHARINE'S ALTAR. S. Katharine's Priory. Kiss of Peace   170–172
LAUNDRESS. Lavatory. Lecterns. Lincoln farthings. Longland's
chantry. S. Lucy's altar   172–175
The MALANDERY. S. Mary, B.V. Mass of our Lady. Com
memoration of B. Mary. Service of B. Mary. S. Mary's
tower. S. Mary's gild. S. Mary's images, etc. S. Mary
Magdalen's chapel. " *Mater, ora Filium.*" Maundy. S.
Michael's altar. Ministrations. Missa matutinalis. Missa
Capitularis, missa in Capitulo. Chapter-houses. Lincoln,
Missa pro defunctis. Missa pro animabus episcoporum. Missa
de die. Missa de Spiritu Sancto. Missa pro itinerantibus.
Missa pro Rege. " *Missus est Angelus.*" Morning (Prayer)
Chapel. Mutatio chori   175–199
S. NICHOLAS' ALTAR. "*Non vos relinquam.*" Nova festa ...   199–201
O (SAPIENTIA). Oblations. " *O Christi pietas.*" Organ. Orna-
ments. S. Oswald's image   201–203
PALLS, carpets, curtains. Paschal. S. Paul's chapel and altar.
Pauperes clerici (poor clerks). Peal altar. Penitentiary.
Pentecostals. Pelliforum, the " Peltry." S. Peter's altar.
S. Peter's relicks. Pillius, or pileus   203–209
PISCINAS AND AUMBRIES : —(1) At *Salisbury*. At the altar
" Salve " of Holy Trinity and All Hallows. S. Peter and
Apostles. S. Stephen and Martyrs. S. Katharine's and S.
Martin's. S. Mary Magdalen and S. Nicholas. The Vesti-
bulum. High Altar of the Assumption. Altar of S. Thomas
of Canterbury, S. Edmund. Relicks altar of S. John Baptist.
S. Margaret, S. Lawrence, S. Michael. S. Osmund. All
Saints. Our Lady of Gesem (Gesina). Morning Altar. Altar
of the Holy Ghost. S. Andrew, S. Mary, S. Denys and S.
Lawrence, S. George. *Altare parochiale*   209–216
(2) At *Lincoln*. High Altar of S. Mary. Le Irons. S.
Hugh. S. John Baptist. S. Mary's. Chauntries. Holy
Trinity. Our Lady's. Burghersh's. S. John Baptist (2).
S. Nicholas. S. Blaise. S. Peter and S. Paul. Revestry
altar. Lavatory. Capella Fundatoris. (?) S. Guthlac, or S.
Edmund's. (S. Anne.) Jo. Evangelist. S. Anne. S. Giles.
Altar of the Holy Rood. S. George. Altar of " Jhesus
Mass " (of the Most Holy Name, or Quinque Vulnerum). S.

PAGE

Sebastian. S. Giles. S. Hugh's, or Le Pele. S. Mary's, or Tom Tower. Morning Prayer Chapel of S. Mary Magdalen. S. Christopher. S. Michael. S. Andrew. S. Denys. Dean's chapel. Camera communis. Domus capitularis. S. Lucy. S. Edward. S. George. S. Stephen. S. James. S. Thomas   216–255
  Note on brackets for lamps or images. Alphabetical reference index to piscinas and altars   256–258

PIX. *"Præciosa."* Processions. Processional stones. Propria hebdomada. Provost (praepositus). Psalter-recitation. Pulpitum. Punishments   258–266

QUERECOPES (cappae de choro). Quirister   266–268

RE ET VE. Relicks. Remigius. *" Requiem."* *" Resurrexi."* Revestry, *see* Vestry. Robert [Grosseteste]. Rood tower and rood altar. *"Rorate."* Rushes   268–273

"SALVE." Scala. Schoolmaster. Scuerariam. Searchers' Chamber. S. Sebastian's chapel. Sempstress. Sepulchre (the Easter Sepulchre). Sermons. Serta. Le Seyney. Ship (for incense). Shrines. Smoke farthings. Spices, *"Species."* [1]Stations. Staves. S. Stephen's altar. Sweepers. Synodus. [1]Stalls. Staple-place   273–288

TABERNACLES. Tabula. Tailor, *see* " Cissor." Tenebrae. Textus. S. Thomas the Martyr. Throne (ordo stallandi episcopum). Tombs of Bishops (tumbae). Torchae. Treasury. Holy Trinity Chapel. Tunicles   288–296

VAT (for holy water). Verger. Vestry (vestibulum). Vigil (*see* " Watchers ")   296–300

WARECTUM. Washing altars. Watchers. William the Conqueror's Chapel. Works chantry house   300–304
  Works,—privileges of benefactors to them (A.D. 1257–1321; 1515)   304–308

[1] See note on p. xi.

INDEX OF HOLY DAYS marked in Kalendars of Lincoln Use   ...   309–313

Mediæval Services.

An Inquiry for the Time-Table or Service-Paper of Cathedral and other Churches in Olden Time.*

INTRODUCTION.

IN a thoughtful and earnest paper, read at the Church Congress in 1895, at Norwich (and recently published by Mr. Bemrose), upon the subject of Our Cathedrals, Canon George Venables made the observation that "it is cruel to the individual himself, and unfair to the Cathedral, if any one be chosen a member of any Cathedral body to whom the daily offices and frequent communions are not delightful and precious spiritual privileges."

The writer of that paper expressed a strong desire that the residentiary canons should include in their number a professor of canon law, that the non-residentiaries should be recognized as the Bishop's council for diocesan matters, and that they should include small bodies (triumvirates) to give instruction in catechising and religious teaching, in the

---

* The papers bearing this title were contributed to the *Church Times*, and appeared in six numbers between June 26th and August 21st, 1896.

B

art of conducting schoolroom services, and in such
parish work as preparing candidates for Confirmation, etc., etc. For the lectures required in carrying
out such a scheme, Mr. Venables proposed that
the side chapels of our Cathedral churches should
be used. And he suggested also, what is already
effected in some instances, that provision should be
made for the needs of those who desire to find a
secluded place for private devotion. The writer of
these lines remembers well searching one day in
vain, at a momentous crisis in his life, for some such
place of retirement, both in Westminster Abbey and
in St. Paul's. This was under the *régime* of twenty
years ago.*

Myself born under the shadow of the Abbey, I
had the privilege of being christened in the south-
west chapel, and I remember being present some
years later at the baptism of a child in the font
which, until later alterations, stood there in front of
the place where the monumental effigy of Keble
now remains. My Father, who, leaving the head-
mastership of Harrow, became Canon of Westminster
in 1844, established the early communion in the
Abbey on Sundays; and he was instrumental also in
reviving the plainly recited early mattins on week-
days, which (like the usual choral service sung at
the ordinary hour) was in the quire at Westminster.
That early week-day service, as I recollect, was
attended by Sir W. Page Wood (Lord Chancellor

---

* St. Faith's Chapel was happily found, and re-opened in the South transept
of the Abbey about a year ago.

Hatherley), except on those mornings when he stayed at home to read family prayers with his household, so as to give Lady Wood the opportunity to attend the church service in the Abbey, and by a few others. And now and then a working man would slip in quietly about 8 a.m. to say his prayers privately to the eastward of the congregation, and after kneeling a few moments on the steps towards the *Sacrarium* would pass out again to his day's work. That was a " day of small things " in St. Peter's, Westminster, but it was to be followed through the wise spirit of Dean Church and others at St. Paul's, London, after an interval of years, by the fuller realisation of the true uses of a great Cathedral or Collegiate Church. Meanwhile, in the cities in the provinces, the Simeons and Annas of the generation before us were now finding the little doors, which had been practically closed for many years, reopened for them in the House of God. In 1869, Dr. Westcott (the Bishop of Durham) became residentiary canon at Peterborough ; and in 1872, Dr. Benson (the Archbishop), already for some years a prebendary, became chancellor and canon residentiary at Lincoln. Then we began to hear of the old ' morning prayer' chapels in our Cathedrals restored to their daily use, and frequent instruction or exposition within strict and punctual limitation of time. These were attended by workmen engaged upon the fabric, as well as by the families of the canons and by students of the theological schools. I write merely from personal recollection of two or

three Cathedral churches, concerning which I had
some natural opportunity for observation, and I
fully expect to be told that there are some two or
three English Cathedrals where side-chapels were
in use and the three week-day services said or sung
daily even in the regency or reign of King George
IV. But it certainly came as a new light to many
in the passing generation, when deans, such as
Trench (Archbishop of Dublin) and Goodwin
(Bishop of Carlisle) with their coadjutors demon-
strated the truth that the minster nave could be
utilised more worthily than as a mere pleasant place
to loiter in, to hear the organ or to study archæology.

Evening services on Sundays and on special week-
days in the nave, great gatherings of country and
city choirs, many of them with surplices and banners;
commemoration of benefactors and worthies, missionary meetings and missionary services, with
children's flower services and the church lads'
brigade at Salisbury, services for teachers and
scholars of church schools and other church workers,
have awakened old echoes in the material fabric,
penetrating in some cases even to the cloister and
the chapter-house. They who have taken part in
some of these gatherings and services, or even they,
I suppose, who may have watched them from the
western gallery or the *triforium*, will hardly ask,
"What is the use of a Cathedral church?" Still
less will anyone who has been present at a funeral
or memorial service of some great hero in the
Abbey, or who had the good fortune to be at a

national thanksgiving service in St. Paul's, have failed to receive some impression in his spiritual character, even beyond the effect ordinarily produced by any great concourse of mankind.

When men like Butler, of Wantage (not to name others before him), who had had exceptional experience in pastoral work and in direct dealing with men's souls, became deans or canons, it was the most natural thing in the world that the Holy Table should re-appear in the side-chapels and retro-choirs or in the crypt of our Cathedral churches.

From suggestions of such a practical nature it is an easy step for the mind to inquire of antiquity, " What was the use made, in earlier ages, of those side chapels and other nooks and corners which, at least at no distant date, were kept sedulously locked, and were only to be visited under a pretext of historical or antiquarian interest or curiosity ? "

There was, it must be confessed, Vandalism rife enough to make some such precautions justifiable and even requisite. And indeed the proper end and purpose for the construction of certain parts of our church fabrics was well nigh forgotten. Even in more recent days we find ourselves strangely un-familiar with some of the simplest details concerning them. More than once the question has been put to me, " What can you tell us about the hours of Divine service in our English churches in the Middle Ages, not simply as regards the *theory* of the eight-fold office and the Christian Liturgy, but as they were carried out in *practice* ? "

I propose, therefore, in the following papers, to offer to my readers such scraps of information as have come under my notice.

Nothing will give me greater pleasure than to find that others can add more interesting information, can correct errors into which I may have fallen, or can fill those gaps, or supply those missing links or needful explanations which I fully expect to be noticed in my sketch.

I propose to give, in the first place, the time-table of services and engagements so far as they were prescribed or used in some of our cathedral churches. Exeter, Lincoln, Salisbury, and Wells have their records of Divine service more or less accessible. The monastic churches such as Durham and Evesham, Westminster and Winchester, and the Brigittine house of Syon have already in part unfolded their domestic annals. Antiquaries will know the sources of my statements if they condescend to read what I have written; and while my private draft contains many references, I think it may simplify our narrative if I omit some at least of them in printing.

In a subsequent section I shall give what little I have observed as to the times of service in parish churches. I wish it were unnecessary to warn any expectant readers that I am myself disappointed in having but a meagre bill of fare to offer. Let them restrain their appetites and I will join them in the hope that a better caterer may presently undertake the business where I fail.

PART I.

Times of Service in Cathedral Churches.

ALTHOUGH the liturgical day (according to Oriental habit and a custom dating apparently from creation) begins with Evensong, we will here take Mattins for our point of departure.

Midnight was the time for Mattins on Advent Sunday at Exeter; and at Lincoln this service was at midnight in summer, and at daybreak in winter. Before this the ringers had their duties to perform. The first of the five peals began with the great bell knolling for half an hour about an hour and a half before service. At Wells there were three peals of several bells (*turbæ*), and one tolling of the great bell or *classicum*. At Exeter three warnings from the bells (*signa*) at intervals.

First and second peals went for half an hour each, the doors being opened and lights lit between the two: then the third and fourth for a quarter of an hour each; and the last for such a time as would allow a residentiary canon to come from the most distant house in Minster-yard.

At Hereford the "hebdomadary" (canon for the week) and other canons, and all the vicars choral, would rise to Mattins at midnight. Midnight

Mattins was abolished in the autumn of 1548, and Mattins at 6 a.m. throughout the year prescribed by the injunctions sent to Cathedral chapters. This custom of an early service went on with more or less regularity till the seventeenth century, besides the ordinary forenoon service in choir. Hollar's plan of Lincoln in Dugdale's *Monasticon* shows the chapel of St. Mary Magdalene at the north-west, still known (and in even the latter part of the eighteenth century, and again, after an interval, in our own time, *used*) as the morning prayer chapel, "where prayers are said (1672) at six o'clock." There is likewise a 'morning chapel' at Salisbury, to the north-east, which is used from time to time when the *Salve* or lady chapel is temporarily closed.

In Lestrange's day, before and after the Restoration, Mattins in choir was at 9 a.m. However, in 1559 the chancellor of the church of Sarum was required to provide a lecture in Divinity in English in a convenient place at least thrice a week at 9 a.m., and all the staff were to attend it. So perhaps Cathedral Mattins in the time of Queen Elizabeth was at 10. The "minister" who was *tabled* (an old-world term carrying us back to the mediæval "wax-brede," on which the officiants' names were posted up in chapter) "to begin the common prayer in quire" for one week, was responsible for the week following for an earlier service in the morning prayer chapel. This was to be at 5 a.m. in summer and from September to April at 6. It had in Elizabethan times an order peculiar to itself:

general confession, absolution, "the litanie until the verse *O Lord arise*," before which verse a chapter from the New Testament in order was read. After that lesson the said "verse" was begun, with all the suffrages of the litany following.* Hence we may gather that in the sixteenth century the prayer, "O God, merciful Father," in the litany was understood to end with an *Amen* (not printed), and the versicle, "O Lord, arise. . . . Name's sake," was still recognised as an antiphon to Ps. xliv., and not, as now, treated as a response to the said collect.

In 1597 Whitgift expressed his approbation of a visitation article for Canterbury, calling upon "the petty canons, singing men, substitutes, or other the inferior ministers and servants of the church," that they "do more daily frequent the first morning service." In 1665, the loyal Denis Granville, son-in-law to Bishop Cosin, and at that time Archdeacon and Prebendary, complained that at Durham they had neglected to have the "six o'clock" prayers "for servants in the Cathedrall for Sundays and Holy Days." But we must return to our account of earlier times.

At Wells, in 1273, Mattins was allowed in the evening *(in sero)* only on Trinity Sunday, the Nat. of John Bapt., SS. Peter and Paul's Day, and Corpus Christi.

It is beyond our scope to describe the services at length, but we may mention that it was the duty of the bellringer to provide lighted charcoal for the

---

* See *Injunctions of the Queen's Visitors*, for Salisbury, 1559, and those for Wells *eodem anno*.

thurifers when there was incense to be burnt at
Te Deum, etc. And meanwhile, one went round on
double feasts to invite certain assistant ministers of
the church to break bread with the principal celebrant at his dinner on the day which was just
begun.* This homely custom of shewing Christian
brotherhood and charity would be said to savour of
irreverence now: but it seemed natural to those
who were accustomed to the Maundy and grace
cup in the chapter, and who spent their days, and
some of them their nights, within the holy fane.

The high altar was censed.

Lauds followed, and some of the vicars-choral
or the choristers sang a melody *(organizabant).*
It was the rule in Sarum choir to recite Ps. *Ad te
levavi* (cxxii.) after Lauds, for the peace of the
church. At York, in Lent, a penitential suffrage
(pro peccatis) was followed by some psalms for the
Minster Confraternity *(psalmi familiares).* At St.
Paul's, Lincoln, Salisbury, and Wells, the recitation
of the Daily Psalter distributed among the canons,
inclusive of the bishop as a brother prebendary,
sometimes with Litany and Old Testament canticles
to eke out the number, was a private act of corporate devotion, which at Lincoln dated from the
time, at all events, of good St. Hugh, and has
at no period since been altogether forgotten.

From the year 1408 till the middle of the sixteenth
century all vicars at Lincoln were required to under-

---

* Archbishop Benson assured me that the *invitatio commensalium inter
sacra* survived at Christ Church down to recent times.

take, upon their admission, to " stand" or attend at Mattins of the Glorious Virgin in choir after Mattins (with Lauds) of the day. Two wax candles of half-pound weight in a basin afforded the light allowed for both these services in choir. The treasurer had to find also a single candle on week-days over the " beam " of the high altar at Mattins ; but two in the small altar candlesticks at Evensong, Compline, and Mass. There was, of course, more light than this provided for holy days, according to their rank. But the single light, to burn " night and day at the north side, near the altar " at Lincoln, was, if we interpret the " Black Book " rightly, a continual light. Very little illumination was provided in the aisle and doorways. But local customs naturally varied in different places as to such lamps, or lanterns and coronas, and even as regards those candles which might be considered as having a ceremonial significance. As to light to read by, the celebrant at the altar sometimes had a taper by his book " on the left half" (left side)* of his altar, which as well as the gospel tapers for the deacon may have served a practical as well as a ceremonial purpose. In choir, Dean, Precentor, Chancellor, and Treasurer were allowed a service-book ; and a single music book for chants and psalmody was allowed on certain days when there was something unusual in the service; and for these, as also for

---

* " Right " is surely a misprint for *left* " hand looking East " in Simmons' *Lay Folks' Mass Book*, p. 174, note (1), to judge from his remarks at pp. 190, 205, 206.

the psalmody of ferial nocturns, candles were allowed.
But for Sunday Mattins " histories," or for any day
in an octave beyond the first, Lincoln vicars choral
were allowed neither book nor light.   For they had
undertaken there (as in other Cathedral churches) to
know their services by heart within their year of
probation.   The service of Our Lady was sung out
of choir on Sundays in Advent, on Passion and Palm
Sundays, Christmas Day, Easter and Pentecost, and
on feasts of B. V. Mary.

At Exeter, independently of any recitation in
choir, the persons whose duty it was to sing Mattins
and hours of the Virgin in her chapel were summoned
" at early morn " by three peals of the same bell
which was to sound presently for the Mass which
bore her name; and again, when the epistle of the
Lady Mass was read in chapel, the first bell for
Prime of the Day in choir was sounded, and, at
Agnus Dei, the second bell.

In 1336, John de Grandisson arranged a series of
daily Masses in the Lady Chapel so that week
by week there might be a remembrance of the
principal Joys of Mary, her Nativity, Annunciation,
Birth of Christ, visit of the Magi, Purification,
" Pity," (' *Compassione*') and Assumption.   At
Salisbury the *Salve*, or daily Mass of B. V. Mary,
was established by Bishop R. Poore so soon as
ever the first or Eastern portion of his church was
ready, at Michaelmas, 1225.

The Sarum rule in the breviary is to say on three
ordinary ferial or simple days each week, if they can

be found vacant, one or other of the three nocturns of *Dirige*, or Mattins of the dead, after Mattins of the day, so that the whole *Dirige* should, if possible, be recited in the course of each ordinary week.

At Lincoln the day-bell was rung and the Morrow Mass was celebrated by a chaplain, for whom the Dean provided a salary, as well as light sufficient to see to read by. This chaplain was excused attendance at Mattins in winter. By the time that half the interval before service had elapsed, a great bell rang the Morning Peal *(pella)* in the south-west tower, known as St. Hugh's. Then the Poor Clerks came in, to be ready to assist the Chantry Chaplains whose low Masses followed in quick succession at various altars from this time to Terce.

Such Masses were numerous, though they never approached the multitude (120 *per diem*, beginning at 4.30), which Dean Stanley found in the great church of the Holy House of Loreto (so he tells us we ought to spell it) in 1852. The number of altars at York was at least two-and-twenty, and apparently at one time nearer thirty. At Lincoln, about 26; at Salisbury, about 22; at Wells, 13 or 14. The chantries at Wells were 11 or 12; and these employed 18 or 19 chantry priests.

The chantry Masses at Salisbury do not appear to have numbered more than eleven, apart from occasional obits or anniversaries. At Lincoln there were more than forty chantries; and, though these varied from time to time, we are able to give a fairly

complete time-table of them in the first half of the sixteenth century. It will be observed that those among the chantry priests who were also priest vicars could not begin their chantry Masses until after the Lady Mass, at which their attendance was required.

Mass of the Blessed Virgin is described as being celebrated " *hora prima*," at the first hour; but this, we believe, in practice was about 7 or 8 a.m. The service was preceded by tinkles *(tinnitus)*. It seems not improbable that this may have been the Ave bell or Angelus. It may not have been until 1492 that Pope Innocent VIII. (or Alexander VI. ?) licensed the devotion of the Ave bell for England at the request of Queen Elizabeth of York, consort of King Henry the Seventh (as the rubric of the Sarum Prymer tells us), so that folk might say "Ave" three times at each tolling of the Ave bell at 6 a.m., at twelve noon, and at 6 p.m. Nevertheless, the signal for such a salutation at least once a day, *i.e.*, just before curfew, by strokes on the great bell thrice over, almost continuously, was ordered for Wells by Dean Goddeley's statute more than a century and a half before, in 1331 in the Pontificate of John XXI. XXII. The late Sir C. Anderson recorded that the six "Lady Bells," in the great rood tower in the midst of Lincoln Minster, were chimed in the belfry on Lady Day to a chant which was probably

A ve Ma ri a : O ra pro no bis.

1. 3.   1.   2. 4. : 1. 5.   1.   5.   6.

We will now give the promised time-table :—

DAILY MASSES AT LINCOLN, A.D. 1505—1545.

ALTAR.	5 a.m.	6 a.m.	7 a.m.	8 a.m.	9 a.m.	10 a.m.	High Mass
The "Irons"							
B. Mary's Chapel		8. Buckingham	14. K. Swinford	*Mass of B. V.*			
St. Hugh				33. Bp. Wells	38. Edenstow.		
H. Trinity			11. Fleming	20. Fleming	{ 37. Colynson & Chedworth		
Hugh & Katherin	2. Burghersh			18. Wolffe		41. Burghersh	
Jo. Bapt. *Salve* altar of B. V. }				{ 21. K. Edw. II. / 22. Tournai / 30. Wynchecumb			
Nicholas	3. Benefactors to Fabric		{ 10. Cantilupe ditto / 11. ditto				
The Works } St. Anne		5. Bp. Lexington		{ 24. Beningworth ditto / 25. ditto	36. Bp. Lexington	39. Fabric	
Jo. Evang.				31. Kent			
Thos. Beckett				{ 15. Ravenser ditto / 19. ditto			
Giles		7. Walmesford		17. Bp. Smyth		40. Faldingworth	
Sebastian Le "Peal"			9. Bp. Wells				
M. Magd.		4. Gynwell	12. Gynwell	{ 27. Lacy / 28. Rowell / 29. Louth			
Christopher					34. Alford		
Andrew	1. Fabric			{ 23. Aveton / 32. Pollard			
George		6. Crosby		16. Caux			
Michael							
Stephen					35. Whitwell		
Assumption							High Mass

Thus we find that about the time of King Henry
VIII., between the three " Morrow Masses," as they
were called, at 5 a.m., and the High Mass, which
was sung about 10 or 11 o'clock, there were at
Lincoln every day no less than thirty-seven Masses,
or, inclusive of these four and of the Burghersh
Mass (No. 41), forty-two celebrations of the
Eucharist. To these we must add the daily
Chapter Mass, which I believe to have been sung
at St. Peter's altar, in the S.E. transept, after prime.
It is certain, moreover, that there were at this
period some other chantries in Lincoln Minster
besides those mentioned above. Such, to go no
further, were those of Barton, Gare, and Thornton,
D'Umfraville, Fitzwilliam, and Bishop Russell. It
is possible that these were not commemorated daily,
but only occasionally, as obits. But the number of
such anniversary Masses was at some periods considerable, and would tend to swell the number of
celebrations in the Cathedral church.

The Morrow Mass mentioned above, and celebrated at one time at St. Nicholas' altar (and in 1492
at St. Christopher's in the nave, and in 1531 at St.
George's altar) had been instituted in 1252 with the
following series of votive intentions :—

On Sunday, Mass of the day.

M., Tu., and Wed., for souls of Bishops of Lincoln
and Lichfield (on account of the founder, Lexington's personal connexion therewith), Deans of
Lincoln, and all Christian souls.

Thursday, Mass of the Holy Ghost.

Friday, for Bishops, Deans, etc., as above.

Saturday, of the Blessed Virgin Mary.

In the 15th century, this Dean's Chaplain's Mass had become a Daily Mass for Travellers.

The Chapter Mass, and other Masses celebrated by the several dignitaries and prebendaries, are likewise not included in the foregoing table; but they were all celebrated between 5 and 10 a.m.

At Hereford, St. Nicholas' Mass began at 5 a.m., and was followed by others up to the Lady Mass at 8.

We must now return to the choir services, which were in part sung simultaneously with sundry of the *Missæ currentes*, which were being said at altars round about the church.

When Mass of the Blessed Virgin had commenced, the bell began to toll for Prime. This ringing continued on week-days till the Lord's Prayer at the end of the Canon of that Mass was said; but on festivals, when there was more music and a fuller ceremonial, the bell would go only till the Gospel was chanted.

The Lady Mass being ended, on double feasts another peal called " Prime into Choir," or " Great Prime," was rung. This was the signal for the service of PRIME, which, at Hereford, at least, was at 9 a.m. At this service the choristers were required to be present. At Mattins only two of the boys, in their weekly course, were expected to attend, except at All Hallows, where there were five, wearing, for that occasion, amices " like nuns."

At Wells, though only two boys were required at
Mattins on ordinary days (in 1507), four or seven
were expected to attend on festivals of less or
greater rank.   Those boys who rose at midnight
were bidden to say their own prayers, and then to go
into choir and there say Mattins of the Blessed
Virgin silently.   The other choristers, who stayed in
bed till the ordinary time of rising, were directed to
say Mattins of Our Lady in couples while dressing
and making their beds.   Then they went for a lesson
in Plain-song in their school until the bell warned
them to " second Prime " or Prime of the Day.
During that peal they had to get their breakfast,
those who were on duty getting into choir before
the bell stopped, and the others going into school
till their hall-time at 11 o'clock.   The choristers at
Lincoln used to have bread and honey with milk
over it as a treat at breakfast on Fridays and
Saturdays; but in 1437 some of them complained
that the seneschal allowed them nothing but bread.

The office of Prime being over, " Prime out of
Choir " rang out, and the choir adjourned (in
orderly procession, according to Exeter rule) to the
CHAPTER HOUSE, and took their places round.
Hereupon a boy (at Lincoln he was the thurifer)
at a desk or pulpit read a few lines from the Martiloge
to announce the date for the morrow, and its list of
saints and blessed persons departed, and to give
notice of any obits or anniversaries of benefactors,
or other local worthies for observance.   A priest
stationed behind the reader responded, " May their

souls and all Christian souls departed, by the mercy of God, rest in peace," and " Right dear in the sight of the Lord." *R.* " Is the death of His saints."

The boy (or, as at Lincoln, the deacon in a surplice) reads another lection. At Salisbury this was almost always a passage taken from the works of Haymo, a 9th century devotional commentator and homilist, pupil of Alcuin. He was a monk of Fulda and Bishop of Halberstadt. During the octaves of the Assumption and Nativity of the Blessed Virgin the homilies, from Jerome and others, provided in the Breviary, supplanted Haymo. Having read his appointed section, the boy stepped down to read the notice-board or wax-brede, which served the purpose of a notice paper or slate. At Lincoln the " board " of readers drawn up by the chancellor, or his deputy the vice-chancellor, and then the " board " of singers made out by the succentor, as representing his lord and master the precentor, were read on greater festivals between the Martyrology and the other reading; on days of an inferior grade the board was read after the lection, the Martiloge, and the publication of any anniversary. It took the following form :—

Table (or board) for Saturday, 25 April, 1500, St. Mark being transferred to May.

Rulers of the Choir: (Canon) Trevelyan, and Weston (represented) by his vicar-choral.

1*st Respond*, (to be sung by) Roby and Borlace.

2*nd Respond*, by Cause and Tregonwell.

3*rd Respond*, by the Rulers of the choir.

Celebrant at Mass : Archdeacon of Totnes.

Gospeller : Young.

2nd Lection in Chapter : More.

Sometimes the list or "table" was much more full and elaborate.

At Exeter, if not elsewhere, some were specially told off to represent the society or Brotherhood of the Cathedral church at Chapter Mass.

The Psalm, *Levavi* (cxx.) was recited standing at Exeter (as at Salisbury) for the Church—or, as it is expressly stated, "for the King, for familiars of the community, for relatives and friends"—before the Chapter proper resolved themselves into a private business meeting. At one period, Saturday in each week was reserved for business. Then the capitular corrections took place *in congregatione chori,* if any delinquent needed to be punished, or pardon to be craved for any offences, or when any arrangements were to be made and announced for the services of the ensuing week. A section of the Custom Book was sometimes read, as occasion served, upon the Saturday (before the vicars and boys withdrew, and left the canons to their private business), so that all might know their duties for the approaching season.

At Lincoln, as elsewhere, Psalm *De Profundis* (cxxx.) was recited for any anniversary occurring, with absolution of the dead, which (at least at Wells) the Bishop, if present, would pronounce.

Leaving the Chapter House, a congregation assembled for the CAPITULAR MASS. This perhaps even more peculiarly than the High Mass constituted the family devotion of the Cathedral body. It was sometimes, *i.e.*, whenever it was to be the anniversary Mass for a Dean or Canon of Lincoln departed* (after notice given at the previous Mattins), celebrated by one of the Canons nominated for this purpose by the Precentor, who in English churches of the Old Foundation is the senior canon next in dignity to the Dean, and who possesses authority over all the musical portions of the service. Deacon and sub-deacon, revested in albes and amices, were in attendance.

At Lincoln the Chapter Mass was, as I infer, sung at St. Peter's altar, which, though situated in a small chapel, had the distinction of being one of the older portions of the structure, and was honoured by having a custodian who ranked next in dignity to the prebendaries (who alone might celebrate at the high altar in that church). In *Durham* monastery, Chapter Mass was always (Elizabethan tradition said) at the high altar at 9 a.m. At *Wells*, it was usually at the high altar, but (in 1240) *sometimes* " otherwise than at the great altar." At *Salisbury*, in the 15th century, it was sometimes (if not always) at St. Peter's (*alias* the Apostles') altar, one (the most northerly) of the three earliest to be dedicated in the chevet (or *capicium*) if it may so be called, 28 Sept., 1225.

At *Ottery St. Mary's* in 1342 (possibly merely as a temporary arrangement, because the church was

---

* Bishops alone (and Kings) had their anniversaries at Lincoln high altar. And by Sarum rules only those persons who were deemed by the Chapter worthy to be entered in the Martyrology had their anniversaries observed at all.

undergoing alterations) funeral Masses were appointed to be said at the parish altar in the nave immediately after Prime " as a sort of chapter Mass " *(quasi missa capitularis)*. In many cathedral churches and for other communities the chapter Mass was no doubt celebrated at the high altar within sight of the ritual quire, or else in some chapel where seats or stalls were provided for the canons, and other members of the community who had already said their own Masses at the other altars, so that they might attend here afterwards and worship as a united body. Chapels so furnished may sometimes be seen in large churches to this day. King Henry VIIth's chapel at Westminster and the Lady chapel at Winchester may serve to illustrate this observation.

As priest-vicars in rotation celebrated the *missa capituli* at Lincoln on days when it did not happen to be a canon's duty to do so, and as no vicar might celebrate at the high altar, it is clear that at Lincoln the high altar was not the proper place for this domestic Mass invariably; and probably it was not ever sung at the 'great altar' of that church. For, according to the old rule there, the anniversary Mass, even for a Dean deceased, was *not* to be at the high altar, but *in capitulo*.

The Chapter Mass was ordinarily a Mass for the Dead; but whenever it chanced that a Sunday (or a fast) was constrained to surrender its claim to *setting* the Mass of the day at the high altar, and was forced to give way, in favour of some festival of higher rank occurring, then the displaced Mass of Sunday (or the *Missa de jejunio,* as the case might be) was said "in Chapter," and not for the High Mass. At *Exeter,* however, only the displaced Mass of Sunday, vigil, or saint appears to have been reckoned as a "Chapter Mass." However, when the office for the dead had to be sung at the previous Evensong, Mass for the dead followed chapter business there. On Sundays, as well as week-days, there was often, if not always, a *Missa in Capitulo* at Exeter, sometimes for the departed, sometimes a Mass displaced from the High Mass. The Exeter MS. gives us a few particulars about *week-days.* "After Chapter and before Terce, Mass in Chapter is said for the departed with deacon and subdeacon vested in albs only. And the like takes place here at all Masses for the dead. Unless, indeed, it be in the case of Bishops of Exeter, or solemn obits, or for a funeral in presence of the corse, and on the morrow of All Hallows'. For then the Mass (of the dead) is said at the high altar after Sext in place of the High Mass, which on that occasion is said after Prime (*i.e.,* at ordinary hour of Chapter Mass): and then let them use black dalmatics and tunicles."

But we must now pass on to HIGH MASS, or to what more immediately preceded it.

If there was to be a festal procession to High Mass, steps were taken to call the congregation, On festivals at *Hereford,* when St. Thomas' bell rang to procession, the Dean sent his verger, or *sompnour,* to give notice to the Mayor of Hereford to send his sergeant to the aldermen at the several parish

churches. They in their turn caused the parochial
clergy to command all freemen to attend on the
Mayor to the procession before High Mass, or (it
might be) to the lecture which took place in the
chapter house during High Mass in choir.

When the chapter and ministers of the church
returned to quire, holy water was blessed (at *Exeter*)
at the choir step in the presbytery on ordinary days.
At *Salisbury* this was done previously at the altar of
St. Nicholas *in vestibulo.* (At *Exeter*, likewise, this
was done out of choir in the vestry on double feasts,
and on Palm Sunday, and sprinkled after Terce.)
The high altar was sprinkled, and likewise the
assistants, clerks, and lay people on either side of
the presbytery. Meanwhile (such at least was the
custom at *Lincoln*) the two great bells in the central
(or " rood ") tower had been ringing for Terce, and
the ringing went on (Lincoln) till the procession
halted. The procession (Salisbury) then went out
of the quire on the north, and went round the
eastern part of the church sprinkling the altars *en
route.* Then down the south side of the church,
past the font near the west end, and up the nave,
halting at the foot of the cross to make a station
with devotions before the rood. At this point a
sermon was preached (Exeter) in Advent and
Septuagesima. The procession then entered by the
western door of the quire, under the rood, a versicle
and orison being said at the stool or form in the
midst of the quire (Lincoln). After this the priest and
his attendants went off to sprinkle the canons' burial

ground, praying meanwhile for those whose bodies
rested therein. (A somewhat similar custom, which
visibly emphasised the Communion of Saints and
proclaimed that "though now divided by the
. . . . narrow stream of death" we are dwelling
as "one family," was in vogue in parish churches,
where when one was lying dead the parson left the
congregation for a space to go out through the
chancel door, and to mark with a cross dug in the
turf the place for the new grave; and then he
returned into the chancel.)

At *Lincoln* the holy water was blessed by the
Treasurer, if the Bishop himself were to celebrate
High Mass; or by the Sub-Dean, if the Dean were
officiating. Other celebrants performed this duty,
usually, themselves.

In the procession the celebrant wore his vestments
ready for Mass, excepting the chasuble, in place of
which he wore the proper processional cope of pall.*
He was flanked by his deacon and sub-deacon, the
second deacon in front carried a precious cross
before his breast, and the second sub-deacon bore
the Gospel-text with Crucifix, Mary, and John
adorning its cover (for, according to time-honoured
custom, the altar ornaments went in the procession,
and were not, as now, "discovered" on the Holy
Table); and, in like manner, young clerks with
relics, surpliced, and thurifers with censers, and
cerofers with "bearing candles," albed clerks also

---

* On the subject of 'ciclatoun,' 'baudekyn,' or 'cloth of pall,' see Rock's
Textile Fabrics, p. 42.

with tall crosses, coped; and, in front of all, a little clerk, sprinkling the holy water, led the procession.

After the "orison" (or collect) in the middle of the choir, where the commodious litany-desk still stands at Lincoln, over the marble stone with its mediæval inscription directing to "sing here," the principal celebrant and his deacon and other attendants went up to the high altar, and put down what they had carried in the procession (text, cross, relics, etc.), and then went off to the vestry to lay aside their copes, and otherwise to prepare for the High Mass, leaving, meanwhile, the Canon, or personage next in dignity, to say the office of Terce in choir, with others to respond.

There appears to have been some difference in different places as to the relative position of the Little Hours and High Mass.

Thus on Advent Sunday, while, according to the *Sarum* custom, the celebrant went out while Terce was in singing, and came back as soon as Terce was over and the introit of the High Mass in repetition, according to the rule of *Exeter* Cathedral (in a passage hitherto, I believe, unpublished) he and his attendants go out during *Sext*, and return from the vestry after Sext is finished, and when the introit began. It was no doubt the rule for the priest to have said Terce, as well as Mattins, Lauds, and Prime, in his stall, or elsewhere privately, some time before he celebrated.

It may be here mentioned that it was the theory of our early Cathedral Statutes in England that (apart from Mass) canons would commonly have other duties to perform besides attendance at the singing of Divine Service in choir. Therefore there must have been a good deal of private or semi-private recitation of their offices. At *Lincoln* so late as the fifteenth century it was considered statutably sufficient (as at St. Paul's from earlier days) that a prebendary (except when bound to do more of the public office in some week of his special duty) should attend *one* hour service in quire each day, *or* High Mass. There was, however, a belief that midnight Mattins were of obligation on Canons at Lincoln. The Vicars were required to attend to the service as their special duty with far greater regularity. A Vicar might miss Mattins twice a week at the most, but this not as a regular habit; and of the other "great" services (Prime, High Mass, and Evensong) he must attend two out of three daily, and of the "lesser" services (Terce, Sext, None, Compline, Commendation, and Chapter Mass) *every one*, unless, indeed, he had kept all four greater services, when he might be excused two of the less. Lenten Compline with the Office for the Dead ranked as a greater office. An older rule allowed the Vicars rather greater laxity, *e.g.*, an occasional week with *four* services excused each day. Choir boys at *Salisbury* had to attend Prime, High Mass, Evensong, and Compline and funeral services, but not as a rule the other offices.　One boy had to attend for his week, because a child's voice was needed, to sing at Terce and Sext in Advent and Septuagesima seasons, and at all the offices in Lent.

On Sundays and semi-doubles at *Lincoln* Terce was followed by High Mass; and Sext and None then were sung after the Mass.　On ordinary days, Sext (and on some feast days None likewise) as well as Terce would precede High Mass.　And *during* this Mass (at least at *Wells*, in the 14th century) it was the rule that no other Mass should be celebrated in any part of the building.　At *Lincoln*, however, there was at least one exception to prove this rule in the cases not excepted, as may be understood on reference to the table of Lincoln Masses; see page 15.　Among the four which are put down as all commencing at 10 a.m., or at all events before 11 o'clock, the last Mass of the Burghersh chantry (which was said in the Angel-choir, north-east of the high altar, and a little beyond the shrine of St. Hugh) was begun as soon as the Gospel at High Mass was finished.

To return to the quire and sanctuary.　Terce (or any subsequent " hour " for that time prescribed) being ended as we have said, the choir began the " office " or introit of High Mass (it was thrice repeated when the choir had " rulers "), after which the celebrant came in from the sacristy, preceded by deacons, sub-deacons, thurifers and vergers.　Going to the altar, they said *Confiteor* with general absolution.　At this point at *Salisbury*, the cerofers having put down their tall candles on the step, one of them went and brought the bread and wine and water to the "place," apparently at some distance from the altar and the choir, where the elements were arranged for "ministration" (or preparation), the other cerofer bringing basins and towel. At *Lincoln* the celebrant, having kissed the texts for the Gospeller and Epistoler, went to the altar to repeat the introit and *Kyrie*, while the choir, having already sung the former, chanted the latter. The succentor came up next and shewed the music of *Gloria in Excelsis* for the priest to begin it. The celebrant himself now passed his cap (it is not called a biretta, but '*pillius*,' or '*pileus*') to the charge of a boy who expected 1½d. for taking care of it till the service was done.

While the choir took up the chant, the first and second sub-deacons (on festivals when there were three)* started on their way by the right (or south) side of the quire, to prepare for reading the Epistle to the people from the pulpit (the *jubé*, or loft, at the choir door beneath the rood). It was the duty of the principal sub-deacon to read this lection, and of the other to carry the book, while a third, the junior sub-deacon, was left to wait upon the altar along with the deacons, the priest, and the other ministers.

After finishing the Epistle in the "pulpit" (we are speaking of a festal Mass) the two sub-deacons

---

* At Lincoln whenever there was a plurality of ministers for the altar they were directed not to wear vestments all of the same suit but to alternate the colour or pattern.

returned the other way (*i.e.*, by the north side), and
at the quire door were met by a thurifer, who relieved
them of the book and carried it to the principal
deacon, who was to read the Gospel. This looks,
by the way, as if in practice at *Lincoln* the proper
use of the two separate texts was not, at the date of
these rules, still observed. Some of the ancient
texts in precious binding may have been less con-
veniently arranged for reading, or less legible, or
may have become frail through age. At Lincoln,
however, another rule prescribed that the principal
sub-deacon and the principal deacon should each
carry his several text when they went with a doubled
procession to the reading of the Gospel. In the
meanwhile, the two sub-deacons passed into the
vestry, where either the sacrist or his clerk delivered
to them a chalice with a corporas-cloth and the
bread. It was now the second sub-deacon's duty
to cleanse the chalice finally for use, and then to
hand it to the principal sub-deacon to carry, with a
special napkin (perhaps of striped silk, like those at
the Abbey, and answering to the modern *velum
subdiaconale*) to the altar, while he himself walked at
the side, carrying the corporas-cloth with another
sudary. On reaching the upper step both these sub-
deacons knelt for a moment to say an *Ave;* and then
they together placed the chalice for a moment
on the altar, designating it, so to speak, for its
use in the current service. The principal sub-
deacon next carried the chalice to the chaplain,
if the Bishop were singing mass, or else to the

celebrating priest, who had been saying his prayers in his *sedile*, after reading the Epistle to himself and to his near attendant at the altar; and the second sub-deacon followed with the cruets with wine and water. The priest, still at the *sedilia*, poured in the (red) wine first, and then a little water, not sufficient however to take away the character or colour of the wine. Then he carried the chalice behind the altar, and placed it in a fit, convenient, and decent place ; and the secondary deacon unfolded the corporas-cloth upon the altar.

Next followed a simple and primitive custom of Lincoln Brotherhood. A clerk in choir habit went round with an invitation from the canon or dignitary celebrating to the deacons and all inferior ministers, down to the two bell-ringers, to bid them dine that day with the celebrant as soon as Mass and Sext and Nones should be finished. Certain others of the community, as we have already seen (page 10), had been previously invited during *Te Deum*.

After the singing of the Grail in the pulpit (by boys at Salisbury, by presbyters at Exeter), the *Alleluia* (by two canons in copes in the pulpit), and the sequence were finished—the last-named having been signalled by two or three bells ringing in the Western belfry at *Lincoln*—the Gospel was read at the *jubé* with still greater honours than the Epistle had been recited, all the three deacons and three sub-deacons and the inferior ministers, with lights and censers, preceding solemnly to the great "pulpit" for that purpose, a thurifer and choir-boy

having got the eagle lectern ready in that place.
The sub-deacon held the text for the deacon while
he was reading, and gave it him to kiss at the
conclusion, and, after the usual ceremonies and rites
of a festal Mass, they returned to the high altar.
On a week-day, when, as the *Exeter* MS. tells us,
some such Mass as *Salus populi* would be said at the
high altar, the deacon read the gospel, not in the
jubé, but at a lectern in the presbytery towards
the north, a cerofer standing on either side, and the
sub-deacon holding the "text" before his face.

The priest censed the chalice and the corporas-
cloth (this would be after the Nicene Creed, when
that was appointed to be said); and on Sundays, as
well as on the other days when this was the case,
the two first deacons censed the altar, the choir, and
the tombs. Arriving in due course at the Preface,
all joined in *Sanctus* with the priest. The principal
deacon, attended by his two fellows, finds the paten
with its napkin; and he hands it ("with the
offertory veil," as the *Sarum* directions state)* to
the sub-deacon who holds it (or gives it to the
acolyte to hold," *Sarum*), till the Lord's Prayer
at the end of the Canon of the Mass, *i.e.*, even
during the Consecration, until the celebrant says
the petition, "Give us this day our daily bread,"
when the deacon, accompanied as before, takes the
paten from the sub-deacon (or 'patener'), and

---

* Although I translate it ' napkin' here and on p. 30, I do not question that
the ' *sudarium quoddam* ' of the Lincoln customs may have been made of silk,
or that it may have been carried on the neck like a scarf, as the *offertorium* or
veil is said to have been worn elsewhere, but I have no evidence to show.

hands it to the priest so soon as he has said the *embolismus* ("Deliver us, O Lord, we beseech Thee, from all evil, past," etc.).

According to the fourteenth century rule at *Exeter*, the boys attending for the service were bound to stand in the choir, or near the altar in the presbytery, while the sacred action of the Mass was in progress, till the priest crossed his hands and bowed while saying *Supplices te rogamus.* Then they were to draw near to assist at the lavatory. And at the Elevation of the Host it was their duty to hold "two great burning torches and two censers."

Between the Fraction and *Agnus Dei* came not only special devotions for the King (at Westminster, and perhaps elsewhere) when they were appointed to be said, but the peculiar ceremonial of the episcopal benediction when the Bishop was performing a solemn Mass. The deacon first bade the congregation bow down, himself bowing westward and holding the staff at the Bishop's left hand, while the chaplain bowed to the right, and the sub-deacon held the benedictional book open at the proper place. The Bishop (according to the pontifical of 1520) rested his forearms* on the shoulders of the chaplain and the deacon while he gave a threefold (or longer) blessing. As there were three *benedictionarii* among the books entrusted to the Lincoln treasurer *circa* 1150—60, it is not un-

---

* "*Cubitos suos*" : perhaps rather his *elbows*, as he was to raise his hands. The Pontifical in question is a Roman book (printed at Venice), but the Episcopal Benedictions, though included in the collection, were specifically noted as not being in use in the Roman Church.

reasonable to suppose that this rite with its curious attendant ceremonial was in use at *Lincoln* as it was in other great churches in England when the Bishop of the place was doing the service.

All repeated *Agnus* three times with the celebrant. Having "finished the sacrament" (such is the phrase used), the second deacon folded up the corporas-cloth, and the second sub-deacon cleansed the chalice. After "*Ite missa est,*" the priest handed the cup to the principal sub-deacon, and the corporal to the secondary sub-deacon, who were holding napkins in their hands to receive them; and so the procession left the sanctuary for the vestry, the deacons leading on one side in single file, and, paired with them, a file of sub-deacons on the other.

The Canon nearest in dignity to the celebrant remained in quire to sing (Terce, if not done already) Sext, and Nones, or either of these offices which had not already been recited publicly. On Sundays at Lincoln, according to the Black Book, Terce preceded, but Sext as well as Nones followed High Mass. At *Exeter*, as we have said already, Nones only remained to be recited.

After that little office, it was time for dinner, except on days of fasting. For folk then kept early hours, and rose early, and High Mass in England, according to the Egerton MS. cited by Gasquet and Bishop, or at all events, at *Hereford*, "was in saying until it was eleven o'clock." And this is like enough to have been true of *Lincoln* also, where, as we have seen, they began High Mass at 10.

One little addition there was (for the priest and his special attendants had said their special office of thanksgiving, after celebrating, simultaneously with the last office which was done in quire after their departure) at least at *Exeter*. After Nones, or, in any case, just before the recess for dinner, it was usual to recite *De profundis* with the accustomed versicle for the Faithful Departed "in the station of the boys." I presume that this means, in the place where the choristers stand in a line at the quire step facing the altar for a few moments before withdrawing. To be told to stand at the end of the row of the boys ("*in ultima statione puerorum*") was a part of the punishment of Canons in disgrace.

As regards the DINNER :—

If the Bishop or Dean were host, the Canons, who had been duly invited in service-time, each of them took with him his chaplain or clerk, and his squire with his cup and cutlery. We have lived to see this good old custom decaying even at school feasts.

Grace was said with some formality before and after meat (in the manner sketched by the late Henry Bradshaw for the Early English Text Society, in Dr. Furnivall's *Babies Book*, or *Manners and Meals in Olden Time*). Drink was served thrice after the meat—ale, wine, and then ale again. If cakes, sweets, pastry, spicery or dessert were to follow, the wine went round first, then ale, then wine and ale together. The host at the proper moment when the meal was over, accompanied his guests to the door (or, if it were the Dean entertaining, he escorted them to the entrance of the hall). There was a fire allowed in the Canons' and the Vicars' halls from Allhallowe'en to Easter Eve.

The CHORISTERS, as we said, went to their dinner at eleven o'clock (at *Wells*) and then back to school till Evensong. In winter they set to work immediately; in summer sometimes a short play-time was allowed.

As to their meals, the boys were to speak Latin, which, not improbably, was on a par with the French which (we have heard tell) is spoken at young ladies' schools under somewhat similar conditions. Forks, as we all know, are quite a modern luxury, and these not being in general use in the 15th century, the choristers were directed—what young ladies would not require to be told—not to use their knives as toothpicks. A direction, similar to that in the first *Boke of Curtesy*, was given to the boys at Wells :—

> Don't bite thy bread, then lay it down,
> That's no manners to use in town,
> Cleanse not thy teeth, at meat sitting,
> With knife, nor with none other thing,
> While meat is in thy mouth, to drink
> A most ill-manner'd trick I think,
> Also eschew (without all strife)
> To foul the board-cloth with thy knife.

An hour or more before Evensong the Dean (or the Canon-in-course) went to wash his hands in the lavatory, for which purpose the sweeper and the sacrist had put out the necessaries. This was the signal for the third bell-ringer (who held also the office of candle lighter) to ring the first of the five peals, just as for Mattins.

Old Wykehamists will remember the various
"peals" which gave them notice for the chapel
services at Winchester, "first peal," "bells go
rotten," "bells go," "bells go double," "gates,"
and then "bells down." How few of those who
remember these customs of a passing generation
could *now* announce the last of these in "gallery"
(the dormitory), and yet find himself in "less than
no time" gliding into his place before the chapel
door is shut! With a greater variety in size and
number, the bells at *Lincoln* chimed to Evensong
and Mattins first peal; for 2nd peal, two small
bells; for the 3rd, two large bells; 4th, two
large bells; and 5th, with large and small together.
Except upon great festivals, the first peal to
Vespers was, at *Exeter*, the sign for *Dirige* with
nine lessons.

The sacrist, while the bells were going, had put,
if the day required it, festal coverings on the desks
(or "forms") before the Dean's, and Precentor's,
and Bishop's seat in *Lincoln* choir, and on the form
in the midst of the quire for the rulers. He also
decked the altar with its ornaments, and put
out the rulers' copes; and the seven-branched
candlestick was lighted up, if there were to be
festal Evensong.

In due course EVENSONG (preceded by the Lord's
Prayer) began; and if the Dean came in too late,
he struck the desk and caused the service to re-
commence, provided the Bishop was not in choir.
The fifth psalm being ended, the Treasurer carried

the book for the Bishop to read the Little Chapter.*
Three senior canons in silk copes, which were
brought to them by a surpliced boy, went to the
lectern in quire, and, from the music book (placed
by the succentor for this purpose), began the
versicle. Two cerofers also sang at the desk, and
then fetched their candles down from the high altar,
lighting them, and waiting upon the dignitaries who
were to go up afterwards to the altar for the censing.
Arrived again at the upper step, they knelt to repeat
an *Ave*, and kissed the carpet on the pavement. Two
thurifers and the sacrist handed them the censers
and the frankincense. The high altar was first
censed, then the tomb of the founder Remigius
(near the central lantern or "rood tower" at
Lincoln, and in the N.E. of the nave). Then they
said *Magnificat* as they went into the Angel-choir to
cense the altar (of St. John the Baptist) where the
Lady Mass, " *Salve sancta parens* " was sung daily at
the hour of prime, due east of the high altar; and
then the tomb of St. Hugh, Bishop and Confessor,
which stood behind the centre of the reredos (or
somewhat northward of that point) and on which
the treasurer placed a light on the obit day of each
and every Bishop of Lincoln as the anniversaries
occurred, and two on St. Hugh's own days. Then
the Dean and Precentor, or some other dignitary
(or the Bishop with the Dean when both were

---

* The Little Chapters were read in the celebrant's stall, and so were the
Collects of the hours, excepting Evensong and Mattins, when the orison was
read at the desk or lectern in quire.

present), and their respective following of attendants, parted company, the former going to the south, the other to the north. They went down the church, censing the altars (where carpets were spread) and the tombs each on his own side (S. or N.), and then re-entered the quire simultaneously.

At *Exeter* the high altar was censed above and on either side at *Magnificat;* then the image of St. Peter and that of St. Paul, and downwards to the lower part of the high altar. On double feasts two small altars in the presbytery there were censed; and the altar in the Lady chapel on festivals of the Blessed Virgin.

In like manner at *Wells,* after the right and left parts of the altar, the image of the patron St. Andrew and the chest of relics were censed. Then all round about the altar, the tombs of Bishops in all parts of the church, the rulers of the choir, and persons in the quire, *decani* and *cantoris.* Where two persons were censing on double feasts at Wells, they went respectively to the east and west ends of the church, and not south and north, before censing the Bishop and one another.

The anthem to *Magnificat* over, the officiant (at *Lincoln*) said the collect at a desk in quire, flanked by sacrist and canon's clerk. Then some skilled singers, chosen by the schoolmaster, and habited in surplices, sang a piece selected by the succentor; and *Benedicamus* concluded Evensong. The principal rulers of the choir went out, and secondaries took their place for the next service, copes being taken off in the vestry ("*capitarium*")*, and staves (the conductors' batons of silver) laid down.

Evensong of the Blessed Virgin was said out of quire on double feasts. But on holidays at Lincoln the officiant in his censing cope began Evensong of Our Lady at the lectern in quire directly Evensong of the day was over, and then put off his silk cope, and said the chief parts of the service in his black choral cope in his stall, if he were on the side *decani* or *cantoris*, which the singers, or rather perhaps their leaders, happened to hold that day. It has been supposed that the singing men and boys (though not so the canons) were usually all grouped on one side, week by week or (at certain seasons) day by day; but this interpretation of the old phrase, "*that side on which the choir is*," may be considered very questionable. Perhaps it means that responses, or other portions of the service attributed to "*chorus*" in the music-books, were on some days taken *decani*, and on others *cantoris*.† If the canon of the week belonged to the contrary side, the senior chaplain-vicar took the principal part in Our Lady's service.

---

* The writer paraphrases or translates "*capitarium*" here as "vestry," because water was to be provided for washing hands in *capitario*. And the Lincoln lavatory is in the choristers' vestry opposite the chapel of St. Peter and St. Paul in the south-east transept, where, perhaps, Chapter Mass was said. The extant Lavatory, however, is dated *circa* 1350, and therefore is later than the regulation cited. But he desires information as to the proper meaning of the word, which looks as if it might have affinity with "*capicium*" and "*chevet*."

† Since I wrote the above I have found in the *Myrroure of our Lady* : E.E.T.S., p. xxxviii., some confirmation of what I here advance as the best interpretation of the phrase, "on that side *on which the choir* is" on such and such a day.

Two great bells in Lincoln belfry near the quire then sounded to Compline, or, on minor festivals, first one great bell for a while, and then a small one. This office was said by the same person who had conducted Evensong. And on ferial days Compline of the Blessed Virgin followed in quire at Lincoln. But at *Exeter*, Compline of Our Lady was said privately, outside, though near, the quire, while certain of the staff sang Evensong and Compline of Blessed Virgin Mary at her altar, and the choristers sang an anthem in her honour at St. Paul's altar, Exeter. There, if it were not a double feast, the office of the dead with nine lessons was said after the first bell for Evensong; then Evensong of the day, Evensong of Our Lady, and, lastly, Compline of the day, with prayer (on ferial days) for the Peace of the Church, Psalm *Ad Te Levavi* cxxii.

At *Salisbury*, at ordinary seasons, Evensong of the day was followed by Evensong of Our Lady, and that again by Evensong and Mattins of the Dead (*Placebo* and *Dirge*).

Compline at *Lincoln* always followed Evensong immediately, except in Lent. Only if a corpse were present, or if an anniversary of some person departed was to be observed, the office of the dead intervened between Evensong and Compline. Ordinarily, like Lauds of the day and of the Blessed Virgin Mary, Compline at *Salisbury* itself (like Mattins of the Blessed Virgin Mary and Compline of the day, when without rulers of the choir, at *Exeter*) was followed by the Psalm, *Ad Te Levavi*, and other devotions, for the peace of the Church.

Compline of the Blessed Virgin (says Mr. Edmund Bishop in his introduction to the Prymer) was recited out of choir by each one privately after Compline of the day.

As a general rule, services of B. V. M. preceded those of the Day, but at Syon under the Brigitine order the hours of Our Lady followed the others.

At *Exeter*, at least in Advent, Compline of the day was said in quire both on Sundays and on week-days.

After Compline at *Lincoln* one of the "little ones of the choir" brought holy water from the south side for sprinkling the choir and the congregation. The Dean in his stall (or the Bishop, if he were present, in his throne) or else the celebrant of the day, or the canon who conducted Evensong, performed this final ceremony. At *Exeter* the aspersion took place during *Nunc Dimittis*.

Ere this the choir boys (excepting one or two who were on duty* in course for Compline, as at Mattins) had finished their choral duties for the day so soon as Evensong was done, and therefore they went to supper, having in summer a short play-time afterwards.

At *Lincoln* the choristers were not allowed to go walking except two and two with a staid man to accompany them.

---

* The writer used the word "*Duty*" in a half technical sense in his first paper. An "Old Blue" who wishes to be anonymous, tells him that "*duty*" was the word regularly used in Christ's Hospital fifty years ago (and perhaps to this day) for night prayers in the wards. "Is it time for *duty?*" "Have you had *duty* yet?"

They had some more schooling after supper, and those who were appointed to take part in Mattins of the following day, had to read over their part to the Master or the Usher. Their day ended with prayers or suffrages in school, with the antiphon *Salve, Regina misericordiae*, without (musical) note. The Psalm *De profundis*, and the Collect *Absolve quaesumus*.

After this the boys went to their dormitory and knelt two and two at the bed foot to say the psalm *Miserere* (li.), the verse "Vouchsafe, O Lord," with its answer, "To keep us this night without sin," and the collect "Lighten our darkness."

The sleeping arrangements at Wells in 1460 were hardly more commodious than those which were described to George Primrose by his usher cousin, or what Nicholas Nickleby experienced at Dotheboys Hall. When they had slipped off their clothes, the choristers jumped into bed in threes, two little lads lying at the head of the bed and a big boy between them, but with his head towards the foot. Such were the primitive arrangements prescribed at Wells in the Fifteenth Century.

In Lent there was some deviation from the order of proceedings sketched above, and in some points also there were variations upon other days of fasting or abstinence.

It has been stated above (page 28) that on certain Holy Days, Terce immediately preceded

High Mass,* and Sext and Nones followed the altar service, and Evensong came after dinner.† But this order was changed on St. Mark's Day and the Rogation Days. Then (at *Salisbury*) mass having been said at the high altar in the cathedral church before Sext, a Procession, with relics, was formed, and the choir walked to a church in the city where another mass was said " in procession " (as the term was); and they returned for Litany to the cathedral quire.

In Lent, and on Vigils and Ember days likewise, the office of Nones followed Terce and Sext before High Mass. Accordingly, the Processional offices for Easter Even begin with None in choir and end with *Missa sine regimine chori.* See Sarum *Processionale* ed. 1882, pp. 74, 90.

The arrangement for ferias in Lent was, I believe, as follows‡ :—

1. Matins and Lauds of the Day (with Penitential Psalms *Miserere* and *Domine, ne in furore,* li. and vi.).

2. Ditto, ditto, of B. V. Mary.

3. Lauds of the Dead.

---

* My friend, Mr. Clifford Holgate, assures me that " *mensam* " (not " *missam* " as I at one time suggested) is clearly the reading of the MS. register at Salisbury, and I understand that the office of None is said after Dinner to this day in a Benedictine House.

† In *Salisbury Statutes,* pp. 73-4, mention is made of a bell rung " at None which is said immediately after *dinner.*"

‡ It will be seen that my table in this place differs in some slight particulars from that given by Mr. Edmund Bishop in the Prymer or Lay Folks' Prayer Book, Part ii., Section i., p. xxxvi., E. E. Text Soc. for 1897, to which I have expressed my obligations.

4. Prime of the Day (with Penitential Psalms *Miserere* and *Beati quorum*, li. and xxxii.).
5. Commendatio Animarum.
6. Chapter Mass. (Brev. Sarum, ii. p. dlxxxix.)
7. Terce (with Penitential Psalms *Miserere* and *Domine, ne in furore*, li. and xxxviii.)
8. Fifteen Psalms of Degrees.
9. Litany.
10. Sext (with Ps. *Miserere* and *Deus misereatur*, li. and lxvii., to avoid reiteration of Ps. li.).*
11. Nones (with Penitential Psalms *Miserere* and *Domine exaudi*, li. and cii.). [Procession on Wednesday and Friday.]
12. Mass of the Day.
13. Evensong of the Dead *(Placebo)*.
14. Evensong of the Day (with Penitential Psalms *Miserere* and *De profundis*, li. and cxxx.).
15. Ditto of B. V. Mary.

After which followed Dinner.

On Saturdays and eves of feasts of nine Lessons in Lent the three last Penitential Psalms were said together at Nones.

It was in connexion with such arrangements when Mass on the fast was followed closely by Evensong before bodily refection was taken, that the rubrics inform us that *Thus enaeth the Order for Mass and Evensong together.* So it was that poor Juliet offered to come to Friar Laurence "at evening Mass" on that unlucky Tuesday (*Romeo and Juliet*, IV. 1), presumably a vigil, as the proposed wedding with

---

* See Dr. Seager's Breviary p. xxxv.

Paris was to be on the Wednesday or Thursday not in Lent.* On the "still days" in Holy Week a single orison did double duty as a Vesper-collect and as a post-Communion for the priest receiving the Pre-sanctified and Reserved Sacrament. On a festival in Lent the Mass of the (ritual) festival came after Sext, and the Mass of the fast as usual after None, both of them at the high altar, unless the Bishop himself had celebrated the former of these

---

* Of course it may be argued that, as the late Sir Augustus Harris introduced the Palm Sunday procession at Easter in order to produce a scenic effect in *Cavalleria Rusticana*, so Shakespeare may not impossibly have taken a poetic or dramatic licence and have over-ridden ecclesiastical rules for the close time for marriages, in favour of the County Paris' hopes. To such a suggestion I would reply in the words of Robert Browning,—

" *Did* Shakespeare ? If so, the less Shakespeare he."

In point of fact there is no need to suppose that, writing in the time of Q. Elizabeth, he had fallen into an error; for 'evening mass' was as regular on a vigil as in Lent. Dr. Wickham Legg has improved upon my argument, and has kindly sent me the following lucid proof to identify the dramatic date of Juliet's visit to the Friar's Cell. This I feel sure will be welcome to my readers.

" Was it before Pentecost ?

'Come Pentecost as quickly as it will.'

—Act i. *Sc.* v. *line* 35.

No, it was Summer :

'The day is hot, the Capulets abroad.'

—Act iii. *Sc.* i. *line* 2.

It was only a fortnight to Lammas (Juliet's birthday being Lammas-eve).

' *Lady Capulet.* How long is it now to Lammas tide ?

Nurse. A fortnight and odd days.'

—Act i. *Sc.* iii. *line* 15.

Therefore the evening mass was on St. James' Eve, July 24th, the only vigil or fast day on which they could have an evening mass in the last half of July.—Q.E.D."

I wish I could add that the 24th of June fell on a Tuesday in 1303, the year ascribed to the tragedy by the people of Verona. But I regret to say it was a Wednesday !

Masses, for in that case the high altar could receive no second celebrant that day, and another altar must be put in use accordingly.

Dirige, or Mattins of the Dead,* was said in the evenings in Lent (Saturday and Sunday excepted), and was then followed by collation and Compline of the day at Lincoln as at Salisbury. But at *Exeter*, Evensong of the Dead *(Placebo)* was said as well as *Dirige*, and Lauds of the Dead at the same time after dinner in Lent.

At *Lincoln* the signal for collation or Lenten readings was the chiming of a little bell, and after a pause, a great bell. The book read aloud at *Salisbury* was either St. Gregory's *Liber Pastoralis*, or else his *Dialogus de Miraculis Sanctorum Patrum.* According to the Ordinal, as quoted in *Crede Mihi* (sec. 75), this reading of *Liber Pastoralis* (nothing is there said of any other book) took place here only when Vigils of the Dead were not being said.

At *Exeter* sometimes Lives of the Fathers were read, or a sermon, or a Homily upon the Gospel of the day, and sometimes St. Gregory's Dialogue, as the Chancellor of the Cathedral might direct.

This Lenten reading took place in the midst of the quire, the whole office of the dead (*Placebo* and *Dirige*) having been said at Exeter while the bell to collation was ringing.

At *Lincoln*, Bishop Alnwick proposed in 1440 to give the Chancellor, or his substitute, discretion as to the choice of the treatise. This was the case

---

* Lauds of the Dead was said apart from its Mattins in this instance.

also at Exeter, and in our own day there is a rule for the Chapter at Truro to the like effect. The reading went on until the Bishop or presiding Canon bade the reader stop, as the Provost used to terminate lessons in King's College chapel at Cambridge two or three generations ago.

In the authorities which we have noticed there are not many direct or specific references to the times of day, excepting the brief description of the Hereford time-table, from which we have already borrowed.*

The following may be thought worth recording:—

In a passage where a rule is given for *Lincoln* that all canons should wear black choir copes of plain Deuxsevers woollen cloth over their surplices, silk copes being worn at the time of procession—and at Terce and High Mass up to *Agnus Dei* on double feasts having a procession assigned—it is said that these choir copes should be used from " the first hour " (meaning either Prime, or less probably 6 o'clock a.m.) on the morrow of Michaelmas, and onwards until Compline of Easter Even (in one place the regulation is thus expressed that black copes are to be worn by canons only at nocturnal Mattins. The canons were to appear in albs from Easter to Michaelmas at the day hours, and at Mattins of Trinity

---

* See above, pp. 7, 17. To this we may add from the Hereford Missal the direction that on Easter Even the Bishop should go in procession to bless the Fire and Incense in the Lady Chapel 'at the sixth hour,' p. 97. Holy Water was blessed on Sundays by the Priest at the lectern in choir before Terce. —*Ibid* p. xliv. Some *Lichfield* notes must be postponed.

Sunday and other holidays, up to the Assumption (Aug. 15), when Mattins was said in the day after Compline. From Eastertide to the Lincoln Audit (Exaltation of the Cross, Sept. 14) surplices without the choir cope were prescribed by the Black Book on feasts of nine lessons, etc., and over the surplice on the shoulders in cold weather, or on the arm in the summer time, a black scarf or amess was worn or carried. This was lined with grey fur. The canon's hair was cut round like a wheel (as, indeed, Dugdale's illustration shows it), and the tonsure *sine stripulo angulari*, made neat, no doubt, with some device such as the curious St. Paul's tonsure-iron described by Dr. Sparrow Simpson. The Lincoln choristers and vicars probably had distinctive linings to their almuces as their *confrères* had at Salisbury.

The rule proceeds as follows :—" But for Mattins when said at *night* they must appear in [black, choral] copes.* Now Evensong shall be always said with Compline directly following it without a break throughout the year, unless the presence of a corse (of any personage or benefactor inscribed in the local martyrology) or the occurrence of an anniversary interferes with this arrangement; for then the Office of the Dead shall be said between Evensong and Compline."

Ferial Evensong in Lent was said before noon. This is a curious vestige of the ancient discipline,

---

* " *Capis nigris.*" So in part iii. of the draft *Novum Registrum* compiled by Bp. Alnwick principally from St. Paul's use: the word "*nigris*" was however marked for excision when he was discussing the statutes in committee. See *Lincoln Statutes* ii. p. 330 *margin.*

for in primitive times the fast was not broken till after sundown, the regular time for Evensong. But, as time went on, the fast was broken earlier, and the fact in a measure disguised by anticipating the hour of the clock and of the sun to say the vesper service. So the Lincoln rule proceeds :—" Also on week-days in Lent, when Evensong has been performed *at the sixth hour*"—here we have clearly a note of the time of day, meaning at 12, *mid-day*— "let Compline be reserved till the evening along with the office of the dead, collation being inserted between that office and Compline, except on Sundays and Saturdays."

Again, a note of time on an exceptional day is supplied by the *Exeter Ordinale* (fol. 45). After treating of Mattins on Good Friday it proceeds :— " On this day let the clerks assemble in the church *after the third hour of the natural day*" *(post horam diei solaris terciam,*" *i.e.,* I presume, after 9 a.m.), " and let them say the hour services of the day in the quire in silence, with devotion and deliberation *(tractum)*, viz., for Terce, Sext, and None, on Good Friday and Easter Even. But let there be a prostration at the beginning of each hour. Also from the Lord's Prayer to the Collect in like manner. Let Evensong also be said at the close of office, privately, before the Sepulchre of our Lord "—where the Host was ceremonially, in a simple sort of Passion-drama, reserved and laid to rest—" all being gathered in front of the high altar."[*]

---

[*] See *Ancient English Holy Week Ceremonial*, pp. 129-177, by H. J. Feasey, 1897.

These Holy Week services were, it need hardly be said, exceptional. But on ordinary days—such at least was the case at Hereford—Evensong was finished at 5 a.m.

Although the last service of the day was finished with Compline, or else with the anticipated Mattins for the following day, the great church was not left entirely deserted.

At sunset in summer, and some time after dark in winter, the curfew was rung. It was tolled on a great bell in the choir-belfry or rood tower at *Lincoln*, or (upon great festivals) on all the great bells, the canons sending their men, and a supply of drink, by way of assisting the regular ringers. We must mention Curfew again hereafter.

After the curfew had been tolled, and any extra ringers had left the minster, it was the duty of the lay-sacrist, the watchman, and the candle-lighter, who were ringers-in-chief, to make the first search or scrutiny, to see that no one was lurking in the church with any felonious purpose. In summer, when Mattins was said at daybreak, there was no need for a second search, as the doors had not been opened, and the nights were shorter. But in winter time there was a second search after midnight Mattins. The three men started from the west door, walking through the building, two of them at right angles to each other, and the midmost searcher diagonally to them straight up the nave. What course the first and second were to take when they neared the south or north wall of the nave, whether straight up their respective aisles, or re-approaching one another, was doubtless a matter of notoriety in the 14th century, but we are left to divine it without the book. The Treasurer provided each watcher with a candle a day in summer, and a double supply in winter. After giving Our Lady's bells forty tolls or strokes in the belfry, the searchers retired to their supper of bread and beer in a wooden structure in the N.E. aisle, within sight of St. John Baptist's chapel, where St. Hugh's bejewelled head was kept (when it was not stolen), and not very far off from his shrine. In old times there were two night watchmen of St. Hugh's, who probably made the Searchers' Chamber their *rendezvous;* and after their searches or ' scrutinies ' two of the three searchers took their rest there likewise. But the night-watchman had to keep awake, and it was suggested by the statutes that, if he had the necessary skill, he should call the hours of the night upon his flute, so that hearing his flute-calls, and the hour striking on the clock, the other bellringers (the lay-sacrist and the candle-lighter) might know when it was time to ring for Mattins.

At *Wells* there was an instance of two clerks, who had no business there, being found in the church after curfew and being in consequence admonished for the misdemeanour in 1507. As regards the exterior of that church, the bishop (as Canon Church informs us) procured in 1285 a licence from King Edward I. to crenellate, or raise an embattled wall round the cemetery of the canons and the " precinct " of the houses of the canons. Inside the cathedral the nave became by day "a place of public resort, of traffic, and often of tumult. Complaints of the noise and disorder there occur in the statutes of 1298, which forbid games, spectacles, and buying and selling in the nave of the church, and enforce on the sacristan greater strictness in keeping order." (*Chapters in Wells History*, pp. 324-5.)

Lincoln having received a royal visit in 1284, obtained a license to enclose its Minster yard about the same time as Wells did their precinct. The canons of Lincoln represented that the place was infested by cutpurses and evildoers, and it was not safe for the clergy to go from their lodgings to the midnight services. Battlements and towers were added in 1319 by the license of King Edward II. It was the rule for the porter to lock the gates of Minster yard every evening, and take the keys at once to the provost, or in his absence to the precentor or senior canon. But in 1425 the porter was charged with opening the gates after curfew for his personal friends as late as 10 or 12 p.m., and for many years afterwards charges were laid against the Dean's servants for tampering with him in this respect. Charges were brought from time to time against the chantry chaplains for playing cards and dice, one of them is said to have sat gambling for eleven hours together. More sympathy may be felt for the vicar choral who gained some notoriety by public wrestling. Indeed it is to be feared that there were too many " idle hands " about the minster : and if " mischief " even of a graver kind was found for them to do, we can hardly be surprised. In the 13th century Grosseteste had set himself to suppress the indecent and irreverent "Feast of Fools," nevertheless we find it practised by the Lincoln vicars in 1390, and public drinkings also in the cathedral church. We have read somewhere of the shaving of a mock-precentor at the west-front of the church in the procession at some Feast of Fools; a performance on a par with "Father Neptune's" on crossing the Line. In the middle of the 15th century, misbehaviour such as talking and laughing in procession, and in choir, and even acts of violence, are charged against deans and other dignitaries, as well as against those who sat below them. Sometimes the priest singing Mass of the Blessed Virgin was left without assistants and had to read the gospel, and the like happened once, at least, at the high altar. Vicars and poor clerks would put in an appearance at the beginning of Mattins in summer, and go out at *Venite;* or come and be marked at the first psalm, and then go out again, and loiter about (with or without their choral habit) chatting in the nave, or drinking in pot-houses, and slip back for the collect at Lauds, or *Benedictus,* or *Benedicamus.* It was at Exeter, in 1330, that the men in the higher stalls used (if the accusation then brought against them may be trusted) to amuse themselves by pouring hot wax upon those who sat below.

We may be glad to think that such improprieties were exceptional, and we may trust that not a few useful and holy lives were lived beneath the shadow of our cathedral churches in mediæval times as in our own days: for, while offenders gain a notoriety, the good and orderly are less observed. At all events such examples of quiet and dutiful behaviour as there may have been (most naturally), did not get reported among the records of misdemeanours which are extant.

The very excellency of the ideal of the constant round of services and the succession of Eucharists as it was intended to be shown forth in the mother church of the diocese, when once the salt had lost (or nearly lost) its savour, as was the case in the 15th century, made the shortcomings the more obvious, and, in some respects, the more deplorable. " *Ruined good*" (as the Latin proverb goes), " *is bad indeed :* " " *Spoilt best, is worst.*" And in spite of all our regrets for the long discontinuance of the old order, and the too close veiling of the outward beauty of holiness, we can hardly be surprised that to certain of the men of the 16th century a reformation, even if inglorious, was thought preferable to a shrine from which the life appeared to be dying or decaying and the glory (if not departed) to be fast departing.

I propose to conclude these papers with some account of Parish Churches, from the meagre notes which have come within my reach.

PART II.

Parochial Services, etc.: their Time-table in Olden Days.

IF the notes of time regarding cathedral services in mediæval days were fewer and further between than we could have desired, our sources for information about the times of Mass and Divine Service generally in parish churches are (so far as the present writer's investigations go) muddy, it must be confessed, and almost dry.

We are constrained, in this condition of drought, to dip first into the pools which lie nearest our own doors, though they may be somewhat distant from the fount of history. The traditions of the parish churches were kept up by the old-world clerks and sextons who tolled their bells at certain hours for no reason than because it had been done so by their predecessors from time immemorial. I remember a large parish church in Mercia, more than forty years ago, where, until within ten years of that time, the churchwardens had actually kept the Sarum Breviary belonging to the church, or to that former parson who had stuck to his ministrations through all the changes from King Henry VIII. till he died in the reign of Queen Bess. There, in my own childhood, the peasant men and women sat apart by sexes, they made a leg or a curtsey on entering the church, they stood up (if I recollect rightly) whenever the Lord's Prayer happened to be recited in the lesson for the day, and one or two bowed at *Gloria Patri*. The May games and Whitsuntide feast had fallen into disuse when Laud fell, but the " Veast " of the Title of the Church was still observed by a small fair; and " king " (or saint) " Jaarge," the Turkish knight and the opportune doctor, and other mummers, as well as the carol-singers and the ringers of the fine peal of bells, helped to make Christmas a marked time for us at Stanford-in-the-Vale.

The ringing of the bell on Sunday was in those days, and in that old-world place, at (or for) 7.30, 8.30, 10.30, and 2.30. Besides this, the bell rang out about noon, after the full morning service, to show forth—so it was explained—that there was to be a service and sermon again in the afternoon. This, until my father, Dr. Wordsworth, became vicar in 1850, had been a rare event. In some places, *e.g.*, Soham, Cambridgeshire, this bell came, from utilitarian considerations, to be known as the *Pudding-bell!* It is just possible, I think, that this may be a survival of the " knolling of *Aves* after service," forbidden by injunctions in 1538.

Mr. James G. Wood, in an interesting communication from which we have quoted above, records his recollection of the times of bell-ringing at

Chepstow (St. Mary's Church, formerly Conventual) some years ago. *Curfew* was rung there from All Saints' to Christmas at 8 p.m.; except on Saturdays when it was rung at 9. Allhallow e'en, by the way, was one of the terminal days or seasons at which the ringing customs and (according to our interpretation of the 13th century custom book) the fires in the canons' and priest-vicars' halls at Lincoln underwent a yearly change. It marked the beginning of more wintry weather. At Chepstow there was also a Sunday morning bell at 8.30, known as the "sermon bell," although any service which may once have been held at that comparatively early hour had been discontinued and forgotten before Mr. Wood's recollection begins.

I remember other places where 7, 9, 11, and 3 were the hours for ringing. Dr. Rock, who took notice of such matters, observed two bells, but at 8 and 9, in country parish churches. (He lived very near us, in Berkshire, about 1850. See *Church of our Fathers*, vol. iv., p. 146.) And I see that Mr. T. North, in his essay on church bells, under the section "Sanctus Bell," attributes to the doctor the opinion that the mid-day bell served to call the people for some instruction usual, as he supposed, in parish churches in olden time, as it was certainly usual in the "Galilee" at Durham on Sundays, at early afternoon.* Among my old memorandums I

---

* At Durham the bell tolled at 12 and afterwards to call people to the Galilee sermon, which was preached "from one of the clock till iij."—*Rites of Durham.* Cp., Dr. Rock in *Notes and Queries*, xi., p. 150.

find " bells rung at Fishlake, Yorkshire, at 6 a.m.,
12 noon, and 6 p.m. ; at Geddington, Northants, at
5, 12, and 8; at 6 a.m. and 8 p.m., at Hawkchurch,
Dorset, in 1828." Such notes, if I recollect rightly,
refer to week-day bells. Pancake bell on Shrove
Tuesday (in numerous places) at 11, and (in several)
at noon. At Cottingham, Northants, the clerk
collected eggs in payment for his services in ringing
daily at 11 in Lent. And at Caldecote, Rutland, a
like bell was rung throughout that season. At
South Luffenham the *curfew* is rung from Sept. 19*
to Lady Day, at 8 p.m., and likewise the *day bell* at
5 a.m., known there as "the morning bell." For
this service the clerk has the rent of an acre of
pasture known as "Bell-ringing close." Bow Bell
(curfew) at 9 p.m., gave the signal for closing
London shops in 1469.

Such notes on bells might be multiplied *ad nauseam*.
But I may venture to comment upon those which I
have mentioned already.

Curfew at 9.—When taverns and shops were
closed at its sound, there was a natural tendency to
make this bell later than its original hour of eight.
Shakespeare, who in " Measure for Measure," iv. 2,
uses the word apparently of some such time, or, at
any rate, before midnight (" 'Tis now dead midnight
. . . who call'd here of late ? None, since the
curfew rung "), evidently knew some *other* use of the
curfew bell. For, when the Capulet household are

---

* Sept. 19, Eve of Nat. B. V. Mary, Old Style. *(J. G. Wood.)*

making preparations by night for the intended
wedding, the old man urges that—

> The second cocke hath crow'd,
> The Curphew Bell hath rung, 'tis *three* o'clock.

So the folio in " Romeo and Juliet," act iv., sc. 4,
the quarto, I believe, has "*four* o'clock." But in
any case he must be here referring to an *early
morning* tolling (upon the same bell probably as that
which had tolled the knell of the past day some seven
or eight hours before). It might be a bell for daybreak Mattins, which would be a common signal for
servants and others to get up for their secular
business, and would serve as permission to revive the
hidden fire in the turf upon the hearth, or, like good
neighbour Pierrot, to strike a light with his tinder-
box " *au clair de la Lune.*"

The bells at 6 a.m., at noon, and at 6 p.m., to
which I have referred, I venture to believe were the
Ave bells. Mr. North dismissed this opinion : but he
did so on the ground that (so far as he knew) the
Angelus was never rung at noon in England. This,
as we have seen already (p. 14), was an oversight;
for the English " rubric primers " speak of the Ave
bell ringing at precisely those *three* times.

The *pancake bell* on Shrove Tuesday has been often
discussed in *The Church Times.* I will simply cite
Tom Hearne's observation made at the beginning of
Lent, 1723, that whereas Oxford scholars *used* to be
summoned to meals at 10 o'clock on Shrove Tuesday
by the pancake bell at St. Mary's, and at 4 p.m. ;
now at St. Edmund Hall dinner was at 12 and supper

at 6, and *no fritters.* " When laudable old customs alter, 'tis a sign learning dwindles." No doubt the bell which rang to summon folk to shrift in the forenoon that day was a convenient signal also for cooks and housewives to make certain preparations which would lead to the seasonable refection of the carnival being duly ready by the time when the last shrived inmate should come home from church.

The 11 o'clock bell, rung in some places on the days of Lent, may, I would suggest, represent the time when Mass was said, after which, if I am not mistaken, many " secular " persons would break their daily fast.

At *Exeter* we find that "every week day all through Lent, whatever the service of the day may be," the bell was to " ring to Evensong, while Mass of the fast was saying. And let Evensong be said directly after the Mass, and before dinner, except on Sundays only." In addition to this rule we find at Exeter the rubric on the " Still Days " of Holy Week, which is familiar to readers of the Sarum books :—" Thus (with a post-Communion Collect and '*Benedicamus Domino*,' or, if the Bishop be celebrating, on Maundy Thursday, '*Ite Missa est*,' or on Good Friday without either of these benedictions,) let (combined) Mass and Evensong simultaneously conclude." I have in a former passage (p. 45) referred to this rule as furnishing an interpretation of Juliet's friar's " Evening Mass," and I have given in a note (on p. 46) Dr. Wickham Legg's interesting observations thereupon.

The rule of fasting for men of religion was no doubt somewhat stricter, and their services accordingly were later. Thus in a famous passage of W. Langland's "Vision concerning Piers the Plowman" (revised *cir.* 1377), William sees in his dream Reason preaching a mission which is attended by the Seven Mortal Sins, who come in turn to confession. Last of them drops in Sloth, a priest of thirty years' standing, who acknowledges his fault in these terms :—

> Vigilies and fasting days : all these let I pass,
> Till matynes and masse be do[ne] : and then go to the freres (*i.e.*, friars' church) ;
> Come I [only] to ' *Ite Missa est*,' I hold me yserved.
> I am not shriven some time (but if sickness it make)
> Not twice in two years and then up[on] guess[work] I shrive me.

The explanation of this is that *parish Mass* was said before noon, but the lazy fellow knowing that the friars had their Mass later, with Evensong, on fasting days, took advantage of it to lie abed till afternoon and scraped in just in time for the blessing at the close.* Being convicted of his offence,

> Then sat Sloth up and signed him swithe (often crossed himself),
> And made avowe before God, for his foul sloth
> " Shall no Sunday this seven year be (but sickness it let)
> That I ne shall do me or day, to the dear church
> And hear Matyns and Mass, as (if) I a monk were.
> Shall no ale after meat holde me thence
> Till I have evensong heard, I byhote to the rode."

---

* It is curious (as Dr. Legg points out to me) that Sloth speaks of this final blessing, or, to speak correctly, dismissal by the deacon, as ' *Ite Missa est*,' instead of ' *Benedicamus*,'—but then as he adds, "it is *Sloth* who says it." Generally speaking, ' *Ite Missa est* ' followed the same rule as *Te Deum* and *Gloria in Excelsis*, and would presumably not be said on fasting days, nor on vigils. The exception to the rule that *Te Deum* is not said on vigils (*Sarum Breviary* i. col. xxx.), viz., ' when the vigil of Epiphany falls on a Sunday ' can hardly be called an exception at all. ' *Ite Missa est* ' was not said in Advent, nor between Septuagesima and Easter Even (unless it were on Maundy Thursday). *Missale Sarum*, cols. 2, 3, 108.

(That is " I swear by the Cross, no Sunday shall pass for the next seven years—health permitting— when I shall not betake me to church ere day-break," etc.)

It may perhaps seem strange to our readers that he says nothing about church-going on week-days. Mattins and Mass quite early, and Evensong after an early dinner, once a week, *i.e.*, on Sundays, was, doubtless, then reckoned to be good, sufficient, church-going. And 7 or 8 a.m., and 2 or 3 p.m., would seem meritorious for *Sloth* to keep; and Sir T. More (cited by Rock, iv. 142) declared, that many laymen in his time thought it " a payne " to rise so early or to remain fasting so long as to " hear out their Mattins," although the service in many parish churches was not begun so early or so long protracted as it was at the Charter-house. Mattins (with an early Mass in places where there were more priests than one), and Vespers in the afternoon will answer respectively to our 7 or 7.30 a.m. and our 2 or 2.30 p.m. traditional bells. The intermediate bell at 9 a.m. represents " Undern " (*i.e.*, Terce), procession, where there was one, and the principal (or in poorly served parishes the only) Mass of the Sunday.

" *Dives and Pauper*," a popular book once, printed in 1536, quoted by Rock and Maskell, speaks of Evensong " at afternoon in the Saturday . . . and in the Sunday," *i.e.*, 1st and 2nd Evensong of Sunday. It will be remembered that the early Oxford Methodists kept Saturdays holy as well as

Sundays, and this was perhaps not merely the spontaneous revival of a primitive observance, but it is quite possible that there was some tradition surviving through such good men as Samuel, the father of the Wesleys. For we have an interesting record (printed for the Surtees Society under the late Canon Raine's editorship) of the rules prescribed to the curates-in-charge of his parishes in Durham, by a brave and loyal Churchman who was Bishop Cosin's right-hand man, Archdeacon (and son-in-law) Denis Granville, whose zeal for the servants' 6 o'clock prayers in Durham cathedral church was mentioned in our opening paper. Granville became Dean of Durham in 1684. Shortly before that date, when already Archdeacon, he informed Archbishop Sancroft that daily prayers and monthly Eucharists were the generally established rule in the parish churches in his archdeaconry of Durham. A weekly sacrament was the one considerable point which the late Bishop, his father-in-law, had left incomplete in his diocese. Granville's correspondence on the subject did much to encourage the revival of weekly Communion. Beveridge (who had been ordained with him by Bishop Sanderson in 1661) had already from 80 to 140 communicants (perhaps at St. Peter's, Cornhill, or at St. Paul's). In 1684 the weekly Celebration was established in Canterbury, and April 26, 1685, at York (where, again, after a relapse, it was revived in 1841 by Archbishop Vernon Harcourt). At length, about Oct., 1685, Granville (now Dean) succeeded in introducing this reform at

Durham. Sancroft's own recommendation as to week-day service was (July, 1688), that the clergy should perform the daily office publicly in all markets and other great towns; and even in villages as frequently as may be . . . . on Holy Days and their eves, on Easter and Rogation Days, on Wednesdays and Fridays in each week, and especially in Advent and Lent. In 1692 Simon Patrick, Bishop of Ely, exhorted his clergy to read daily services "publicly" in their own families at least, if they could not procure a congregation in the church. This, and the similar evidence which Canon J. C. Robertson adduced ("*How to Conform*"), appears to us who have grown up to value the privilege of daily offices in parish churches and college chapels, a somewhat unsatisfactory standard to put forward. Nevertheless, I believe that it will be found, so far as public or congregational recitation of the Divine office went, to differ but little from the general practice of mediæval times in England.

The Mass, no doubt, was in many places very *frequently* offered, but in some places not more than three times; in *others* hardly once a week, but only on occasional Sundays. And *reception* of the Sacrament (one of its principal ends and benefits) was, as is well known, rare. To quote a well-known instance, the most devout Lady Margaret, who died in 1509, was considered quite a wonder of sanctity in that she "was houselled fullnigh a dozen times a year." And this infrequency of Communion was so fully established a defect, that the Devonshire people, already discontented about secular matters, in 1549 protested that they loved to have it so, and when an attempt was made under the first Prayer Book to secure that *some* should always communicate with the priest, they demanded that *none* of the lay folk should be allowed to receive the Sacrament at Mass except at Easter.

To return to Archdeacon Denis Granville's directions to the curates in his parishes of Sedgefield and Easington in 1669:—He charged them that " Mattins " be said daily in the chancel of each parish at 6 a.m., Evensong likewise at 6 p.m., as these hours were " the most convenient for labourers and men of busyness." But there were exceptions on special days :

All Wednesdays and Fridays at 9 a.m. So also throughout Advent and Lent, and on Ember Saturdays as well.

Rogation Days, at least an hour earlier by reason of the perambulation.

Evensong at 3 on all vigils and holy-day eves, " also on all Saturday afternoons (which anciently were half holy-days").

At the Sunday and holy-day afternoon service there were to be instructions, viz., catechising after the second lesson, and exposition after the third collect, for a quarter of an hour or more. This was sometimes to be a reading from the Canons. The Homily on Obedience, *t.* i. *no.* 10, or that on Disobedience (and Rebellion), *t.* ii. *no.* 21, to be read; but not oftener than to " countenance the book, or assert the King's supremacy." There were to be readings also in the forenoons, either from the desk between first service (*i.e.*, Order of Morning Prayer) and Litany, or between Litany and second service (*i.e.*, Order of Holy Communion), or else from the pulpit before or after sermon, omitting in that case "the psalm then usually sung" (doubtless Sternhold and Hopkins). These readings sometimes consisted of such rubrics and canons as were most neglected, the canon on excommunication in particular, and such an explanation of the service as the King's directions to preachers indicated, and likewise those directions once a year, and excommunication to be denounced (*i.e.*, published). Young persons, as a *rule*, were not to be admitted to communicate before the age of 16 years.

Granville, as we have seen, was zealous for the Sunday Eucharist in cathedral churches. For his country parishes he prescribed, in 1669, Sacraments at Christmas, Easter Day, Holy Thursday, and Pentecost; also New Year's day, 1st Sunday in Lent, 1st Sundays in July, in October, and November. This arrangement left February (and sometimes March), August, and September without a celebration. But ten years later "at the combustions" (what were these?)* he made the Communion monthly.

---

* Is this a misreading of "Combination," a word frequently found in Laud's Instructions, as at Cambridge more recently? Parishes (or Colleges) *combined* to supply a cycle of preachers, whence (it is said) the common-parlours at Cambridge originally took their name of "Combination Rooms." We shall have occasion to refer to the Brackley Combinations on page 72, below. Or were there conflagrations in Durham?

These late seventeenth century arrangements for teaching bear some affinity to those which were promulgated by Bishops and Archbishops in the latter part of the reign of King Henry VIII., in or about 1538. In the pulpit at High Mass time, *Pater, Ave,* and *Credo* were to be published in English immediately after the Nicene Creed. And parsons once in three weeks had to declare what were the Seven Deadly Sins and the Ten Commandments. Shaxton (omitting "Ave Mary") added the recitation of Epistle or Gospel, or both, in English, from the pulpit, and the declaration of the Royal Supremacy, and he directed the parson finally to bid the Beads. Edward Lee, Archbishop of York, was more explicit in ordering recitation of *Pater* and *Ave* "at Mattins time, between Mattins and Laudes"; the Apostles' Creed in English, piece by piece, after Nicene Creed at Mass; and, for the afternoon, to "reherse the Ten Commandments everie one by it selfe, between Evensonge and Completorie" (*i.e.,* Compline). He was to hear his parishioners repeat the same (after the true intention of *catechizing*) on each occasion.

Doubtless there was a reforming spirit in these regulations; nevertheless they were founded on earlier precedent. The Lambeth Constitutions of Archbishop Peckham, in 1281, obliged parsons to *expound* once in a quarter in English the Creed, the Decalogue, the Two Precepts of the Gospel, Works of Mercy, Deadly Sins, Seven Virtues, and Seven Sacraments. And the individual teaching

of the Lord's Prayer was insisted on from the days of
Bede and Egbert to the Synods of Norwich, Exeter,
etc., in the 13th century, as Maskell shows in a sort
of *catena* (Mon. Rit. iii. pp. l.-liv.). Some of the later
directions prescribed public instruction on the use of
the Angelic salutation and the sign of the cross, in
addition to the older course of teaching. In 1480,
an Archdeacon of Dorset inquires whether the eight
Beatitudes (as well as the General Sentence of
Excommunication, the Articles of the Faith, the
Ten Commandments, the Seven Deadly Sins, the
Seven Works of Mercy, bodily and ghostly, and the
four Cardinal Virtues), are published quarterly.

But we must carry our record back more gradually.

I have noted from the *East Anglian N. and Q.*,
1888, iii., 389, but without recording the date, on
the authority of " Mr. Kirkpatrick's MS." of the
Order of Funerals, Ringing, etc., at *Norwich*, that
there were prayers thrice every week-day at the
cathedral—viz., at 6 a.m. (changing to 6.30, and
again to 7, in colder and darker seasons), at 11
o'clock, and 3 p.m. ; the Sunday morning service in
choir ; the Sunday afternoon service in St. Luke's
chapel, or on chief festivals in quire. Defoe, in
1728, found a congregation of 500 people at 6 a.m.
service at Durham.

In a paper written and read in 1730, Fr. Peck
mentioned that long after the Reformation the
Litany was kept as a distinct service " in the middle
space between Mattins and the Communion Office,"
and was so treated at Queen's Coll., Cambridge,

within times then recent. And it was still the custom at Christ Church, Oxford, for the students on Wednesdays and Fridays to go to *Mattins* at 6, and again to *Litany* at 9.

In 1714, the date of Paterson's *Pietas Londinensis*, an eighteenth century forerunner of the Rev. C. Mackeson's well-known *Guide to the Churches of London*, the general rule for London churches is stated to be *on Sundays*, 10 a.m., Morning Prayer and sermon ; 9.45 on Sacrament Day, viz., first Sunday in the month, and at Christmas, Easter, and Whitsuntide.

In St. Lawrence Jewry there were *daily* prayers constantly at 6 a.m. and 8 p.m. ; Holy Communion at 6 a.m. every Sunday, excepting the first Sunday in the month, when it was at noon. In addition to the 6 o'clock week-day Mattins, there was a *second daily Mattins* on Monday, Wednesday, Thursday, and Saturday at 11 ; on the two remaining days this was at 10, because of the Tuesday and Friday lectures, on which days T. Morer discoursed, as also on Thursday afternoons at 3. This lectureship was at one time held by Tillotson, at others by Sharp, and other eminent divines. There was also a special Sunday afternoon lecture at 5. St. Lawrence was, perhaps, a church above the average. Nevertheless, daily Mattins at 6 a.m. was quite common in town till the Hanoverian decadence prevailed. Paterson gives also as the rule in 1714 :—Afternoon service between 2 and 3 p.m., and on " Sacrament Day " a quarter of an hour later than other Sundays.

What a comfortable notion this gives us of a con-
descension to human weakness as to Sunday dinners!
The parson, in his cassock, wig, and band, is dining
with the churchwarden—where else *should* he live?—
in the city. The clerk sends in, with his duty, to
know when his reverence will have prayers. Mistress
Gilpin suggests that honest Roger may as well take
a glass of ale to drink to Church and King, as bell-
ringing is such dry work, or she sends Betty down
with a glass of "the liquor which she loves"
(because, you know, it is Christmas), but leaves a
modicum of "daylight" for fear, of course, of spilling.

Paterson mentions (as many of our readers know)
a considerable number of exceptions to his general
rule. We may instance the great Churches:—

A.D. 1714.	ST. PAUL'S.	WESTMINSTER ABBEY.
6 (or 7)	Mattins in Chapel daily.	Daily throughout the year.
9	*(Nil.)*	2nd Mattins, Sundays & Holydays.
10	Mattins in choir.	2nd Mattins, on week-day.
12 noon	Holy Communion every Sunday.	Holy Communion occasionally.
3 p.m.	All days (on Sunday a sermon).	Evensong, on week-days.
3.30		Evensong, on Sunday.

"I am well assured," says J. Johnson, in 1705,
"that long since the Restauration in the Metropoli-
tical Church of Canterbury, Morning Prayer was
read at 6 o'clock every Sunday in summer, at 7 in
the winter. At 10 they began the Litany, and, after
a voluntary, proceeded to the Communion service
and sermon. And so it is, or lately was, at the
Cathedral of Worcester."

Scudamore, Robertson, and others help us to

carry the record further back. In 1659, on the eve
of the Restoration, L'Estrange remarked that "the
hour of Morning Prayer with us is 9 in the forenoon." Sparrow, two or three years earlier, had
stated that to be the canonical hour for the Eucharist.

In his *History of the Sabbath*, 1636, and to the like
effect in his *Antidotum Lincolniense* in 1637, Peter
Heylyn stated that there had been two services for
the morning on Sundays and holy days, Mattins at
6, or between 6 and 7, the second service or Communion service at 9, or between 9 and 10. He
remarked that people had become now too slothful
to go to church both times in the forenoon, so the
two were done by accumulation, but the old use still
was kept up "in the Cathedral Church of Winchester, in that of Southwell, and perhaps in some
others." Also, that in some places, "while the
litany is saying, there is bell tolled, to give notice
unto the people that the Communion service is now
coming on." In his orders (preserved by Prynne,
p. 379) for the Wednesday Combination sermons
for St. James's Chapel, Brackley, in 1639, J. Towers,
Bishop of Peterborough, directed that from 8.45 to
9 the bell should toll. The Morning Prayer and
Litany, said in surplice and hood, metrical psalm
sung, "second-service" (ante-Communion), to be
said by the preacher for the day in surplice and hood
at the Communion table, to go into the pulpit, using
only the bidding prayers according to Canon 55,
naming his University and College if he please, and
(if he be chaplain) his patron. Sermon limited to

the hour, to be ended with "Glory be to God" (*sic*) etc. Return to the Communion-table for prayer "for the whole estate of Christ's Church," etc., and one or two of the Collects which stands (*sic*) after the Communion service, and so shall dismisse the people with that blessing there, The peace, etc." Somewhat similar directions for a 9 o'clock service at Bury, on Monday, Wednesday, and Friday, had been issued in 1636 by Matthew Wren, Bishop of Norwich, *ibid.*, pp. 374-6. His ideal service seems to have included *all* the occasional offices except a funeral.

It was probably about the same time, or rather earlier, that Cosin lamented in his note ("third series") that Morning Prayer, instead of being, as in old times, at an early hour, had come to be said "towards noon." Laud instructed the Dean of Christ Church that morning service should be over by noon "at farthest"; "vespers" strictly between 3 and 5. Isaak Walton says that George Herbert went to church "strictly at the canonical hours of 10 and 4." In 1561 and 1571 respectively two Elizabethan Bishops, Parkhurst of Norwich and Scambler of Peterborough, ordered that morning service in town parish churches should end by 9, so that the congregations might resort to sermon in the principal church. This was a curious inverse development of the old "stations" and processions.

It was stated on oath at Laud's trial* in 1644

---

* On the testimony of "Mr. Le Greese and others." Prynne's *Canterbury's Doome*, p. 208.

that Cosin's *Devotions* (printed three or four times in 1627 for the use of Anglican courtiers and persons of leisure, on the lines of the " horæ "), or, at all events, the canonical hours in some form or other, were introduced at Peterhouse in the University of Cambridge when Cosin was Master (*cir.* 1638). But whether these were said at seven times a day (Ps. cxix. 164), or at the *minimum*, "at even, and morning, and at noonday" (Ps. lv. 17) is not clear. The college chapel had been consecrated in 1632 in Dr. M. Wren's mastership, partly on the ground that, being up to that date dependent on the use of the parish church of Little St. Mary's, the college had been driven to have morning service unduly early, Evensong unduly late, and Celebrations at inconvenient times. It is remarkable that in the first year after its dedication the chapel was furnished with *eight service books in Latin* (Willis and Clark).

It seems to me hardly so likely that these were copies of the *Preces Privatæ* printed "in studiosorum gratiam" by Seres, with Royal authority, in 1568, or even of the *Horarium* of 1560, which followed the lines of the Canonical hours more closely, as that Wren, and Cosin after him, should take advantage of the Letters Patent issued by Queen Elizabeth to the Universities, Colleges, and Royal Schools, in answer to a petition in 1560, whereby the rubrical permission for *private* recitation of the daily office in *any* language was extended to the corporate or collegiate use of the service in Latin, and to Walter Haddon's version of 1560 in particular, also including

Celebrations at Funerals, and the terminal Commemoration of Benefactors. Another version followed in 1574. In 1632 Richard Crashaw was still an undergraduate at Pembroke; in 1636 he went to the "house" over the way (across Trumpington-street, in just the contrary direction to that which was to be taken by another poet, Gray, in 1756), and soon he became Fellow of Peterhouse. From time to time Crashaw went into retreat with the Ferrars at Little Gidding, and when he returned to Cambridge he would keep similar night watches in Little St. Mary's church (so says Pickard) which, though no longer serving for the College services, still had a private door of communication to which the poet had (presumably) procured the key. Being deprived of his Fellowship, like other royalists in 1644, he went abroad; and, falling perhaps more under the influence of Henrietta Maria's friends, he despaired of the Church of England, and he died among the canons of Loreto. His "Song" on "The Bleeding Wounds" was printed in 1646. The "Flaming Heart" appeared in 1648 with metrical versions of the Hours of the Cross and several of the Psalms and Latin hymns, etc.

Archbishop Laud, when answering his accusers, pleaded that Latin prayers for Ash Wednesday were an established custom at Oxford. He was, however, charged with the innovation of carrying them on through Lent.

In 1625-26 the *Sunday* services attended by the Ferrar family at Little Gidding (apart from those

private exercises which had specially attracted
Crashaw some years later, were morning service at
9; second service, with sermon, at 10.30; Evensong,
with sermon, at 2 p.m.   But on *week-days*, Morning
Prayer at 6.15 (or at 8, so long as they were beholden
to the neighbouring parson coming over); Litany
(every day, by Bishop J. Williams' licence) at 10;
and Evening Prayer at 4, or 4.15.   It seems
probable, indeed, that as they were saying part of
the psalter as each hour struck at home, the church
bells must have *begun* at the hour, or after it, and so
all the services were rather later than the clock.

In Sept., 1559, a diary quoted by Strype ¹(*Annals*
1, 134), records the fact regarding the Prayer Book
of Queen Elizabeth ; " there began the New Morning
Prayer at St. Antholin's, London, the bell beginning
to ring at *five;* when a psalm was sung after the
Geneva fashion ; all the congregation, men, women,
and boys singing together."

Reformatio Legum Ecclesiasticarum, designed under
King Henry VIII., and drafted in his son's reign
in 1552, proposed that in cathedral churches and
colleges (with some relief for students in the latter)
there be daily morning service with Litany on
Wednesdays, Fridays, and on Sundays and Holy-
days, followed by Holy Communion on Sundays and
Holydays, but with no sermon in such churches lest
people should make excuse to forsake their parish
churches for such attractions, Evensong to be daily
in the afternoon.   A sermon at 2 p.m. (probably
only on Sundays and Holydays), followed by prayers

at 3. (There has been a sermon at this time in Lincoln nave from time immemorial, and until Dean Butler's time, Evensong in quire followed at 4 p.m.) For town parishes *Reformatio Legum* designed the same Sunday and Holyday arrangement as in cathedral churches, only with addition of sermon in the morning. Holy Communion in no place as a rule unless on Sunday.

At 1 p.m., catechising; and after sermon and Evensong disposition of alms (from poor-box, etc.) for "pious uses"; and exercise of penance or discipline.

In country parishes, sermon at the Communion in the forenoon; and afternoon as in town parishes.

It will, doubtless, be remembered that the *Reformatio Legum* never came into use, and I have here referred to its provisions not as a sure evidence of custom, but as an indication of what was thought suitable and practicable at the time of its composition.

In 1547, Oct. 27, Rd. Holgate, Archbishop of York, ordered for his Minster :—

SERVICE.	SUMMER.	WINTER.
Mattins	6 a.m.	7 a.m.
High Mass	9 a.m.	9 a.m.
Evensong with Compline ...	3 p.m.	2, or 2.30

The Third Hour (9 a.m.) is specially named in Canon Law as the canonical time for Mass. *(De Consecr.* dist. 1, cap. *et hoc.*, following the 14th canon of the 3rd Council of Orleans, A.D. 538.)

The English parish priest was required (*Constit. Provinc.*, A.D. 1322), to say his office of Mattins, Prime, and Terce, before celebrating his Parish Mass.*

About 1540, a Rationale or Book of Ceremonies was drawn up, probably by some member of the committee on ritual appointed co-ordinately with the committee on law and discipline which resulted in the draft *Reformatio Legum ;* there is an interesting statement as to the difference of practice then existing in English churches. It speaks of " the service used in the church *dayly in some places*, or upon the *Sundays and other feasts* in *al places;* that is to say Mattins, Prime, Hours, Evensong, and Compline." (*Cap.* 5-6, " of Mattins, Prime, and other Hours.")

Of an important parish church in the City of Salisbury (St. Edmund's) it was asserted in the time of King James I. that morning prayers had always been " about 6 a.m." for the last 60 years, viz., *cir.* 1547-1607, *i.e.*, at least, since the time of King Edward VI., excepting one week, then recently, when the minister had scandalously neglected this service. In 1548-9 candles were provided for ringing at 5 a.m. and 7 p.m. The (? next) year, in

---

* According to Lyndewode's gloss here, (*Provinciale*, lib. iii. tit. 23,) Terce was said to occur at, or in, Mass on Festivals,

> On ordinary days, Parish Mass was ' *in sexta*,'
> On Fast days,   ,,   ,,   ' *in nona*.'
> On Ember Saturdays, ,,   `,,   ' *in Vespera*.'
> On Easter Even,   ,,   ,,   ' *in noctis initio*.'

Custom allowed private Masses in the early part of the day, and public Solemn Mass on any day between Prime and Nones in Lent, and on Ember Saturday ' *usque ad Vesperam*.' Never before day, except on the night of our Saviour's Birth, and that of His Resurrection.

which the high altar there was pulled down, in the reign of King Edward, there was a payment for these candles, and likewise payment for ringing None on holy-day eves (some 28 in number). In 1560 ringing "None" on All Hallows' Eve, Christmas Eve, Our Lady Eve, and Easter Eve is mentioned.* In 1562 it is "ringing to morning prayer, ringing on Saturdays and saints' eves, and ringers on Monday in Rogation Week." In 1592 we come to "ringing *at noon* on Saturdays for the whole year, 6s.; ringing on Ascension, Whit Sunday, Christmas Day, and Easter Day, 2s." Under the Puritan ascendency in 1650 it was agreed that "if there be any need of the bell called the saints' bell [or *Sanctus*], he be made use of to the casting of the two bells (the 5th and treble), and that the bell called the 5 o'clock bell be preserved : and to stand in the same place and to be rung daily at 5 of the clock in the morning by the sexton." In 1652 "some strangers" pay an "extraordinary" fee of 1s. "for ringinge for pleasuer;" but in the course of the year (on the ground of necessary repairs) the sexton is bidden to ring no bells except one for a knell or a sermon, or (by later order) the great bell to call the people together, and the treble to ring at 5 a.m. (as before).

---

* In the accounts for the same year (viz., 1560 and 61) there were entered also payments for "ryngyng to the mornyng prayer," for "a comvnion booke," "ryngers when my lorde byshop cam in," "lone of a book namyd the pharasyres" (Paraphrases of Erasmus), "holly agaynst crystmas," "John Atkyns for carryeng off the latyn bookes to our lady churche," for "a boke of the homyles," Beckyngam, "for hys kowe that dyed in the pounde," etc., etc., p. 105.

The accounts of the fraternity of Jesus Mass in the same parish church of St. Edmund's in the city of Salisbury at an earlier date, viz., in 1500, show that the "first Mass," or "Jesus Mass," was said daily at the altar of the Holy rood at 6 a.m. The celebrant there was called "the morrow-mass chaplain." "*Salve de Jhesu*" was sung there on Fridays in Lent. (Was this the special version of "Salve festa dies," the rhythm of Fortunatus adapted, or rather re-written or imitated, for the feast of the Holy Name, as printed in Henderson's *Processionale Sarum*, pp. 152-3? Or was it "Salve mundi Salutare?" Sequences beginning with the word "Salve' are found in such profusion that it would be rash for me to pretend to decide among them all. Its name shows it to have been something different from Salve de B.V. Maria.)

In 1557 Card. Pole had inquired *(Cardwell)* whether taverns and ale-houses opened their doors on Sundays and Holy Days in time of *Mass, Mattins,* and *Evensong.* These evidently were the services of general obligation. As Dr. Rock says (*Ch. of F.* i., 70-71 *n.*), people went to church not only for Mass daily, but "on Sundays and holidays at early morning for Mattins and Lauds, and in the afternoon for Evensong, and for hearing the sermon after dinner." He is here speaking of the benches, of an age anterior to the Reformation, which are found in some old churches, and these, he tells us, were required in churches in old time for other services, but were not (in his opinion) used at the Low Masses

(p. 68) which then had become common. However, his own authority, a poem wherein "freemasons" were instructed in behaviour at daily mass, not only bids them stand for the Gospel, and kneel, generally, before it and after it, but *repeats* the instruction (from Myrk) for young and old to kneel at the sacring, or consecration. This seems to me to imply that, in practice, a certain allowance was made, at least, for the aged and weak to sit, even at Low Mass, though not at the Consecration. The custom of sitting for the Epistle is mentioned by Rupertus Tuitiensis (of Deutsch, near Cologne, A.D. IIII.) Some ancient English benches look as if they were constructed for kneeling high, on a sort of broad book-board, with the toes resting on the seat, thus giving men in the nave a view of the altar through the screen. But so many old benches have been cut away or abolished that it is hard to speak positively.

Dr. Rock, in the place cited above, does not actually mention Sunday and Holy-day Mass (where he speaks of Mattins and Lauds, and Evensong and Sermon), but he takes that, no doubt, as a matter of course. Daily attendance at the Eucharist,* when

---

* Even of William the Conqueror it has been told by Robert of Gloucester to a later generation that—

"In Church he was devout enow ; for him none day abide
That he heard not Mass and Mattins, and Evensong, and each tide."

Did he make an exception "upon the Pope Callixtus' day," in October, 1066 ? Perhaps not. The devout example of K. Henry V. at Agincourt before and after the battle is immortalised by Shakespeare. And in more recent times it is remembered that our Commander in the Sikh war went down upon his knees upon the ground to thank God the moment that news was brought him that one of his companies had routed the foe.

possible, was, it appears, customary, if not with
King Arthur's knights themselves, yet, at all
events with those in the fifteenth century who
loved to write or read or hear about them, with
the devout nobility and gentles, with persons of
leisure, and with the "more noble" artisans and
plowmen, who would *make leisure* because they
knew well the adage that "*Meat—nor Mass*"—
and some would add, "*Manners, nor Medicine—
marreth no man's Matters.*"

In a copy of the Sarum Custom-book,* as slightly
revised for use in parochial and conventual churches,
it is directed that at the choir-entrance on the west
the stall of the chief person in the church should be
on the right hand side (corresponding to that of the
Dean at Salisbury), and on the left, the place of the
second in command, corresponding to the chanter
or precentor. "Next to the chief person on the
right side, let priests and other clerks be ranged,
who as their ages and character demand are
admitted on tolerance (*ex dispensatione*) in the upper
row of stalls. Next them, towards the east let
other minor clerks stand, and be styled 'clerks of
the second form.' If there are any boys in the
quire, let them be set to stand on the floor of the
church and (be styled) 'clerks of the first form.'
And the other side of choir in like manner."

---

* The Rev. Walter Howard Frere, who kindly lent me his notes on Sarum
Consuetudines some years ago, is at present engaged in preparing the text for
the Cambridge University Press.

This mention of two principal persons sitting in the stalls leads naturally to the question, How many clergy were there in an ordinary parish ?

Taking the returns for Somersetshire and Yorkshire at the accession of King Edward VI. we find that in almost every church where there were chantry chapels there was a priest for each chantry in addition to the parson.* Often these chaplains, varying in number from one to five, helped the priest at the time of the general Easter Communion, and assisted in ministering sacraments and sacramentals where the parish was scattered, or where the sick were numerous. In large parishes the vicar provided an assistant priest to serve the cure (or, especially if he were himself non-resident, a second one, and occasionally three). Sometimes the parson employed one or more of the stipendiary chantry priests for such purposes, but also in frequent instances a curate independently of them. To take one instance : in the large parish of Thirsk there were four chaplains to three chantries. All these four had to do Divine service ; three of them

---

* The chaplains then as now were of necessity for the most part in priest's order. Now and again there is reference to a deacon. Provision was made for the deacon and sub-deacon for the Lady Mass at Prime in the ordinance of the Normanton and H. Lexington Chantry at Lincoln. Early in the 15th century it was the *deacon's* duty "to see that the holy cake (*pain béni* or *eulogia*) be cut according to every man's degree," and to "bear the holy bread to serve" the people in the north side of the church. (Has the document detailing the duty of a deacon at Trinity Church, Coventry, mentioned by Maskell, *Monumenta Ritualia* (1882) I. p. cccxx. *n.*, as preserved in the vestry there, ever been printed in full ?)

helped the parson, and one taught in the Grammar
school. It is, moreover, frequently noted concerning
a chantry priest or chaplain that it is his regular
duty "to maintain prayer" or "to do Divine
service" (as well as to say his *requiem* Masses, his
placebo, and his *dirige* for the souls, and to keep
obits), and to sing in the high quire on Sundays and
holydays. In *York* itself the phrase is added,
"in his habit of a parson," or "as other parsons
use." In many cases he kept a grammar school for
the children of the parish. At Topclyff the gild
chaplain "kept" the quire with six children on
holy and festival days, providing the said choristers
with books as well as with instruction. By no
means unfrequently the stipendiary priest was to
pray for the *living* parishioners, and to say the
Morrow Mass for servants, labourers,* and travellers.
Sometimes he had to attend a chapel of ease, and to
celebrate there for parishioners cut off by floods or
by long distances and bad roads from their parish
church, and sometimes for aged and impotent folk.

In a large church, as at Wakefield, where the
annual communicants were 2,000 (population, say,
3,630), there were five priests to two chantries, one
of these being the Lady Chapel on the South.
Four of these priests were, however, to sing (Mass)

---

* At *Lichfield*, in the second quarter of the fifteenth century, Morrow Mass
was at 5 a.m. (the celebrant there being excused midnight Mattins). In a
poem on the Art of Masonry (or, in the Latin, " Gemetria ")—cited by Rock,
i. pp. 68-70, from Halliwell—the craftsman or freemason is bidden to " hear
his Mass each day," or at least to pray at his work when he hears the church
bell, that God may make him partaker of the service to be done in church.

in the high quire once a day, and the other to " do Divine service there, and to help the curate in his ministrations." It must not, however, be supposed that there was daily service in every church. In a small parish, Aller, in *Somerset*, where there were 124 communicants (population, say, 200) on the roll, a doctor of physic who held the parsonage provided a curate in charge, and there was a chantry priest besides. At Wincanton, with 280 communicants (population, say, 465), Lord Zouch, the rector, found the curate, and there were two chantry priests beside. At Shepton Mallet there was a staff of four (parson, curate, fraternity priest, and chantry priest). At Bedminster, with the free chapel of St. Katherine, where there was Mass thrice a week, and 320 " houselling people," there were five priests (parson, vicar, curate, and two chaplains).

In Mr. Page's " Yorkshire Chantry Surveys" (Surtees Society, 1894), we notice the following particulars relating to *Yorkshire :—*

The " Rookeby " priest to say Mass *one* day in the week in the parish church of Scruton.

Lord Scrope's chaplain to say Mass three days a week in Kirkby Fletham parish church, and three days in Great Fencote's chapel. Similarly a chaplain in Wathe parish, founded 1505.

Chaplain of Lord Scrope of Uppesall to say Mass on Sunday, Wednesday, and Friday, in St. Edmund's chapel in Patrick Brompton.

Tadcaster (1505), chaplain to sing at the altar of

St. John Baptist in the quire on Sunday, Tuesday, Thursday, and Friday, and on Monday, Wednesday, and Saturday in the chapel of Todecaster Tonnesande.

At Bankenewton, in Gargrave parish, Mass on Wednesday and Friday, and every second Sunday.

The rood chantry priest at Giggleswick, etc. (and the like at Tykhill), to be " sufficiently seen in Plainsong and grammar," and to sing Mass of the name of Jhesu on Fridays (at 9 a.m. *Tykhill*), and of our Lady on Saturdays (at 6 a.m., *ibid*).

Our Lady's chantry in the northsyde of Rothwell church (1494), followed the older foundation of her chantry on the opposite side (1273), it being the duty of the ' incumbent ' of each of these chantries to celebrate Mass daily in chantry and other Divine service, and be in the "high quere" all festival days at Mattins, Mass, and Evensong, and to help minister sacraments in the parish.

The gild-priest at Whitgift was directed to say Mass in the parish church " at his plesure."

At St. Agnes' chantry, Foss Bridge, in St. Denys' parish, York, a Mass was founded in 1425 to be between 11 and 12 o'clock, but was altered in the time of Henry VIII. " by the advice of the parishioners there, as well for their commodity as [for] travelling people," to an earlier time—viz., between 4 and 5 a.m.

There was Morrow Mass in St. Michael's chantry, York Minster, for "strangers labouring in their journeys, and other artificers and young folk."

At Doncaster were above 2,000 communicants, 8 priests (including the St. Nicholas' chantry chaplain), who had their hands full in Lent hearing confessions. There then was daily Mattins, Mass, and Evensong by note, and six other Masses, *one at every hour*, from 5 a.m. to 10 a.m., after which probably the aforesaid *missa cum nota* was sung.

At our Lady's altar in Rotherham church "divers well disposed persons" founded a chaplaincy "to sing mass of our Lady every Saturday at 8 of the clock."

At our Lady's chantry in Cawthorne church (1452) mass on Sunday, Friday, and Saturday.

The rood chantry in Skipton church was founded for a priest to say Mass "every day when he is disposed" at 6 a.m. in summer and 7 in winter, for the purpose that, as well the inhabitants of the town as Kendalmen and strangers should hear the same.

Margaret Blade, widow, endowed the chantry of our Lady in Kildewick parish in 1505 for a priest to help divine service in the quire, to help the curate in time of necessity, and also to sing Mass of our Lady on Saturday and Sunday "if he have convenient help."

The mayor and his brethren at Pontefract put in a chaplain to survey the amending of the highways, and to say the Morrow Mass, which was over by 5 a.m. Also a chaplain for the chantry of our Lady, to say Mass at 8 a.m., and another in St. Rock's chantry to say Mass at 9. Also another in the chantry of our Lady in St. Giles' chapel-of-ease there, to sing Mass daily "for the ease of the inhabitants." There was also a "Rushworth chaplain" at St. Thomas's chantry in the parish church.

In Wakefield church the parishioners ordained a Morrow Mass at 5 a.m. for all servants and labourers in the parish. The three Rood priests in Ripon said Mass (presumably in rotation) before the image of the Rood about 4 a.m. and 7 respectively. There was also a Mass said in St. George's loft by another priest.

Dr. Rock says concerning the wakes or vigils, as the OFFICE OF THE DEAD was called in England, that the dead were buried commonly on the third day. Over night *Placebo* (Evensong) was sung; on the early morrow, *Dirige* (mattins and lauds of the Dead), followed by two Masses, one of the Trinity, the second of the Blessed Virgin Mary, accompanied by the organ, and chanted in pricksong, or, as we would call it, with florid music.

In 1463, J. Baret, of Bury, directed that on the day of his burial there should be a Mass of prickedsong of B. V. M. at 7 a.m.

After breakfast the mourners returned and took their places round the hearse when the third Mass, a solemn High Mass of *Requiem* began.

Chaucer in the *Pardoner's Tale* tells of three boon companions in a tavern hearing

> "A bell clinke
> Before a corse [which] was carried to his grave,
> *Long erst ere prime rung of any bell.*"

As to the season of prime Chaucer's Nun's priest gives a cryptographic indication which, perhaps, some astrologer will kindly expound. At *Prime*, early in April, as Chanticleer reckons, the sun has climbed 41 degrees, or more. What time of day was that?

Meanwhile, sly Reynard is lying in wait in a bed of herbs in the kitchen garden, and stays there till it was past *undern* of the day. Undern here, as in nine places out of ten, means *hora tertia*, and Dr. Skeat says of it that it means " a particular time in the morning—either about 9 a.m. or somewhat later. (Also applied to signify mid-afternoon.)"

And thus we come to ask about the time of WEDDINGS. Here and there no doubt you might find (like Biondello) an " old priest at St. Luke's church " ready to marry a couple " in an afternoon " when the bride is supposed by her friends to have just stepped out into the garden " for parsley to stuff a rabbit." But, whatever was the case in the times described by Shakespeare, we must suppose that Chaucer's " Markis Walter " (in the *Clerk's Tale*) was doing nothing *outré* when he married Griseldis at " the time of *undern*."

It was at the same hour some years later that this patient wife had got the house ready for her disagreeable but penitent husband to bring home (as he pretended) another bride (really their daughter) to a wedding breakfast.

The *Myrroure of our Lady*, written perhaps in

1430 and printed in 1530, though treating, of course, of a "religious" house, mentions incidentally the diversity of custom about the times of Mattins— (bed-time, midnight, a little before day, and morrow-tide). The notes of time in that treatise are as follows:—

At *Mattins* time (some say) the shipmen's "Star of the Sea" rises. These "are said in the night" (pp. 90, 150).

Pryme, the hour when our Lord was led to Pilate. A star appears before the sunrise. "By morrow, at the pryme time," is apparently intended (p. 12) to paraphrase "*mane*" (at morning) in Ps. 53. Prime belongs to the first hour of the day after sunrise (p. 138).*

At the hour of *Terce* (probably kept at Syon strictly at 9 a.m.) our Lord was scourged and mocked, and at Pentecost the Holy Ghost came down. At this hour "labourers desire to have their dinner." (After Terce the Sisters said *De profundis* in procession by a grave dug and left open for the purpose) p. 142.

At the hour of Sext the sun waxeth more hot. The time of the crucifixion (between 9 a.m. and noon).—*Blunt*, on the *Myrroure*, p. 341, &c.

---

* A friend asks me whether I think that *prime* was sung or said in *parish churches* under the head of "Mattins." It certainly was my impression that prime was a comparatively popular service, but I cannot at this moment cite any authority. It is a curious fact that where our old-fashioned text of Chaucer's *Persone's Tale* speaks of "general confession of *Confiteor* at masse and at prime and at complin," Dr. Skeat's more scholarly text (Student's edition, p. 687, sec. 22, end) *omits the words* "and at prime."

At the hour of *None* the sun is highest. The service of None was said before meat (p. 90).

Before *Evensong* the Sisters said "*Indulgete*" (a special service of mutual confession) in chapel (pp. 153-5).

This service is said "after noune" when the sun faileth much. (After 3 p.m., towards the end of daylight. *Blunt's* note on the Myrroure, p. 341.) *Compline* is the end of the day (just before bed-time, *id.*) which, says Blunt (*ibid.*), was doubtless (at Syon in the 15th century) as at Durham (in the 16th) about 6 p.m., supper being ended by 5, and followed by collation.

In 1452 parochial clergy were required to say the office on Sundays and all feasts of the Church in their own churches; likewise on ferial days if they could manage it.

W. Langland in his *Vision concerning Piers the Plowman* hears Gluttony confessing that he has drunk too much, or, as he expresses it, "forgotten" himself at his *supper*, and some time at *Nones*. Also that he "hied to the meat ere none, when fasting days were." In vi., line 147, the same poet speaks of anchorites and hermits, "that eat nought but at *Nones*." On these passages Dr. Skeat has some important notes from various sources. "The day's work was supposed to be completed at the ninth hour—three in the afternoon, according to our reckoning. This hour was called *high noon*, and the meal then taken was called a noonshun or nun-cheon (*Timbs*). It is certain that *Nones* originally meant about three o'clock in the afternoon at the equinoxes, but it was afterwards [advanced to about two p.m., Haydn, *Dict. of Dates*, cited p. 195, *Skeat*, and again] shifted so as to mean midday, our modern *noon.*" (See Wedgwood, *s.v.* 'Noon.')

" There seem to have been two principal meal times, viz., *dinner* at about 9 or 10 a.m., and *supper* at about 5 or 6 p.m. (*Piers the Plowman*, passus vi., li., 262, 265). See Wright's *History of Domestic Manners*, p. 155. But there is here reference to the *one* meal at 12 o'clock, to which the anchorites and hermits restricted themselves. In this they adopted the rule for *fasting-days*, viz., to have *dinner at 12 instead of* 9, and *no supper.*"*

Dr. Rock quotes (iv. 141) two other passages from Langland to the effect that it was the duty of the plain layman to labour, and of lords to hunt, but that they ought to desist on *Sundays*, in order

> " God's service to hear,
> Both *Mattins* and *Mass;* and, after meat, in churches
> To hear their *eve-song* every man ought.
> Thus it belongeth for lord, for learned, and lewed (*i.e.*, lay),
> Each Holy day to hear wholly the service."

And the poet asks concerning the slothful—

> " Where see we them on Sundays the service to hear,
> As *Mattins by the morrow*, till Mass begin
> Other (? Either) Sundays at eve-song ? "

Holy days (says *Pauper* to *Dives*, 1536) ought to

---

* The *Vision of William concerning Piers the Plowman* (revision cir. 1377), ed. W. W. Skeat for the Clarendon Press, Oxford, 1893, p. 150, note on vi., 147.

be kept from evening to evening. And where people begin to ring the bells at mid-day on Saturdays and vigils, that is only a reminder of the coming of the feast in the evening, not an obligation to leave off working at once. In fact, we may work till sunset on Saturdays (though not on Sundays), though first Evensong of Sunday be done on Saturday afternoon (before sunset).

The time of COMMUNION for lay folk was (according to Maskell, *Ancient Liturgy*, p. 184) after the priest received the chalice and before purification or rinsing. Rock, however, says (iv. 169) that very commonly, if not generally, it was after Mass was done, as *Do Best* says in Langland's poem :

> I " did me to church
> Tho hear wholly the Mass,
> And be houselled after."

The Lambeth Constitutions in 1281, while forbidding the cup to the laity in parish churches, apparently left it open for some in the greater (cathedral and conventual) churches to communicate in both kinds with the celebrant. (Lyndewoode, *Provinc.* tom. 3, p. 27, ed. Oxon, 1679.)

The order in parish churches was for the Sermon to follow the Creed or the Offertory. (At the Offertory, according to the *Rationale* or Book of Ceremonies, *cir.* 1538-42, " the Minister, laying the bread upon the altar, maketh the Chalice, mixing the water with the wine.") After the Gospel, indulgences, excommunications, and banns of marriage were proclaimed. (Maskell, *A. L.*, pp. 70-73.) The Bidding of Beads, which in cathedral and collegiate churches was given out on Sunday at the procession for sprinkling holy water before the west door of the choir, was *in parish churches* after the Gospel and Offertory, either from the pulpit, or from before an altar. The celebrant proclaimed in English the holy days and the subjects for intercession, " Pray we for the Church of England," &c., &c. (Rock ii. pp. 361-7.) The Bead-roll of Morebath may be seen in *Somerset Records* iv., 210-218, and others are given by Maskell, *Mon. Rit.* ii., 373-8, 412-13.

In 1500, chantry priests about the time of the "lavatory" after the Offertory, used to exhort the congregation to pray for the souls commemorated by their foundation. The names were posted up on the south side of the altar. The priest invited the people to say *De profundis* and orisons with him, either before the lavatory or else after the last Gospel at the end of Mass. (*Rock*, iii. 129.)

By the Constitutions of Oxford 1322, a priest was required to say Mattins with Lauds (and if he were a parish priest, Prime also and Terce before his Mass). (A synodal of Norwich, 1257, says that Prime must be over before he begins celebrating.) Peccham's " Lambeth Constitutions," in 1281, bids every priest to celebrate *at least once a week;* and the gloss, in *Provinciale* (*Lib.* iii., *tit.* 23, gloss ' *saltem semel,*' p. 232, ed. 1679), adds "*on Sunday, if possible.*" By Bishop Cantilupe's " Constitutions "

(Worcester, 1240) *Chaplains* were required to attend Divine offices and Mass in the parish church, and no priest was to presume to begin Mass before Prime was canonically done.* Priests were not, as a rule, to celebrate more than once a day. (Council of London, Canon 2, A.D. 1200.)

In 1241, Walter de Grey, Archbishop of York, gave statutes to St. John's Hospital, Nottingham. He prescribed that Mattins should be sung by the brethren in time to finish before day-break from Easter to Michaelmas, and to begin at dawn (*ab ortu auroræ*) between Michaelmas and Easter. The lay-brethren and sisters were to recite 25 Paternosters in lieu of Mattins, and 7 for Prime: 7 likewise apiece for None, for Evensong, and for Compline. Also a Credo and a Pater before Mattins, and a Pater and a Credo after Compline. Their Mass came between Terce and Sext. (*Monasticon,* ed. 1846, vol. vi., part 2, p. 679.)

In 1300, the chaplains and clerks of St. Elizabeth's, Winchester, were directed to rise not later than dawn, and then to say Mattins of the B. V. Mary in a distinct voice. Then Mattins of the day, *cum nota.* Then (after Prime of the day) Mass of the B. V. M., *cum nota.*

---

* An instance *(apparently)* of High Mass *before Terce* may be found in the Exeter *Ordinale,* fo. 109aa, A.D. 1337, in the Parker MS., in a rule for All Souls' Day. It was, however, a peculiar case, and it must be read with the *proviso* on fo. 100 (= 76, ed. Reynolds) that "all the Hours be said before Mass."

In 1096, the " Little Office " of B. V. M. was enjoined on the clergy generally. They induced the laity likewise to adopt its recitation as a devout practice. Not only did the Brigittine Sisters of Syon, near Kew, sing each hour of B. V. M. in their own chapel, so soon as the Brethren of their community had finished the corresponding Hour of the Day in *their* chapel adjoining, but many pious women were observed in our churches repeating Paternosters on their rosaries, while they and their husbands and brothers were attending Mass on week-days ; or (if they could read) opening their Prymers, which they had taken with them, and repeating the Office of Our Lady in church in a low voice with some companion, verse and verse, " after the manner of Churchmen." They always heard Mass on Sundays in their parish churches, and gave liberal alms. Such was the testimony of an Italian who visited England about the year 1500.*

Italian Relation of England (Camden Soc.), p. 23.

Postscript.

THE rules or customs of *Lichfield* Cathedral Church belong by rights to the former section of these notes. Having, however, overlooked them while the earlier sheets were in the press, I will now give a summary of that part of them which concerns the subject of this book.

Drawn up originally in the time of Bishop Hugh de Nonant (1188-1198), they have hitherto been known to us principally through a much later revised edition supplied for the information of Cardinal Wolsey by Bishop Geoffrey Blythe, Dean Denton, and Chapter in December, 1526, and edited in Dugdale's *Monasticon*, along with other statutes of Lichfield of various intermediate dates. About twenty years ago Mr. J. F. Wickenden, then prebendary of Lincoln, drew my attention to a 14th century transcript of Hugh de Nonant's Lichfield statutes which some Lincoln scribe had taken pains to enter in the register which John de Schalby had begun.* Though as a composition it shows signs of some modification at least as late as 1240, so that it cannot be taken to represent the customs of 1190 in an absolutely unadulterated form, nevertheless,

---

* It has now been edited for the Cambridge University Press in the second part of the collection of *Lincoln and other Cathedral Statutes* (from the late Henry Bradshaw's papers), pp. 14-25, Cambridge, 1897.

this less known copy differs in some interesting particulars from that still later recension which, as I said, was communicated to Cardinal Wolsey in the 16th century. Some of the diversities which such a lapse of time occasioned will be brought before the reader's notice.

At *Lichfield*, then, cir. 1190-1250:—

From the Nativity of B. V. Mary (8 Sept.) to Easter, *Mattins* are to be said about midnight;* from Easter to Trinity Sunday, at daybreak; from Trinity onwards, on feasts of Three Lections, Mattins likewise at daybreak.

From Trinity until the Nativity of the B. V. Mary (8 Sept.) on Feasts of Nine Lessons, Mattins in the evening immediately after Compline.†

[*Morrow Mass* celebrated by Chaplain of St. Chad at 5 a.m.—(Statutes cir. 1420-47.)]

Bell rings for Mass of B. V. Mary, thus being the first bell of the day.

Mass of B. V. Mary celebrated.

(Chaplains say their Masses from 6 a.m. to 10.)

Bell for Prime. [During this bell-ringing, according to Lichfield Statutes cir. 1256-95, there was on Fridays a Chapter-business meeting.]‡

---

* Another way of expressing this is ' *In æstate, quando cenam matutinæ præcedant.*'

† The Statutes of Bp. Heyworth, cir. 1420-47, restricted the feasts in the summer and autumn when Mattins was to follow Compline to the following seven: Trinity Sunday, Corpus Christi, Nativity of St. John Bapt., St. Peter and St. Paul, Thomas the Martyr, Feast of Relics, and Feast of the Assumption. At one period, as will be seen at the close of this Postscript, Curfew here preceded Mattins.

‡ It is hard to say whether this was distinct from the Saturday meeting, or whether we have here the vestige of the varying customs of two different periods.

Then *Prime* said in choir.

Choir enters Chapter[-house]* and *Martiloge* is read there. ' Præciosa' and orisons. Ps. *Deus misereatur* (lxviii.), Gloria Patri, Kyrieleison, Pater noster, Versicles. Oratio. *Ecclesiæ tuæ*, etc., *et nos famulos tuos ab omni adversitate custodi. Per Dominum.*

Memorial for the living. Ps. *Levavi* (cxxi.). Gloria, Versicles. Oratio. *Prætende Domine.*

Obits of the departed. Ps. *De profundis* (cxxx.). Kyrieleison, Pater noster, Versicles. Then (if it be an Anniversary Day, Oratio. *Deus indulgentiarum,* and, in any case, that is to say, with or without the aforesaid) the orison *Fidelium.*

The principal person present first says *Benedicite.* R. *Dominus.* On a Saturday, or on the Vigil of a double feast, the *Board* (or service-list, ' tabula ') is read. The succentor orders the service of the ensuing week in the presence of all the staff. Then *Chapter-business* follows.

In Lent:

Commendatio is said ' in capitulo, in prostratione.' Then

Missa pro fidelibus defunctis. (Was this the ' Missa in Capitulo ' ?)

Then the clergy go into choir.

---

* The Chapter-house at Lichfield was built cir. 1240. It may be questioned whether in this and like instances ' *capitulum* ' had as yet acquired its connotation of locality. On the other hand these words may be supposed to have been added in the interval between 1188, the time of Bp. Hugh de Nonant, and 1385, the approximate date of the Lincoln transcript.

On ordinary days *(profestis)* Bell rings for Terce.
Terce.
Sext (without any bell-ringing).
High Mass.   After the Sacring, perhaps about 10
a.m., a chaplain says a Mass for Wayfarers ('*pro
viantibus*,' Stat. Lichf. cir. 1420-47.)
Nones in choir (immediately after Mass).
Bell (*classicum*) after Mass.
Dinner.

On Feasts of Nine Lessons :—
Bell for Terce.
Terce.
High Mass.   After which immediately follows :
Sext in Choir, and *Nones.*
Bell (*classicum*) after Mass.
Dinner.*

---

* In the rule which St. Gilbert, of Sempringham, gave to his Canons in
Lincolnshire and elsewhere, circa 1140, and which his successors revised, (see
Dugdale, *Monasticon*, ed. 1846, tom. vii.) the festal services at which they
were to wear linen copes are mentioned in the following order:—First Evensong, Mattins, Prime, Morrow Mass, Terce, High Mass, and Second Evensong.
When the lay brethren of the order received Holy Communion it was to be at
the Morrow Mass if possible, but if that were impossible, then at High Mass.
They and the lay sisters of the order were to communicate eight times in the
year as a rule, viz., at Christmas, Candlemas, Assumption, Nativity of
B. Mary, Maundy Thursday, Easter, Pentecost, and All Saints' Day.   Novices
of either sex received the Sacrament *three* times a year, viz., on Christmas
Day, the Dies Absolutionis, and at Easter, as well as at times when they were
ill.   The *conversi* might communicate at different altars as the prior might
direct.   A *calamus argenteus* and a chalice of tin were provided for the
Communion of those who might be suffering from leprosy, etc.
The time for funerals varied according to the hour of death in each case.
On holy days Chapter followed the Conventual Mass.   On ordinary days *in
winter* the brethren went back to the dormitory after Mattins.   At daybreak
the bell rang for Prime.   After Prime, Mass was sung, followed by private

As to the order of these services in Lent, when Sext and None did not follow Mass, reference was made to provisions of the Lichfield *Ordinale* and *Consuetudinarium*, which are unknown to me.

High Mass always begins *circiter horam terciam*, 'about the third hour' (after 9 a.m.),* according to the seasons of the year : so says the older copy of 1190-1390. But the later recension of 1526, as printed in *Monasticon* vi., p. 1255, says, 'inchoata semper *ante horam nonam*, secundum anni tempora.'

After Dinner :	After Dinner, in Lent :
[Bell (*'classicum'*)† for one dead, if required.]	Bell rings to call the clerics.
Bells (*'pulsatio'*) for Evensong. The fourth peal (*'classicum'*) for Vespers and Mattins not to sound until it had	*Dirige* (Mattins of the Dead) up to Lauds of the Dead. Collation read in the midst of the choir (ex-

Masses until the bell rang for Terce. After Terce, Chapter, Refection, Grace in Church, Office of the Dead, Study in Cloister, Bell for Evensong.

In Summer, Prime was followed by Chapter, Labour, Terce, Conventual Mass, Study in Cloister, (? Nones and Office of the Dead,) Refection, Grace in Church, Mid-day rest, bell for Evensong.

The Lay brethren had an 'Evening Chapter' on Wednesdays after Evensong in Winter, and *post cenam* in Summer.

* The varying times for *mass* to which I have more than once referred in these notes, ought to be compared with varying times for *fasts* and *"stations"* upon certain days in earlier time. ' "Stations" were fasts till None, whereas *ieiunium* was till Vesper (*cf.* Bona *de horis*, cap. iii). Gregory the Great assigned certain churches at Rome for their observance, and on more solemn days (*statis diebus*) ordered stations till Sext. But the practice of Stations was earlier than Gregory: *cf.* Tertullian *de Oratione* xiiii, de *ieiunio* 10, 13, 14 (where stations on Wednesday and Friday till None are referred to) and Apostol. Constit., 69.' *Sacramentarium Leonianum*, ed. C. L. Feltoe, Cambridge, 1896, p. 187, n.

† *Classicum*=a clash of bells.

been ascertained whether the Dean was to be expected.

Evensong, so timed as to finish some while before dusk.

The bell for Compline, the last bell of the day, unless an alarum bell be required.

Compline in choir.

cept on Sundays, Vigils, and St. Chad's Day), ending with ' *Tu autem.*'

Curfew. Only it comes before Mattins on feasts of nine lessons in summer. (The copy of 1526 expresses the rule about Curfew somewhat differently, thus:—It is to be sounded every night at 7 p.m.— ' hora septima post meridiem '—except on those holy days on which Mattins are said after Compline, when it is not the custom to ring Curfew.)

Here I must end this series of my notes, leaving it to others to supplement them, and where necessary to correct any false inferences which I may have drawn. I shall be well pleased if any of my readers who have had patience to peruse what I have gathered can restore from the heap the true structure of the Time-Table of Services (1) in a Cathedral, and (2) in a Parochial, Church.

PART III.

An Account of some old Lincoln Customs and Ceremonies, with Notes on the Dedications of Altars and Chapels in Lincoln Minster, alphabetically arranged.

I HAVE put here in alphabetical order some notes illustrating old customs of Lincoln Cathedral Church, or bearing upon the various portions of its interior arrangements. They have been gleaned from some of the Chapter Muniments and other sources.

I had at the outset abstained, as far as is possible, from entering upon the difficult questions which beset the task of trying to identify the relative positions of the various altars, &c., in our Minster. I simply marshalled under the names of the individual Saints or other dedications such facts as I have gathered. Having reached the middle of my collection I have (under the head of "PISCINAS, &c.") been compelled to some extent to hazard several conjectures, though I believe I have always apprised the reader where I know the ground to be uncertain.

If after my index is finished, when experts in Lincoln topography and antiquities have supplemented and corrected it, I shall be glad if it should prove that any sound decision can be reached.

Although it has fallen to my lot to handle and to glance at most of the books and other documents in the collection of the Dean and Canons, the number of Act Books and Accounts which I have hitherto perused from end to end is comparatively small ; but the result is such as to assure me that, as others are doing their part towards a thorough examination of the rest of the collection, knowledge both solid and interesting is certainly being acquired.

A summary of the contents of at least the earliest of the 35 volumes of Chapter Acts, which reach from 1305 to 1876, is a *desideratum.* It would be sufficient to make an intelligent summary of the marginal rubrics which the Chapter clerk has written, or to supply them for any volume where they have not been given, with the addition of the dates from the Acts themselves, and to give a few longer extracts for the most interesting entries.

I rejoice to hear that the Rev. A. R. Maddison, F.S.A., Succentor of Lincoln, has been paying special attention to this branch of the enquiry.*

---

* I will take this opportunity of recording my obligation to Mr. Maddison and likewise to Mr. Gibbons for help which I have derived, not only from their printed writings but from their kind services as correspondents. To Mr. Freemantle, at Salisbury, and (naturally) still more to Mr. Logsdail, at Lincoln, I owe several kind suggestions in answer to enquiries which I have made, and which few (if, indeed, any) are so well qualified to answer. To the Rev. John Kaye, Junior, for a survey of the Minster and several other researches and communications, whereby he has saved me sundry journies to

For the *compotus* Rolls and books of accounts, it would probably be enough to transcribe one of the earliest and one of the latest specimens entire, enriching and illustrating them by additional or parallel passages from the audit accounts of intermediate years. These range (fairly consecutively) from 1304 to 1577, 1601-41, and 1661 onwards.

CHRIS. WORDSWORTH.

ALLELUYA. A payment of 6*d.* is charged (*e.g.*, in 1452, 1476) in the attendance Rolls of " Re and Ve," claudentibus alleluia, *i.e.*, for the singers of the last Alleluia on Saturday before Septuagesima, when there was to follow "a close time" for joyous singing until Easter. Even so late as 1617 we find an entry of the payment, " pro excludend' *Alleluya,* vj.d."

ALL SAINTS. At this festival the choir and high altar were decked with rushes or mats (" in nattez empt', vnacum cariag' eorundem 11*s.* 11*d.*).

ALTARE MAGNUM, MAJVS, SIVE SUMMUM. The High Altar. Here High Mass (*missa major*) was sung with deacons and sub-deacons. Likewise the funeral mass of a canon, *pro corpore præsenti ;* but the anniversaries of none less than a King or a

Lincoln or to libraries elsewhere, I desire to express my obligation. Likewise to Canon Fowler, editor of the *Lincoln Diocesan Magazine,* in which the following index or series of notes has been appearing from time to time since September, 1894. Last, but not least, Dr. J. Wickham Legg, F.S.A., has suggested some of the improvements which I hope may be noticed by those who read these papers in their original form.

Bishop of Lincoln (including among the latter Geoffrey Plantagenet, who had been Bp. *elect*) might be performed here. Mass at the high altar was usually celebrated by the Canon in weekly course *(hebdomadarius)*, and none might ever celebrate here excepting a Bishop or a Canon of Lincoln, or some other Bishop present on a visit. (Black Book, pp. 293, 389.) In Jordan de Yngham's accounts, 1271, occurs a payment "custod' magni altaris 26*s.* 8*d.*" On the high altar, and in charge of the said "keeper," stood customarily in the 15th century, "one silver candlestick with [3 branches, 3 'boles,' and: *add.* 1536] three pricks ('pykes') for candles, with one knop in the midst, having figures of Mary and Gabriel, and a pot with a lily, (*i.e.*, the Salutation) and the Nativity of our Lord beneath figures of Mary and Joseph, and the Resurrection of our Lord. Also the images of the Deity, and of Mary, in the similitude of a coronation in the midst of the style, silver-gilt, and 8 angels of silver-gilt above the foot." This, when somewhat broken, weighed 80½oz. See below, under "*Candlesticks.*"

AMICTUS. The Amice, a white linen Mass-vestment, placed for a moment on the priest's head while vesting and then allowed to lie as a collar to his alb and chasuble. I do not recollect the occurrence of this word often among Lincoln records, but no doubt the thing was implied, for example, in the inventories where they speak of "albes with all other apparrell" (e.g. *Inventories*, pp. 34, 59). But in one instance we have (*ibid.*, pp. 26, 51) 'a chasuble of red, called peace, with one small orfrey of cloth of gold with two albes,* three *ammesses*, without tunacles,' where the reference must be to *amictus* rather than *amitia*.

ALMITIA *(Almutium)*, or

AMITIA. A canon's almuce of black cloth lined with grey fur, worn in choir on the neck and shoulders or carried on the arm. It was put on, with a surplice, by the Bishop of Lincoln (as canon) on the occasion of his installation, before he was led to his stall. He took also his mitre and staff. He resumed the same canon's habit after his Pontifical Mass on the same occasion. *Statutes* ii. 554, 555. See also 'Choir Habit.'

ALTARS. For a list of thirty-five altars at Lincoln, see below at the end of the long article on "Piscinas and Aumbries."

ST. ANDREW'S ALTAR. Here was Oliver Sutton's Chantry. In 1527 Dionisius Brodhed was admitted as Oliver Sutton's Chaplain. D. ii., 64 (i) No. 28.†
It appears from J. de Grantham's book (cir. 1500)

---

* A plain instance of the distinction between the (choral) *almuce* and the (altar vestment) *amice* is supplied by a passage in Salisbury Cathedral Statutes (p. 31), where dignitaries ('personæ') and canons are specifically allowed, when there is danger of taking cold while celebrating, 'sub *amictu* lineo *almuciis* suis libere, cum voluerint uti,' to protect their throats.

† It may be well to explain here at the outset that the principal presses in the Dean and Chapter's Muniment-Room in Lincoln Cathedral Church are lettered from *A* to *D*: whereof *C* and *D* have four compartments each (besides practicable gables, C.v. and D.v.),—Thus "D. ii., 64 (i.) No. 28" must be interpreted to indicate "in Press D., compartment ii., the 64th pigeon-hole, 'Stone's patent' box No. i., article packet or document No. 28."

that a chaplain celebrated here for the soul of Nich. Hych, Sub-dean, who died about 1270. (Grantham makes St. Andrew's altar distinct from St. John Evangelist's.) At St. Andrew's in 1531 W. Foreman, chaplain, celebrated for the souls of Geoff. Pollard, W. Aveton, and W. Hemmyngburg, and received 4*l*. 13*s*. 4*d*. But in 1420 these last were commemorated at St. Michael's altar, and Hyche, etc., at St. Denys'.

St. Anne. It is said that the dedication of the southern altar in the south aisle was latterly changed to that of St. Edward the Martyr. Here was the Duke of Lancaster's Chantry, and at this altar the Works' Chantry chaplains said mass at 5 a.m., and at 10 o'clock in 1531. The festival of St. Anne was not published for England until 1383. In 1500, and later, the porter of Lincoln Close performed some ceremony of "crowning Mary" (perhaps placing a garland on the principal image), and was rewarded for that service, and for attending to the clock. See below "*Curialitates.*"

Apertura. The audit or periodical opening of money boxes, stocks, or other receptacles for offerings at certain shrines, altars, and images or relics in the church. Thus in the accounts for 1420—1421 we find :—(1) At the High Altar, opened on the morrow of St. Denys in October, 75*s*.; of St. Lucy in December, 104*s*.; of the Annunciation in March, 4*l*. 17*s*. 2*d*.; and at the audit in September, 115*s*. in gold and silver, besides the smaller sums a dividend from the broken metal, 2*s*. 6*d*. " de pondere croni auri," which, I suppose, means gold at troy weight; silver, 1s. 6d. (2) Apertura 'of the image at the Dean's tomb.' (3) Opening of the stock (*stipitis*) of the Image of the Blessed Mary of Grace, 20s. 2d. (4) Stock of St. Christopher, 5s. 1d. Offerings at St. Christopher, 16s. 4d. (5) At the image of Blessed Mary on the south side of the choir, 45s. (6) Offerings at the tomb of Little Hugh, 10½d. (7) Offerings on the north side of the choir, 11d.

The late Precentor Edmund Venables has given us a paper on the *Shrine and Head of St. Hugh*, 1893.

AUMBRY. See below, "*Piscinas.*"

AURORA DIEI. See "Missa Matutinalis."

AVERIUM. An animal used in husbandry. Usually in the plural 'averia.' The word [Anglo-French, *aveir (aver)*, Fr., *avoir*, Lat., *habere*,] is said to mean "property, chattels, stock, cattle." It has survived in Scotland and in Northumberland and North Yorkshire in the forms *aver, aiver, afer, haver* or *hawfer*, and has come to be applied to a sorry, worn-out, horse. See Dr. Joseph Wright's *English Dialect Dict.* s. v. 'Aver' and 'Average.' The in-coming Canon of Lincoln was to have on his prebend, during the year while the estate of his predecessor remained in possession, a cow-house *(bovariam)* where he could stable "boves suos vel averia ad arandum vel ad warectandum necessarios." *Black Book*, p. 277.

BANCVS, a bench, anglo-latin. 'Bancum in choro,' *Stat.* ii. 158. I have often heard workmen use the term 'bank' for a workman's bench.

BEAM. The beam along the altar (*trabs secus altare*) is mentioned in the *Black Book*, pp. 289-292. It was an early custom that the treasurer should provide 16 tapers, each weighing ¼-lb., to burn thereon at mattins on principal feasts, and on Lady Day, All Saints, and St. Hugh's Day. These, I suppose, were identical with the " 16 small wax candles " which the three Cathedral carpenters were bound to light and put out there duly. On Sundays, moreover, and when there was service of the Blessed Virgin, and when the choir had " rulers," the treasurer had to provide, besides the two lights " on the little candlesticks before the altar " for vespers, compline, mattins, and mass, one likewise " above the horn (or corner) of the altar towards the north." This last is glossed in Bp. Alnwick's MS. " above the *beam* of the altar towards the north." Similarly, where the old custom spoke of three candles on, or over, the altar during the octaves of St. Martin, St. Agnes, and St. John Baptist, and one only on ordinary days, Bp. Alnwick wished to express this more clearly, " *super trabem*," in each instance. The present reredos, or altar screen, is a restoration by Essex about 1770. The late Precentor Venables has explained (*Linc. Dio. Mag.*, ix., p. 160, Oct., 1893) that this screen represents the eastern-most of two long parallel walls which made a narrow but convenient passage, chamber, or sacristy behind the high altar, and supported the tabernacle on its roof or verge. In very early times altars were covered by a solid canopy not unlike an Elizabethan four-post bed. See sketch of a *ciborium* at Ravenna in *Dict. of Christian Antiq.*, i., p. 66.

About the time when Remigius built his church at Lincoln, it became the fashion to remove the front, and perhaps the side members, of this structure. Thus the eastward frame remained :— a beam (over the back of the altar) supported by two upright posts or pillars. An excellent illustration of this arrangement may be seen in the early 15th century sketch of the altar, &c., of St. Augustine's, Canterbury (reproduced for Dugdale, *Monast.*, i., 121, and others), where the beam, supporting the tabernacle or reliquary of St. Ethelbert, and the precious texts or MSS. of St. Augustine, rests on two uprights at the altar ends, and in its turn supports a higher tier with other relics and images. St. Hugh's church contained, no doubt, such a structure. The Sarum beam supported 8 lights. With a little imagination we may represent the westernmost beam of the old *ciborium* (which Dr. Rock tells us was removed from the front of the high altar about St. Osmund's time) as having been brought down westward to make the rood beam between the choir and the nave.

BELLS. Black Book, pp. 273, 286, 292, 295 (at excommunication, 332). Statutes ii., 461.*

---

* In this work I cite as " Statutes ii." the collection of " *Statutes of Lincoln and certain other Cathedral Churches* " which I have recently edited in two *fasciculi* for the Cambridge University Press (8vo, 1897) as a continuation to " *Liber Niger : the Lincoln Black Book* " which I edited from the late Henry Bradshaw's papers (Cambridge, 8vo, 1892).

BELLRINGERS. Black Book, pp. 364, 387. Statutes ii., pp. 414, 415.

BENEFICIA ECCLESIÆ, LINCOLN. See "Confraternity" and "Psalter."

BENEFACTORS. By the order of St. Hugh in chapter, cir. 1195-1200, a daily mass and psalter with suffrage was said for all Benefactors living and departed. On the stone screen outside the northern chantry, or Founders' chapel, in the great south transept is the legend, " *Oremus pro benefactoribus istius ecclesie*," *i.e.*, Benefactors of the Fabrick. See ' Missa pro Benefactoribus.'

BISHOP'S EYE. A name for the circular window in the great south transept facing the Palace, which may be traced back to the early 13th cent. metrical life of St. Hugh. See " Dean's Eye."

BLADUM. Growing corn.

ST. BLAISE (Bp. and Martyr, 3 Feb.). The dedication of the altar in Bp. Russell's Chantry, about 1495. (See " Williamson's Guide," p. 92.)

So in the Obit List of 1527 (fo. 31) Bp. J. Russell's Chantry pays " to the clerk of St. Blaise's chapel for finding wax to burn in at least two candles of sufficient size about the tomb of the said reverend Father, all the time of his obit, both during the ' exequies ' and at mass, 18*d*." Browne Willis likewise identified this chapel with ' Russel's Chantry,' on the authority of MS. Cotton *Tiberius*, E. 3.

BOARD RENT. The office of Receiver of these rents was mentioned incidentally as held by T. Lowe in 1437 at the time of Bishop Alnwick's Visitation.

Statutes ii., 409. Board Rent Rolls of the years 1460, 1733, &c., are preserved among the Chapter Muniments. Were these connected with the feudal custom of landlords charging certain lands with the duty of providing the maintenance of their table?

BOOKS. Statutes ii., 404, 424. With certain reservations, the use of service-books in choir was forbidden, because the singers were required to know their service by heart in their year of probation. See *Black Book*, pp. 392, 393, 399.

BOROUGH'S CHAPEL. The northernmost of the three chapels at the extreme east in the retro-choir. See Sanderson's notes, ap. Peck's *Desid. Curiosa*, p. 294. 'Borough' and 'Burwash' are among several forms in which the name Burghersh appears. The surpliced choristers are called in a document of 1624, 'Burrischantryes.'

BOUNGARTH, a Danish name for a homestead *(Bunde-gaarde)*. It appears at Lincoln as the name of a piece of property given to the community of Vicars.

BROTHERHOOD, BRETHREN. See 'CONFRATERNITY of the Church of Lincoln.'

BREAD. A loaf or manchet of bread was presented to visitors, as it is to wayfarers at St. Cross, near Winchester, but not so much here to *bonâ fide* travellers as to personages of distinction. The accounts of 1271 have 14 entries "in pane," *e.g.*, presented to the Justices, for the Bishop of "Dulkend," for the Countess of Lincoln, for Master de Sempringham ; presented to the Earl of Warren ;

sent to the Viscount; the price varying from 5½d. to 7½d. In bread presented to the Justice(s) of our lord the king on Thursday after St. Peter "ad wincal" (*i.e.*, Lammas or *ad vincula*) 26d., wine from the commune, 12 pitchers (lagenae) to the porter, 3¼d.

According to the early 13th century custom of Lincoln the Bishop used "a loaf or a book" as the ensign by which he conferred a prebend "in his chamber, or where he would."

BROAD TOWER. A corruption of "Rood Tower."

BUCKINGHAM CHANTRY. See 'Altars of St. Hugh and St. Katharine' under the heading of "*Piscinas.*"

BURNET. A dark brown woollen stuff, forbidden as a material for Lincoln choir copes, which were to be of black Deuxsevers cloth, manufactured originally at Niort, or some other of the towns in that department of western France, in Poitou, between the two rivers Sevres. *Black Book*, p. 391.

BURSA DOMINI EPISCOPI. The three carpenters at Lincoln used to receive their stipends (about 18 or 20s.) in half-yearly payments at the synod on the morrow of Holy Trinity, and at the synod after Michaelmas Day, 'from the purse of his Lordship by the hand of the Archdeacon or his official from the farm (firma) of the archdeaconry.' *Black Book*, p. 293. Cf. "Camera Episcopi."

CALEFACTORY. Under the head of "*pelves, et cetera,*" the Lincoln inventory of 1536 has five pair of "basyns" and three "spowtes" belonging to three of the sets, a holy water "fatte" and "strynkell," two sawsers, sacryng bell, two sconses with handles, two "fioles" or cruetts, and "*Calefactorye* sylver and gylte, with leves graven, weyng 9½oz." This was doubtless like the pila calefactoria at Westminster, or the "*pomum de cupro ad calefaciendum manus*" at Lichfield or Salisbury, a "pome" or metal ball, with hinge and clasp containing an iron heater, for thawing the hands of the celebrant on frosty mornings. The Lincoln calefactory was "in custodia sacriste" in 1536. It had apparently been taken away before 1548, possibly in the 4,285 oz. of silver which went to Henry VIII. "shortly after his returne from Bulloygne" in 1540.

CAMERA COMMUNIS. A long chamber on the right hand of the passage from the Church to the Chapter-house. In the upper storey is now the clerical library. Here cloth was stored for distribution to the poor. Cloth appears to have been sold. In J. de Fotherby's accounts for 1294-5 we find, "de 21*s*. receptis de panno vendito, qui prius emptus extitit per dominum R. . . ." In the accounts for 1458-9 occur, under the head "pro distrib. panni," 20 doz. of linen cloth of the colour "musterdevillers" (viz., 4 doz. broad cloth, and 16 doz. narrow, "viz., lez streytes") bought of W. Gale, at various prices, at Sturbridge Fair (near Cambridge), with 4*s*. paid for the expenses of Rob. Hide, who bought the said cloth and rode from Lincoln to "Stirbrig" and back, 14*l*. 14*s*. 4*d*. In 1452-3 the cloth bought was of "moulderusset" colour.

CAMERA EPISCOPI. This phrase occurs in the Black Book, p. 303, in the title of the prebend, ' Decem Libræ de Camera Episcopi percipiendæ.' No psalms were assigned to this stall of *Decem Librarum* in the Black Book. Cf. " Bursa."

CANDLESTICKS. At the end of the 15th century there were entered in the inventory two great and fair gold candlesticks given by John of Gaunt, Duke of Lancaster, circa 1396-9, weighing together (in 1536) 450 oz. ; two silver gilt candlesticks, weighing about 70 oz. each, given by Bp. Bokyngham, cir. 1362—1397; two large silver candlesticks (averaging 33 oz.), given by J. de Rouceby, cir. 1375; two plain candlesticks given by P. Dalton, Treasurer, cir. 1405; and one silver candlestick with three pricks, or pykes, for three tapers, which stood on the high altar, and was in charge of the keeper of that altar. (*Invent.*, pp. 9, 10.)* This three-branched

---

* "*Invent.*", i.e., a collection of *Inventories of Lincoln Cathedral Church* reprinted, or extracted as a " short-copy," from my paper in the *Archaeologia*, liii., 4to, Lond., 1892. As some interest has been shown with regard to the three-branched candlestick which in the fifteenth century used to stand on the high altar in Lincoln Minster, it may be well to give the Latin description from the late 15th century inventory, together with the corresponding entry in the English inventory of the revestry taken by Treasurer Lytherland in 1536.

Under the head of ' *Candelabra* ' : "Item j candelabrum argenteum cum iij Pykes pro iiij cereis superponendis; habens ymaginem Marie et Gabrielis ac urnam continens unum lilium, et nativitatem domini sub ymagines marie et josephi ac resurreccionem et ascencionem domini necnon ymagines dei et marie ad modum coronacionis in medio stili totaliter fabricat. cum uno Knopp. deaurato et bene inferius supra pedem habet viij angelos de argento deaurato. Et solet stare super magnum altare sub custodia custodis ejusdem altaris et nondum ponderatur." Lf. 7a=*Invent.*, p. 10. The English inventory some 40 or 50 years later supplies the weight, etc., as follows:—"Item, a Candelstike, sylver and (' parcell gylte ' *altered to*) gylte wyth one knopp yn the myddest

candlestick which was wont to stand, not on a shelf, but on the high altar itself at Lincoln in the latter part of the 15th century was no doubt something far more dignified than the poor and paltry brass candlesticks which are sometimes offered for sale. It was of silver gilt and weighed 80½ ounces after some of its ornaments had been broken away.* In the list of candlesticks in 1536 there were also a pair, weighing about 90 oz. each of silver, purest gilt, given by Bp. Chadworth, cir. 1470, and a pair in memory of Richard Smyth; but Dalton and Rouceby's candlesticks were not noted, so that the total at both these dates alike is three pair of ordinary size, John of Gaunt's large pair, and the triple light placed on the high altar. (*id.*, pp. 19, 20.)† In 1548 only two pair are left (Bokyngham's and Smith's) besides the triple light (p. 46). In the Marian list of 11th May, 1557

wyth dyverse Images, the Coronacion and Salutacion of owre Lady wyth iij braunches, iij boles, iij pikes, weyng iiij score unces et dimidium, the hightes (? highest) bole wantyng two flowres, the second bole wantyng iiij flowres, and the thyrd bole wantyng halfe the crest wyth the flowres." The marginal note on this item indicated, I suppose, its destination when the royal visitors were taking away the Lincoln treasures : " *extrahitur per capitulum*," ms. A.D. 1536. Lf. *G.=Invent.*, p. 20.

* See the note to the preceding entry.

† It may give some notion of the relative weight of silver vessels if I state that the average weight of the Elizabethan Communion Cups runs from 5 to 6 oz. without the cover. Each of the fairly massive silver candlesticks (figured on plate vii. of Andrew Trollope's *Church Plate of Leicestershire*, 4to, 1890) made in 1701, and given to Swithland Church in the reign of George the Second, measures 9¾ inches in height, and weighs a trifle over 12 oz. The more elaborate silver-gilt candlestick made in 1654, and belonging to the Church of Staunton Harold in Leicestershire (*ibid.*, plate iii), weighs something over 77 oz., and stands 18 inches high.

(Dugd. *Monast.*, vi., p. 1290), there are in the revestry only " one pare of bearing candylstyckes of lattyn " (to be carried by the *ceroferarij* in the procession for High Mass, and set down on the step before the altar). " Item a nother pare of a larger sworte standyng of the altare in our lady chore. Item a nother pare of bearyng candylstycks broken." (See " Judas.")

At Ottery St. Mary, so late as 1342, Bishop Grandisson, of Exeter, ordered *one* candle to be provided for every altar. *Registr. Grandisson.* p. 131. So John Myrc instructs the parish priest when saying mass to take his candle of wax and ' set her, so that thou her see, on the left half of thine au*l*tere ' (line 1876).

At Westminster Abbey there were only four pair of candlesticks in 1388, afterwards increased to six pair. In 1540, only four pair. (J. Wickham Legg's *Inventory of the Vestry*, in *Archaeologia*, p. 34.) And it appears from the drawings in the Islip roll that the ornaments were not kept on the high altar there, but put on specially for Mass. It was never considered right to celebrate the Eucharist in darkness :* but the burning of " two candles, or at the least one and a lamp," at Mass time, became actual English Canon Law only after the Council of Oxford under Abp. Stephen Langton, in 1222. It was repeated by Walter Reynold just a century later, only with

---

* " A sy byrnende leoht on circan thonne man maessan singe " (*semper lumen ardeat in ecclesia dum missam cantet*). Laws Ecclesiastical under K· Edgar (A.D. 967), cap. 42.

the omission of the lamp. Lyndw. *Provinciale* iii., 23, *Lintcamina*, and app. pp. 7, 40. In the Constitutions of Bp. Grosseteste, for his parochial clergy, parishioners are bidden to do reverence when the Sacrament is elevated, or is being carried to the sick, ' *semper lumine precedente,* cum sit candor lucis eterne ;* . . *tintinnabulum semper precedat.'*— E. Brown, *Fascic. Rerum Expetendarum,* ii. 410. Langton's time was that of Bp. R. Poore at New Sarum, and Hugh de Welles and Grosseteste at Lincoln. By a curious coincidence we have records of the ornaments, not only at New Sarum itself, but in several of its prebendal churches and chapels for the years 1222-4, the exact period of the Oxford Council. Out of nine churches visited by Dean Wanda in 1222, *only one* (Mere, see Osmund Reg. i., p. 291) has a pair of candlesticks, and they are of copper. But two years after the Council the Dean begins to *take notice of the defect* (pp. 311-3) at Swallowcliff and Horningsham. At Hill Deverel he finds one small pair of bronze, and a lesser pair of iron. As for the Cathedral itself, the Treasurer takes over at Old Sarum in 1214-15 one pair of silver, one pair of tin, one pair of iron, and nine candlesticks of enamel (*id.* ii., pp. 128-9), and exhibits them to the Dean and Chapter in 1222. He delivers over for the altars in the rising Cathedral at New Sarum (ii., pp. 139-141),

---

* Lyndewoode the canonist, who was a canon of Lincoln, has on the words of Abp. Walter's constitution ("tempore quo missarum solennia peraguntur, accendantur duae candelae vel ad minus una ") the gloss, "Candela namque sic ardens significat ipsum Christum, qui est splendor Lucis aeternae," with a reference to the Roman canon law, which he quotes, though not *verbatim.*

for the altar of St. Peter *none*, for All Saints *none*, but Bp. Poore makes up this deficiency by offering a silver pair, a legacy from Gundreda de Warren, on the dedication day, 28th Sept., 1225, and himself made provision for keeping the light (*luminare*, p. 39, not on, but) around the said altar; for St. Stephen's altar a pair of copper candlesticks; for St. Nicholas, *none*; for B. Mary Magdalene, *none*; for St. Thomas the Martyr, one brass pair. Approaching the subject from another side, we find the Bishop, in his famous Custom Book of Salisbury, requiring the Treasurer to find two candles above the high altar (the earliest text gives " *in superaltari* "*)

---

* Duos scilicet (in superaltare, *altered to*) in superaltari, et alios duo in gradu coram altari, *Dublin MS.*, now at Cambridge: 'in superaltari' *Osmund Register*, at Salisbury, fo. 1*b*. The printed editions give an incorrect reading, or, at least, they misrepresent the MSS., although something may be said in favour of regarding the reading given by the editors as a possible emendation. The interpretation is somewhat difficult. The late Henry Bradshaw supposed the *beam* (*trabs* is specified at Lincoln) to be intended by 'superaltare' at Salisbury. It is, however, the opinion of some antiquarians that the 'beam' ran right and left, and not behind, the altar. The usual meaning of *superaltare* is a movable hallowed slab. One which belonged to Card. Bessarion, to Count Cicognara, and subsequently to Dr. Rock, of late 12th century work, measures only about 12-in. by 7½-in. (see *Church of our Fathers*, i. p. 257) inclusive of the border. This would only hold two candlesticks with base of 6-in. diameter placed close together. Although the 'superaltare aureum,' which belonged to Salisbury in the early part of the 13th century (Reg. Osm., fo. 85*b*), may have been a little larger than that which belonged to Dr. Rock, it seems highly improbable that in olden time two small candlesticks should have been crowded together upon such a base, even if the portable altar were ever placed at the back of the high-altar as in a position of honour and security. All that we know is that there was in the charge of the Treasurer of Sarum circa 1214-22, besides the chest or box (archa) for books and relics, well bound with iron, near the principal altar, "another long box in like manner in which the golden superaltar used to be laid up in days gone by" (*in qua antiquitus superaltare reponebatur*. And Dr. Rock supposes that the *superaltare* was occupied by the

and two on the step before the altar (and the like on some days at evensong and mattins). On Christmas Day, and when there are processions, eight about the altar *(circa)*, two before the image of our Lady, six others on high *(in eminentia)* before *(coram)* the relics, crucifix, and images there, five in the corona before *(ante)* the choir step, and five above the wall behind the lesson-pulpit *(super murum post pulpitum lectionum,* i.e., the *ambo* at the rood screen, *id.* i., p. 8). From Whitsuntide to the Nativity of our Lady inclusive, tapers on a seven-branch candlestick of brass. On ferial days, one at mattins at the choir step, and two at mass, besides two tapers at the Sepulchre for Good Friday,* and the great Paschal candle ; also a mortar (or great night light) every evening before St. Martin's Altar (N.E. of the choir), and another at the W. door of the choir during mattins.

The directions given to the Treasurer at Lincoln

---

chalice (northward) and the host (southward), '*calix ad dextrum latus oblatæ,*' at least in Italy (*id.* p. 261). He mentions such a stone represented as 'standing up conspicuously from beneath the cloth overspreading the papal altar' in one of Raffaelle's frescoes, shown in *Vaticano Descritto*, ed. Pistolesi, t. vii., tav. xxiv. Du Cange cites Matthew Paris, *Vitæ Abbatum S. Albani*, pp. 71-80, and J. Beka *in Egilbodo Episcopo Trajectens*, 13, as using *super-altare* in an unusual sense, equivalent to an 'upper frontil,' as Dr. Rock calls it, *Ch. of our F.*, i. 237n. Happily we are not bound to copy minutely in practice every custom that was in vogue in Italy in Raffaelle's days (in church or out of it), nor even to attempt to restore every detail of ceremonial which may or may not have been introduced in the illustrious and Anglican church of Sarum in the reign of K. John or of K. Henry the Third.

* The second of these Sepulchre lights was to be put out at night, and only the one to be kept burning through Easter Even until the procession before mattins on Easter Day. *Registrum Osmundi.*

early in the 13th century were no less explicit. *Black Book*, pp. 288-90.   Ant. Beek's Book, fo. 6.

On the principal holy days, seven candles weighing 12lb. are to burn on the 7-branched brass candlestick, at evensong, or mass, or both.   Also 5 candles above the altar, and 2 on the bearing-candlesticks which the boys bring in the procession and set down on the pavement before the footpace of the altar. Also one candle ("in a candlestick near the altar" *Nov. Reg.*)* on the north side by the altar, to burn by day and by night; and 16 on the "beam" along (or beside, '*secus*') the altar, to burn only at mattins. These last were four to the pound.

On Sundays and certain other days, one candle at the corner or "horn" of the altar towards the north.   The *Novum Registrum* subsequently explained that this was "on the beam towards the north, and 2 on the little candlesticks, not on, but before the altar.

On week-days 1 above the altar (on the beam), 2 on the little candlesticks.

He had also to provide lights at the tombs on Bishops' anniversaries, also 2 candles for Chapter Mass, or whenever Dean, Precentor or Chancellor were celebrating.   When the Bishop pontificated at evensong or mattins two cerofers were to stand

---

* *Nov. Reg.* i.e. Novum Registrum, an attempt made by Bp. William Alnwick, circa 1439-42, to codify Lincoln rules and customs on the model or skeleton of Statutes of St. Paul's, London.   A convenient edition was printed for my Father, 8vo, Lincoln, 1873, from such MSS. as were then accessible. A text from an earlier and original manuscript, subsequently identified by H. Bradshaw, will be found in "Statutes ii.," pp. 268-363, Cambridge, 1897.

before him, and to walk before him, carrying two
lighted tapers in taper-holders *(in cerofarariis.)* It
is possible that the "Iudaces—of brasse" which
remained till 1556 had been used for this purpose.
See below "Judas."

The Decretals of Gregory iii. ti., 41, cap. 10.
Sane. where Honorius III. says, "*Semper lumine
præcedente, cum sit candor lucis aeternae,*" referred
originally to carrying the Eucharist to the sick.
These words (as I have said already) occur in the
constitutions issued by Bp. Ro. Grosseteste for his
parochial clergy in Lincoln diocese, where he bids
parishioners to do reverence when the Sacrament is
elevated, or when it is carried to the sick, for which
purpose a bell *(tintinnabulum)* is to be carried in
front to give warning. Micrologus, c., 11, and
others cite the *Ordo Romanus* for lights at mass.

"CANTATE HIC." A marble stone with this inscription in old Lombardic letters marks the place in
choir where verses of responds were sung at *Dirige*,
and where the Litany Desk still is placed. It is
mentioned in the late 14th cent. MS. of a late 13th
cent. custom book, but with the slight inaccuracy
"Canite" for "Cantate." It is sad to think that
the floor of the nave, once scored over with similar
directions for the procession, in roundels or processional stones, had all its ancient landmarks
obliterated in the last century.

CAPITARIUM. Here the sweeper of the church
was bound to provide water for washing hands after
dinner, and likewise for filling the chaplains' mass

cruets.   Here the relays of rulers of the choir
changed their silk copes, and put down their staves
when changing over between vespers and compline;
and the vicars who had to read or sing found their
silk copes put out for them.—*Black Book*, pp. 365,
369, 382.   See below, pp. 137-8.

CAP (pileus).   The celebrant's cap was handed to
one of the assistant boys at *Gloria in Excelsis* at
mass, who received 1½d. for holding it.

CAPICIUM.   The *chevet* or east end of the church.
(Giraldus Cambrensis, *Vita Remigii*, cap. 43.)

CAPITULUM.   The *chevet*, or eastern head of the
church.   In later times the name was applied to the
Chapter House, "the council chamber of the bishop,
the parliament house of the diocese, the daily home
of the chapter, *domus capitularis*."   (C. M. Church.)
See "Missa Capitularis."   The word is, of course,
used also most commonly for the "Chapter" or
body of Canons or Prebendaries who form the
Bishop's Council, and with him as their head (*caput
principale*, as the Canonists say)* constitute the body
of the Cathedral Church to serve as a consultative
body for the welfare of the diocese.   In like manner
with the Dean as their head (*caput numerale*) they
transact as a resident body the ordinary routine
business necessitated by their ordinary corporate
existence.

I am inclined to suspect some connexion of the

---

* See De Bouix, Part i. and ii. c. 2, cited by the late Abp. of Canterbury,
in his essay on *The Cathedral, its Necessary Place in the Life and Work of
the Church*, 1879, pp. 55, 59.

term, *Missa in Capitulo* with the old "*capital maesse.*" In an antient latin conversation-book, the *Colloquium Monasticum* of Aelfric, the pupil is made to tell his master as follows:—

"I have done many things this night: When I heard the bell ('cnyll'=*signum*), I arose from my bed, and went out to church, and sang night service ('uhtsang'=*nocturnam*) with the brethren. Then we sang [the office] of all Saints, and mattin lauds. After these, Prime, and Seven [Penitential] Psalms, with Litany and first mass ('capital maessan'=*primam missam*). Then terce ('undertide'); and we did mass of the Day. After this we sang Sext ('middaeg'), and did eat and drink and go to sleep, and got up again and sang Nones; and lo now here we be, in thy presence, to hear what thou hast to teach us."—Cotton MS., *Tiberius*, A. 3, fo. 62ᵇ, quoted in Hampson's *Kalendars of the Middle Ages* [1841], ii. pp. 382-3.

CARPENTARII. Workmen are mentioned in the *Black Book*, 291, 293; Statutes ii., 409, 435, 462.

CARUCATA BOUM. A team of eight oxen, *i.e.*, sufficient for working a carucate (eight oxgangs).— *Dimock.*

CATHERINE, SAINT;—*See* "Katharine.'

CEROTECAE, CHIROTHECAE, *see* "Serotecae" (Gloves).

CHANTER'S AISLE. An old-fashioned name for the aisle to the south of the choir, where some of the Precentors were buried. See Bp. Sanderson's account of the monuments. (Peck *Desid. Curios.*,

p. 296.)   It is the contrary side to the *pars cantoris*
in choir; but in parts of the church other than the
choir, the northern side belongs to the Dean, whose
" chapel " and " lodgings " are to the north.   However, in the ceremony of censing the Dean took the
south and the Precentor the north.   (*Black Book*,
p. 368.)

CHILDERMAS.   We have tantalising references to
some obsolete customs relating to various seasons
of the year.   That there was a boy bishop at Lincoln
as well as at Salisbury, at York, and elsewhere, may
be inferred from the appearance in the inventory of
1536 of " a coope (cope) of Rede velvett with rolles
and clowdes, ordenyed for the barne busshop, with
this scriptur, ' *the hye way is best.*' "   A pretty full
idea of the ceremonies may be gathered from the
re-printed service books, and from the *Camden
Miscellany*, vol. vii.

CHORISTARUM DOMUS.   A house in Minster Yard,
next the Chancery, where the boys of the choir used
to live under their master.   It is now the Organist's
house.   For *Ordinatio Puerorum sive Choristarum*,
see Black Book, p. 410.   There is a cartulary of
their property written about 1400.   (A. 2, 4.)

CHRISTMAS.   We find in the accounts (1406)
" In thak empt. pro choro ad fest Nat. Dñi 4*d*."
For gloves bought for the Mary, Angels, and
Prophets on Christmas morning (" in aurora ") 6*d*.
This is a customary payment (" consuetudo ") also
in 1452 and 1531.   It probably referred to some
dramatic representation of the Nativity performed

by the choristers or clerks. Straw (stramen) was bought also by the Chapter for the Church of St. Nicholas on All Hallows and Christmas Days. In early times (cir. 1270) it was an established custom for sailors to resort to Lincoln to ring for the service of prime on Christmas Day. (*Black Book*, p. 374.) In 1420 tithes to the amount of 8*s*. 8*d*. were assigned to Thomas Chamberleyn for getting up a spectacle or pageant ("cuiusdam excellentis visus"), called "*Rubum quem viderat*," at Christmas. An anthem sung at lauds on New Year's Day, and in the memorial of the Blessed Virgin at ferial vespers, begins thus:—"In the Bush which Moses beheld, and it was not consumed, we recognise and praise thy virginity." This, no doubt, suggested the title of the Representation.*

CHOIR HABIT. Excepting at the time of the procession, terce, and high mass on double feasts having a procession, when silk copes were worn until *Agnus Dei*, the regular *habitus chori* for all who took part in the choir service was a black cope of plain Deuxsevers cloth over a surplice. This habit was worn also at mattins in all seasons, and vigils of the dead throughout the year. At *Agnus Dei* they changed their silk copes for the black choir-cope on procession days, in their stalls; and conversely on Easter Even and Whitsun Eve they threw off their cloth copes at *Gloria in excelsis*, and appeared in their white

---

* A corresponding representation of the Three Maries and the Disciples is mentioned as being performed in other places at *Easter.* See Mr. J. H. Feasey's *Ancient English Holy Week Ceremonial*, pp. 170, 172.

surplices. *Black Book,* pp. 390, 391. The vicar, clerk or chaplain, who attends a Canon when he goes to read or sing, or when he enters choir or chapter house, wears the black habit, except when silk copes are ordered for all the choir (pp. 382, 392). The officiant began the sacerdotal versicle before lauds in his black cope (p. 372). From Eastertide to the Audit (Exaltation of the Cross), in the middle of September, surplices were worn without the choir cope on feasts of nine lessons, etc. (p. 391, cf. 383). This choir cope is still preserved at Lincoln in the black dress of the four choir boys of the cathedral foundation, excepting that sleeves have been added in modern times. Over the surplice was worn a black scarf, the "almuce" or "amess" lined with fur. At Salisbury, canons had a privilege from K. Edward I. to have their almuces of grey fur on the outside, with a lining of minever (a kind of ermine). The Sarum Sub-Dean and Succentor, when not canons, had theirs of (black) Calabrian fur externally, lined like the canon's with miniver, while vicars choral had theirs of black cloth lined with lambs wool or goats hair, and these were not to extend below the waist. *Sarum Statutes* (ed. Dayman and Rich. Jones), p. 30; J. Wickham Legg *on the Black Scarf, in transactions of St. Paul's Ecclesiological Society,* Vol. III., p. 42, 1892; W. H. [Rich] Jones, *Fasti Sar.,* pp. 255, 266, 277. See above, pp. 48, 49. In 1437 Chancellor Patrick desired that Bp. Alnwick should direct that the canons at Lincoln should as a rule *(omni tempore)* wear only surplices and almuces, and not black choir copes except when the custom of the church required them to wear these copes *in matutinis de nocte.* (Statutes ii., pp. 374-5.) The Bishop of Lincoln wore surplice and amess as a canon when he was installed. *See above*, "Amitia."

The Vicar's dress is not specified in the Lincoln *Novum Registrum* part 5, only it is implied that it varied with the season; so, presumably, they wore the cloth copes only in summer. And from the white borders in the front of the chorister's gown at the present day we may infer that the boys, and *à fortiori* the Vicars Choral, wore some kind of amess. But of the Canons it is said (part 3) that they are to wear (1) white linen *surplices*, and (2) grey almuces, *almicias de griseo*, and (3) black woollen cloth *copes*, of reasonable length. Their hair is to be cut round like a wheel, and the tonsure " *sine stripulo angulari.*"

St. Christopher's Altar in the Nave. It was probably near the N.W. door, or at the other end of the north alley of the nave near the choir screen. See Maddison's *Wills*, p. 19, no. 43, cf. id. p. 11, no. 22.* In 1531 Thomas Alford's chaplain said mass here at 9 o'clock. An order had been made 19th Oct., 1492, that in future Morning Mass should be sung here instead of at St. Nicholas' altar Maddison's *Vicars Choral*, p. 68. Among relics at

---

* " St. Christopher's Altar in the nave " may have been, perhaps, under the Rood tower: but, at all events, it would in all probability stand in some conspicuous place. The authority to which I refer in the text is " *Lincolnshire Wills*: First Series, A.D. 1500-1600, with notes and an introductory sketch by the Rev. A. R. Maddison, F.S.A." ; Lincoln, 8vo, 1888.

Lincoln was a tooth of St. Christopher in a crystal and silver gilt ampulla, and another relic in a silver gilt double cross florée. See also "Gilds" and "Apertura." St. Christopher had a 'new image' about 1399.

CHURCHES IN LINCOLN. I take the following list from the late J. F. Wickenden's papers. See also the map of Lincoln parishes in the Muniment Room:—All Saints, Hungate; All Saints, in the Bail; St. Anne, Thorngate; St. Andrew; St. Andrew above hill; St. Andrew; St. Augustine, or Austin; St. Bartholomew (now in St. Martin's); St. Bartholomew's Chapel in the Close; St. Bavon; St. Benedict; St. Botolph; St. Clement; St. Clement; St. Cross ("the prebendal church of Holy Rood"—*Venables*); St. Cuthbert; St. Denys ("the prebendal church of Thorngate"—*Venables*); St. Edmund; St. Edmundi iuxta Minores (*Statutes* ii., 393); St. Edward; St. Edward; St. Faith (Fides); St. Giles (Egidius); St. Gregory; St. James; St. John Baptist; St. John Evangelist; St. John Evangelist; St. Katharine without the gates; St. Lawrence; St. Leonard; St. Margaret (in Minster Yard); St. Margaret ("the Chequer Church"); St. Mark; St. Martin; St. Mary Magdalen; St. Mary, the Cathedral Church; St. Mary, Crackpole [*i.e.*, Creek Pool, Brayford]; St. Mary-le-Wigford; St. Michael-on-Hill; St. Michael; St. Nicholas; St. Paul *(olim Paulinus)* in the Bail; St. Peter-in-Eastgate; St. Peter-at-Pleas *(ad placita)*; St. Peter-at-Arches ("the Corporation Church");

St. Peter's Superior; St. Peter stanhegate al's stantheked; St. Peter at the Chine Market; St. Peter le Wigford; St. Peter-at-Gowts; St. Peter; S. Petri ad Pelliforum (Skin Market [*Statutes* ii., 393]); St. Rumbold, or Rumwold; St. Stephen in Newland; St. Stephen; St. Swithin; S. Thomas of Canterbury; St. Thomas' Chapel on the High Bridge; Holy Trinity above Hill; Holy Trinity; Holy Trinity. *Lincoln Prebends* are:—St. Botolph; Sanctae Crucis, St. Cross or Holy Rood; St. Martin; Omnium Sanctorum, Hundegate; Omnium Sanctorum, Thornegate. (Precentor Venables says: " St. Denys, Thorngate."—*Guide*, p. 31.)

CIMITERIUM (Coemiterium). The Cathedral Yard requires from time to time to be cleared from beasts depasturing. *Stat.* ii., 391.

Arms not to be borne there. *Black Book*, p. 331.

CISSOR, or SISSOR, or SCISSOR, a tailor. These spellings are found in the Lincoln Succentor's book of 1527. The former is right in this sense, though our common word " scissors " is a mistaken spelling for " cisars." (See Skeat, *Etymol. Dict.*) " Sutori sive cissori lineorum, 3*d.*," on the principal feasts. "Sutori vel cissori pannorum lineorum pro tota septimana [sc. S. Trinitatis] preterita, 2*s.* 3*d.*" A

※ In the foregoing list I cannot say for certain whether the names repeated in duplicate without further distinction (viz., Andrew, Edward, John Evang., Peter, and Holy Trinity) were intended by Preb. Wickenden to imply that he had found so many churches of the same dedication, for I do not know precisely the circumstances under which his list was made. He may, for example, have meant that he required a supplementary box as a receptacle for more numerous documents concerning the parishes in question.

mender of vestments, "reparitor," was also provided by the Treasurer : a poor person to repair vestments, copes, and cloths, the Treasurer finding his thread (silk, linen, or hemp, as required). *Nov. Reg.*, part i.

CLOCK. The old clock being in a sad condition, the treasurer T. of Louth, 31st March, 1324, undertook to present a new clock, under the proviso that he and his successors should not have the charge of its repairs. It was by written custom the duty of their office to keep, regulate, and repair the Minster clock. *Black Book*, pp. 285, 350. T. de Luda died in 1329. About fifty years later one of his successors, the beneficent J. de Welbourne, presented a new clock, which was in existence until the 18th century. A sketch of it is in the Gough collection at the Bodleian, showing three quarter jacks or figures of men, one at the top striking the hour, and two at the sides for the quarters. One of these has been preserved in the Cathedral Library. The original 14th century clock case (having done occasional duty as a pulpit canopy at Messingham, whence Bp. Trollope rescued it) has been restored to its old place in the north transept for the clock which has been erected at Lincoln in memory of Mr. Arthur Blakesley, of Bishop's College, Calcutta, by Miss Alicia Blakesley.

COLLACIO. A reading in choir (at Lincoln) selected by the Chancellor from some patristic or devotional treatise, and brought to an end when Bishop, or senior, gave the word (as almost within living memory a Provost of King's used to terminate the daily lessons *ad libitum suum* in College Chapel).

Every evening in Lent (Saturday and Sunday excepted) when Evensong had been celebrated 'hora
sexta' (*Nov. Reg.*, p. 331) the office of the dead came
later, then collation, and compline last of all. There
were also "collaciones sanctorum Patrum" read in
the Chapter House. See below "*Præciosa*," cf.
Novum Registrum, part 3 and 5.

At Salisbury the collatio, after dinner in Lent on
week-days, consisted of a piece from Gregory's *Liber
Pastoralis*, or his *Dialogus de Miraculis Sanctorum
Patrum*, or else was superseded apparently by Vigils
of the Dead. *Tracts of Clement Maydestone*, p. 48.
See above, p. 47. The Sarum Breviary and Legenda
provide the special *Lectio ad Primam in Capitulo*
for the Feast, and throughout the Octave, of the
Assumption and likewise of the Nativity of the
B. V. Mary.

COLOURS. The rule for liturgical colours given
for Saints' days at Lincoln in the latter half of the
13th century in the days of Bishop Gravesend may
be translated as follows :—

(After certain preparations have been made in
quire for first evensong of a double-major feast)—

"Let the Sacrist or his Clerk cause the high altar
to be made ready with ornaments proper for such an
altar for a solemn festival.

Then let him make ready also the silk copes for
the rulers of the choir, and let him see to it that
the copes be such as the feast demands, that is
to say,

If a Martyr (of whatsoever rank, whether Apostle,

Evangelist, or Virgin), let there be copes of red
['rubie,' *i.e.*, rubeae] silk for the main part.*

If a Confessor, green or dark coloured *(fusci)* :
(perhaps for the latter 'brown' or 'russet' would be
a better rendering.)†

If a Matron or one Betrothed *(sponsa)*, saffron.

And the said copes ought to be worn by the
principal rulers of the choir, forasmuch as a thing
must always take its description from its principal
[part or feature]."

The rulers of the second rank *('secundarii')* might
wear copes or vestments of a different set or suit
('sectae').—*Black Book*, p. 367.

Two out of these three Lincoln rules or customs,
which relate to Saints' Days only, do not tally with
the Sarum colour rubric which may be found in
missals of Sarum use.‡   In the Sarum rule saffron is
the only colour assigned to confessors, and its prayer

---

* *Red worsted* was provided for Somerby Church, Lincolnshire.

† Sir T. Cumberworth provided in 1440, for Trinity chapel in Somerby
church a *black* suit "to sing in of *requiem*, or for Confessors." And "for
holy days" black bawdekin (brocade) with green work. In other Lincoln
records we find whole cloth of gold for principal feasts. Red velvet on satin
for the 'highest feasts of Holy Kyrke' (in Somerby Church). Another suit of
red velvet for those feasts which are to be ministered in red, next principal
feasts. White for our Lady and Virgins (not Martyrs). For Lent and Vigils
white "demyt." A double cloth of white and red for Lent, with a plain altar
cloth with frontlet of the same suit. For ferial days (when prayers were said
flexis genibus) white fustian, with black martlets. For Good Friday red. For
week days bord Alexander; *i.e.*, a textile fabric of various coloured stripes in
eastern style.

‡ I ought perhaps to say "do not tally *absolutely*," for to the ceremonialist
yellow and green were interchangeable; and, as Mr. St. John Hope has
pointed out, blue 'almost certainly' was in like manner reckoned the same as
violet or purple, and these last might be used for black.

books moreover knew nothing of godly matrons as forming any distinct class, until (at a comparatively late date)* the church of Sarum undertook more definitely to cater for other dioceses than its own in the form of supplement or appendix ' de communi unius matronæ.' York breviary prescribes certain forms for SS. Batild, Anne, Martha and Pelagia to be supplied de *communi matronae.*

Bp. Thomas Beck left by his will to Lincoln Minster in 1346 his *purple* velvet vestment for the use of the celebrant at solemn exequies of the departed. (*Testamenta Eboracen.* i. 24. Surtees Soc.)

A complaint brought at Bp. Alnwick's Visitation in 1437, declaring that some had worn red instead of white, shows that white was considered at Lincoln, as in other places, the proper colour for the 'Lady Mass.' *Statutes* ii. p. 402.

I have given a list of the Minster altar cloths in

---

* *i.e.*, when printing was applied to produce service-books. I leave this passage about the ' *Commune Unius Matrone* ' as I wrote it, because I believe it to be right in the main, although I find that I was mistaken at the time in thinking that 1519 was the earliest book of Sarum use in which this supplementary (non Sarum) office was provided. I find it in fact to be included in the rare and early printed edition of 1494 (3 id. Feb.) by P. Levet, Paris, whereof an interesting copy, long in hiding in that neighbourhood, at Sawston, has been happily quite recently purchased for the University Library at Cambridge. It contains after the *Commune Sanctorum*, besides ' *Vnius Matrone*,' the 'Commemoratio beati Thome martyris'; and after the *Sanctorale* the three lists of Sundays and of simples with Rulers on which the final Respond at Mattins, or that at first Evensong, was to be sung by two. Then, after a blank, the Translation of St. Chad for Sunday before Ascension Day, and on sig. xx10*b*, a convenient table *De Capitulis dicendis in festis sanctorum secundum vsum Sarum.* Dr. Seager has some observations on the *Commune Vnius Matronae* among the notes on § 94 (pp. 163–5) of his unfinished Sarum Breviary Annotationes breviores (1855), p. xxxij.

Lincoln Inventories (Archæol. liii., 1892), and *Linc. Dioc. Mag.*, No. 21, Jan. 1888, p. 136. Cf. *id.* No. 22, p. 154. Dr. Henderson's *York Missal*, I., p. xxi., and *Manual*, pp. xx.-xxv. Dr. J. Wickham Legg, *Notes on Hist. of Liturgical Colours*, 1882, p. 48, reprinted from the Transactions of St. Paul's Ecclesiological Society, vol. i. W. H. St. John Hope, *English Liturgical Colours* (St. Paul's Eccl. Soc.), 1889, pp. 34-5. E. Peacock, *Engl. Church Furniture*, 1866, pp. 180-185.

'Colours' (probably in the sense of pigments for the paschal taper) were to be provided, among other requisites, by the Treasurer at Lincoln (as elsewhere), according to *Novum Registrum.* See *Statutes* ii., p. 303 ; cf. ii. 98.

CONFRATERNITY OF THE CHURCH OF LINCOLN. The title "confrater et concanonicus" was of old given to each member or the Chapter in relation to his brethren. But "fraternity" was not confined to those who held a prebend or dignity with stall in choir and voice in Chapter, nor was the bond of familiarity confined within the limits of the clerical order or of the male sex. Canute and his brother Harold were received into fraternity at Canterbury, and Athelstan and others at St. Gall. (Rock, *Ch. of our F.*, ii. 321-337.) As early as the 12th century obits of "our sisters" Outhild, Goda, and Merewen, were entered in the Kalendar of the great Latin Bible at Lincoln, still visible in the Chapter Library. A few years after Worcester Cathedral had been dedicated, a confraternity was started there on

St. Wulstan's Day, Jan. 1225, but it was destined to last only for seven years. (*Anglia sacra* i., p. 487.) The Lincoln brotherhood had greater vitality. We find, for instance, K. Edward III., with the Black Prince, D. of Clarence, J. of Gaunt, and E. of Lancaster and Lincoln admitted in 1343. And there was still occasion to write out forms of admission in the two following centuries. *Black Book*, pp. 408. 409. The benefits of fraternity granted by St. Hugh, his contemporaries and successors (such as 33 masses weekly in Lincoln Minster alone—Dimock *Girald Cambr.* vii., appendix F) were duly set forth, apparently by Grosseteste.

CONSISTORY COURT FOR ECCLESIASTICAL SUITS AND ARCHIDIACONAL VISITATIONS. The large chapel at the south-west end of the nave was granted in 1609 to Dr. Hill, Vicar Gen. of the Diocese, for his court. (In Coney's map in the *Monasticon*, 1817-30, it is wrongly called "St. Hugh's" Chapel.) The Dean's Consistory Court was in the central chapel of the S.W. transept.

CONSTABLE OF THE CLOSE. His chamber was entered by a step ladder and small door in the first bay of the Chanter's aisle.

COPE BELL. This was rung as a signal for putting on copes. See Archd. Southam's complaint at Bp. Alnwick's visitation in Oct., 1437. Vicars changed their copes in the *capitarium*, but Canons in their stalls. *Black Book*, 382. See also *Statutes* ii., pp. 355 *margin*, 377. At St. Paul's, London, when there was a procession with copes, the rule

(A.D. 1506) was for the vergers to place a table in the midst of the choir. The copes were laid upon the table and the ministers came in their proper order and took each man his cope quietly, without noise or disturbance. Colet's *Statutes for Chantry Priests*, &c., edited by Dr. Sparrow Simpson, 1890, in *Archæologia*, vol. lii., p. 21. When saying their chantry masses they were to go in clean surplices each to his appointed altar, "et super ea sacerdotalia vestimenta induere," *ib.*, p. 19.

CORONATION OF MARY. See above, "Altare Magnum," and below, "Curialitates."

CORPUS CHRISTI. This term sometimes means the consecrated Host. So in the accounts for 1420, 20s. is the annual payment to John Rouceby for making wax (tapers) for part of the communa, and great tapers for the elevation (leuacione) of Corpus Christi and of Blessed Thomas the Martyr at Christmas. Among the images inventoried by the Treasurer in 1536 was an image of our Saviour, silver and gilt, standing upon six lions, void in breast for the sacrament for Easter Day, having a beryl before, and a diadem behind, with a cross in hand, weighing 37 oz.* There were also among the pyxes a round pyx of crystal, having a foot of silver and gilt, with one image of our Lady in the top, having a place for the sacrament for Rogation Days, weighing

---

* Compare the acoount of the like ceremony described in the *Rites of Durham*, pp. 10, 11, as re-edited for the Surtees Society. Mr. H. J. Feasey has a chapter on ' the Burial of the Cross and Host in the Easter Sepulchre' in *Ancient English Holy Week Ceremonial* (London, T. Baker, 1897), pp. 129 foll.

$21\frac{3}{4}$ oz. Item a round pyx silver and gilt, with the sacrament, weighing $10\frac{5}{8}$ oz. The festival of Corpus Domini, originated in 1264, was enjoined by Abp. Simon Mepham upon the Province of Canterbury in 1332 (Wilkins, *Conc.* ii., p. 560). It is mentioned as of recent introduction in the compilation of Statutes collected in 1523 (? date of document). The celebration of this feast and its octaves not unfrequently gave rise to doubts and difficulties even in the 15th and 16th centuries (see Clement Maydeston's Tracts, and Wilkins' *Concilia* iii., 683), and at Lincoln in 1434 there was apparently some doubt whose duty it might be to read the Epistle and Gospel. Canons J. Marshal and T. Ward threw themselves into the breach and read, lest the high mass should be brought to a full stop, as in point of fact was like to have been the case *("prout alias de veritate cessaret"),* and in order to avoid scandal and an outcry of the people ; but they subsequently (June 12th) protested solemnly in Chapter that their reading then was not to be taken for a precedent or an acknowledgment of any obligation so to do. Of the existence of a Corpus Christi Play at Lincoln we find the following slight indication among "curialitates," charged (among "allocations") in 1478-80, "In commun' canonicorum existent' ad videndum ludum Corporis Christi in camera Johannis Sharpe infra clausum, $17s$. $11d$."

CRUCIFIX. Lights before the Crucifix in choir are mentioned. *Statutes* ii., 403.

ST. CRUCIS. Before the altar of the Holy Rood

Remigius the founder was buried, according to Matthew Paris. The "*Rood* Tower" has been vulgarly corrupted into "the Broad Tower." *(Venables.)* The metrical life of St. Hugh describes the great Crucifix, Mary, and John at the west of the choir. I suppose the Rood Altar was on the floor of the '*pulpitum,*' or rood-screen, answering to the present organ-screen. At Durham the entrance at the west of the choir was not by a single central door, but through two Rood-doors, right and left, with the Rood itself high upon the wall between them. On the western side of the lantern, facing the Rood, was a Jesus Altar *(Durham Rites).*

CRUETS. There were in 1536 "two fioles of silver and gilt" in the custody of the Sacrist. One was in memory of J. Walpole, cir. 1445, the other had "Ihs" engraved on one side, and "Xps" on the other. One of these was "taken out by the Chapter." Later on, Bp. Longland gave a pair for this chapel. *Invent.*, pp. 21, 72. And in 1566 there were "Cruettes—ij. of silver and gilt re- mayning" (*Lincoln Inventories*, p. 80).

CURFEW. Tolled on a great bell in the choir belfry or Rood Tower, or, upon great festivals, on all the great bells, the canons sending their men and a supply of drink, by way (as it was thought) of assisting the ringers. This was at sunset in the summer, but after sunset in the winter. *Black Book,* 370, 385.

CURIALITATES. These payments by courtesy, not of debt, occur in the *compotus* rolls and old account-books at Lincoln. Thus in 1327-8 the said R. [de Carleton, Clerk of the Communa] accounts as paid for the work of the poor of Glentham parish by the hands of John, the present vicar (or in 1334 "of Mr. T. Beek") 7s. Item do. T. de Carleton, clerk vicar of Lincoln, for divers pains expended for the chapter, of courtesy, 6s. 8d. Item to the men who carried the spear-staff ("lanceam" in the 15th century usually called "hastam") from Nettleham (the Bishop's manor) to Lincoln at Whitsuntide, to drink, 6s. 8d. Item to J. de Rothewell for helping at the mass of Blessed Mary at the first hour, 20s. To W. Moghan for charge of the organs (in 1452). To J. Lytyll, junior vicar, for charge and playing (*lusu*) of the organs of the said church, 13s. 4d. To Rob. Dove for organ at Christmas and Nativity of John Bapt., 13s. 4d. Again, to the verderer (*parcario*) of Bytham sending two does, with the expenses of a man bringing the said venison (*ferine*) at Christmas, 3s. 4d. (in 1480). And from 1500 to 1531 I find paid to T. Watson (or other), porter of the Close, as a reward (regard') for the clock, and for Coronation of [the image of] Mary at the feast of St. Anne, 12s.

CUSTURARIA, see "*Sempstress.*"

DALDERBY'S SHRINE. The late J. F. Wickenden has written the history of the overtures made for the beatification of Bp. John de Dalderby, who died 12th Jan., 1320, and has printed it with the scheme for a service in his commemoration. In 1321 J. Wisheart, Bp. of Glasgow, granted 40 days' indulgence to devout worshippers at his tomb, which is in the great south transept at Lincoln. The stone base of his shrine is still to be seen. It is on record that the shrine itself "was of pure silver, standing in the south ende of the greate crosse Ile, not farre from the dore where the Gallyley courte ys used to be kepte." (Memorandum relating to the letter of Henry VIII., 6th June, 1540, written on the inventory book of 1536.)

DAY BELL. Called also, in Latin, "campana diei," and "signum matutinale," thrice tinkled on a great bell by a clerk in choral habit, after lauds, as a signal for the morrow mass.

THE DEAN'S AISLE. By analogy to the "Chanters Aisle," this should be the north choir aisle, parallel to the choir; but apparently Peck, in his addition to Sanderson (*Desid. Curiosa*, p. 304), applies it to the great north transept, or "cross isle," by which the Dean passes to the Deanery. However, the context shows that this is a mere blunder.

THE DEAN'S CHAPEL. On the left hand side as one goes from the church to the Chapter House. Here was formerly an upper storey lighted by windows which looked into the north-east transept. There are structural cupboards, or *apothecæ*, where drugs for the poor, it is said, were stored. There is a piscina or drain in the floor, which is sometimes said to have been used by the dispenser of drugs. It is however possible that it was used by the clerk or sacrist for clearing the mouths of cruets *(phialæ)* for the altar service, which (as Mr. Micklethwaite tells us) was the purpose for which such drains were intended. I have suggested below (p. 148, *n.*) that the Dean's Chapel may have been the chapel which was dedicated in honour of St. George.

DEAN'S EYE. A name for the circular window in the great north transept.

The *Metrical Life of St. Hugh* has the following passage on the circular windows known as the Bishop's Eye and the Dean's Eye:—

Prebentes gemine iubar orbiculare fenestre
Ecclesie duo sunt oculi: recteque videtur
Maior in hijs esse presul, minorque decanus.
Est aquilo Zabulus,* est Sanctus Spiritus auster:
Quos oculi duo respiciunt. Nam respicit austrum
Presul, ut inuitet: aquilonem vero Decanus,
Vt uitet: uidet hic ut salvetur, uidet ille
Ne pereat. Frons ecclesie candelabra celi
Et tenebras lethes oculis circumspicit istis.

DEFUNCTIS. See "Benefactors," "Missa pro Defunctis," and "Works Chantry."

ST. DENYS. (Dionysius, Bp., 9 October.) At this altar was the chantry of W. Lexington, Dean, who died c. 8 Sep. 1272, and was buried in the great north transept, close to the entrance to the Cloisters. Here in 1420 mass was celebrated for Dean Lexington's soul, and for those of J. Wydynton and Nicholas Hyche, but in 1500 at St. Andrew's altar (*computus* fragment). On the position of this chapel see *Williamson's Guide*, p. 73.

THE DOVE. Probably a representation of a dove let down by a string from a hole in the roof in the

---

* *Zabulus* a mediæval form of *Diabolus.* Evil was commonly associated with the north.

ceremonies of Whitsuntide.   See Hone's *Every Day Book*, i. 685, ii. 663.

M. E. C. Walcott's *Traditions of Cathedrals*, p. 195, cites a reminiscence by the lawyer and anti-quary, W. Lambarde, born in 1536, that as a child he had seen at St. Paul's a white pigeon let fly out of a hole in "the roof of the great aisle." In the Whitsuntide distributions, as recorded by J. de Schalby, Canon of Lincoln in 1330, "Clericus ducens columbam" is to receive 6*d*. E. Venables tells us that in later times 1*s*. was the fee. So it is in the *Black Book*, p. 335. "Ducenti" may imply either that he *brought* or produced a tame pigeon, as at St. Paul's, or (as I think more probable) that he *drew* a live dove, or an image of a dove, *with strings*. As Barnaby Googe says:

> On Whitsunday whyte pigeons tame,
>   In strings from heaven flie;
> And one that framed is of wood,
>   Still hangeth in the skie.

Thus at St. Patrick's, Dublin, in 1509, 4*s*. 7*d*. was paid for the cords.

DUPLIFESTARII. It was part of the system of brotherhood in the Cathedral body that invitations to dine should be sent round by the canons or dignitaries to the assistant ministers in time of divine service while *Te Deum* was sung at mattins, or while the chalice was being mixed or "made" for the oblation at mass. *Black Book*, 372, 378. Any canon, however, might give to any minister he pleased a standing invitation, serving for all Double Feasts in the year, once for all. This was arranged on All-hallow e'en, and his guest was called "*duplifes-tarius*" (in the vernacular, perhaps, a *double-feaster*).

EDWARD THE MARTYR'S ALTAR. See St. "Anne."

EGIDIUS. See "Giles."

FABRICK. See "Works."

FERTORY. A portable shrine, a hand-barrow, or bier on which chests, tabernacles, or reliquaries ("phylatoria," "capsule reliquiarum," &c.) were carried in procession, or were at other times allowed to stand. See St. "Hugh." Four "feretra" are noted in the Lincoln inventory of 1336.

LY FFOLCFESTE. A feast at Christmas mentioned in Canon J. Marshall's complaint at Bp. Alnwick's Visitation in 1437. *Statutes* ii. 388.

FLAGELLUM. "Switches" or "flails" of timber ("meremium") were made by the three cathedral carpenters, and put on the great bells. They were of sufficient size or value to be treated as perquisites. (*Black Book*, p. 292.) Whether they were "stays," or chiming hammers, or what, some campanologist will perhaps explain.

FLEMING, RICHARD, Bp. of Lincoln. Ob. 1431. Founder of Lincoln College, Oxford. His chantry chapel is annexed to the Angel Choir on the north of the church. (On its dedication see *Williamson's Guide*, pp. 91-2.)

FLUTE. The night watchman was allowed, if he had the requisite skill, to mark the hours "per fistulacionem." (*Black Book*, p. 386.)

FORMS. There were four moveable benches (formæ) which the sacrist or his clerk had to cover

(? with decent white napkins, "manutergia") on greater double feasts before evensong: one before the Dean, another before the Precentor, a third before the Bishop's seat, when he was present, and the fourth—this last a long music stool rather than a desk—for the Rulers of the Choir to sit on in the midst of the choir. (*Black Book*, p. 366.) It was at the last, or at some other "form in the midst of the quire" that the officiant at procession stood to say the collect or orison in the suffrage, *post introitum chori.* (Ibid. 376.) The "first" and "second" forms, below the stalls or higher step, were occupied by choir boys and vicars; but the latter seem to have sat in their "lords'" (the canons') seats, the stalls, when their respective prebendaries were absent. (See Bishop Alnwick's Visitation, A.D. 1437, *Statutes* ii. p. 409.) According to the famous Sarum Custom-Book the term "*prima forma*" is assigned to the boys of the choir, and "*secunda forma*" to men whose age and deserving had advanced them to the middle rank.

"FRATER, ASCENDE SUPERIUS." When an Archdeacon or dignitary is to be installed, he is first placed in the stall of any prebend to which he is collated (if none be assigned to his office), and presently the person installing him (after shewing him the Psalms of his prebend noted on the tablet hanging above his head) leads him to the stall of his office, saying, "Brother, go up higher." (*Black Book*, p. 275.)

LE GALILEE. The greater southern porch, built

as an entrance from the Bishop's Palace about the time of Grosseteste, has a room above it where now the Chapter muniments are stored, and where formerly the Dean and Chapter took cognizance of offences committed in the precincts in their court of jurisdiction, "*curia vocata le Galilee.*" I believe that the name may have been derived from some incident in the half-dramatic Paschal ceremonies, such as the sequence "Victimæ paschali" (appointed for Friday in Easter week in Sarum use, and sung in five parts), containing the jingling metre—

> Die nobis Maria, quid vidistis in via ?
> Sepulchrum Christi viventis, et gloriam vidi resurgentis.
> Angelicos testes, sudarium et vestes.
> Surrexit Christus, spes nostra : præcedet vos in Galileam.

Missale Sarum, 377. See also the Tuesday sequence "Prome casta contio" (p. 368), which likewise mentions Galilee, as do the Alleluia verse for Thursday and the Easter Day Gospel (374, 362). And compare the first respond at Mattins on Easter Monday and Thursday (Brev. dcccxxiv., dcccxxxviii.), the grail verse at the Thursday evensong, the anthem at lauds on Friday (dcccxli.—iv.), and other references to Galilee in the Breviary for that week. On the Christmas and Easter dramatic dialogues, "Quem quaeritis in praesepe" and "Quem quaeritis in sepulchro," see the *Winchester Troper*, edited for the H. Bradshaw Society by the Rev. W. H. Frere, pp. xvi.—xviii., 17, 145. The *name* of the court occurs at Lincoln at least as early as the reign of K. Edward III. See *Black Book*, p. 110. (At *Durham* the "Galilee" is to the N.W. of the lantern. It contained the altars of Our Lady of Pue,* and Ven. Bede. There, about 1430, T. Langley founded the daily mass of our Lady with organ accompaniment.)

ST. GEORGE. Here, in 1531, Morning Mass was said at 5 a.m., by a priest of the Works Chantry. Mass also was celebrated here at 6 by J. Crosby's chaplain. (Maddison, *Vicars Choral*, 40, 41.) W. de Skipworth gave to the church an ivory chest, with copper handle, containing a relic ("juncturam," a joint) of St. George, for which Lady Joan de Willoughby bequeathed money to make a gold box or cover. There was also a portion of this saint's breastplate enclosed among other relics in a small gold crucifix, and part of his collar bone ("de service," *sic*,) in a 10⅛ oz. gold and silver double cross florée.†

---

* 'Our Lady of Pue,' the old name for our Lady of Pity or Compassion. Thus, Ant. Woodville, Earl Rivers, says in his Will, in 1483, "I will that my heart be carried to our Lady of Pue, adjoining to St. Stephen's College, at Westminster, there to be buried by the advice of the Dean and his brethren ; and in case I die south of the Trent, then I will that my body also be buried before our Lady of Pue."—*Testamenta Vetusta*, p. 380. A representation of the Blessed Virgin sitting with the Body of our Saviour taken down from the Cross and extended in her lap, *Madonna della Pietà*, was a favourite subject for Italian painters. The "ymage of pyte," which appeared as a woodcut, with an indulgence, in Caxton's primer (circa 1487) and elsewhere, and which is fully described in Henry Bradshaw's *Collected Papers*, pp. 89-95, is a different thing, representing our Lord with the marks of His Passion as He appeared in the vision known as ' the Mass of St. Gregory.'

† Mr. Maddison finds that in 1457 the late Dean Mackworth's chantry mass was in "capella sancti Georgii." At first sight it is natural to suppose that this was near Mackworth's tomb, by the S.E. pier of the nave. But it has occurred to me that what is commonly known as the Dean's chapel may have received this dedication in the 14th century, when the cultus of St. George received an impetus.

GILDS. Miss Lucy Toulmin Smith has edited her father's account of six Lincoln Gilds (No. vii. in *English Gilds*, E. E. Text Soc. 1870), and I gather brief notices of four or five others from the *Lincoln Wills*, edited by Mr. Gibbons and Mr. Maddison.

Gild of St. Anne, Lincoln. Ro. Huddleston, citizen, bequeathed 3*s*. 4*d*. to this in 1487. (*Gibbons*, p. 195.) "Gilda s'ce Anne in civitate predicta (Lincoln) vocata *le great guilde* in ecclesia sci Andree Lincoln," 1545. *Chantry Certif.* 33, No. 5. Pageants or Sights of St. Anne's Gild are mentioned in 1514-21, etc., 1555, 1568. Leland says, in the Church of St. Anne.

Gild of St. Benedict, founded (like hardly any other) in honour of "*God Almighty* (and of the B.V.M. and our Lord Jesus Christ"). *Engl. Gilds,* p. 172. Chief days the Purification, and (for morn speeches) Sunday after St. Michael, and Sunday after Epiphany.

Gild of St. Christopher. In 1392 W. Wayte left 6*s*. 8*d*. to this; and in 1416 J. de Kele, Canon residentiary, gave a bequest to the same. (*Gibbons,* pp. 86, 127.)

Gild of St. Clement, the Lincoln Bakers' Gild. Charter 28 May 1523.

Gild of Clerks* of Lincoln. Mentioned 1381. Ro. Appulby, in 1407, gave a bequest to that gild "while it lasts; whenever my name shall be recited

---

* For Clerks' Gilds see Hone's *Every Day Book,* i., pp. 753-4. Rock, *Church of Our Fathers,* ii., 418 *n*., 444, 486 *n*.

among names of the departed, with this antiphon,
Alma Redemptoris," &c.   Ro. Huddleston gave
20*d.* to it in 1487. (*Gibbons*, pp. 107, 195.) Peter
Efford, citizen and notary public, in 1540, who
desired to be buried in the chapel of St. Peter-in-
Eastgate Church, gave 3*s.* 4*d.* to "the Clarks'
Gylde, for to say or sing this antiphon, *Domine
non secundum actum meum Noli me judicare,* &c.
Cum [Ps.] *De profundis clamaui.*" (Maddison's
Wills, No. 61, p. 24.)   Stock and plate lately
belonging thereto mentioned 13 Feb., 1549.

The *Cordwainers*, or Shoemakers, so called
because Spanish leather was supplied from *Cor-
dova*, were under the patronage of St. Blaise
(3rd Feb.). The Cordwainers' Company and that
of the Weavers were the only trading companies at Lincoln distinguished by having a Royal
Charter.   The brethren and sisters accompanied
their graceman yearly in procession from St.
Thomas' Chapel on the High Bridge to the Minster,
each offering ¼*d.* *(Venables.)* In 1519 it was
ordered that so far as possible every man or woman
in Lincoln should be brother or sister, and that they
should pay for each man and wife at least 4*d.*

Gild of Corpus Christi. Founded Easter Even,
1350, for folk of middling rank.   In the will of
P. Dalton, Treasurer of Lincoln in 1401, it is
mentioned that he and the Mayor of Lincoln, and,
apparently, Geoffrey Lesthropp, or Le Scroop,
sometime Prebendary of Heydour, who had died in
1380, had been brethren, and had worn garlands

(probably of silver) when holding the office of "graceman" of the Gild. (*Gibbons*, p. 97.) Gild of Corpus Christi in St. Michael's-on-the-Hill, 1383. *Ibid.*, p. 32.

Gild of the Resurrection of Our Lord. Founded at Easter, 1374. This company keeps herce for the departed, and lights for the Easter Sepulchre. Has Mass and offerings on Wednesday after Easter. Grace after dinner with Ant. *Regina celi, letare. Pater noster.* Recitation of names of brethren and sisters departed. *De profundis.* (This Lincoln grace has more affinity with York, or with Westminster, than with Sarum use. See my *Tracts of Clement Maydeston*, p. 155; Westminster Mass-Book, ed. J. Wickham Legg, iii., col. 1379.) Members of this Gild, and that of St. Benedict, contributed ½*d.* each to palmers going on pilgrimage to Rome, or to St. James of "Galacia," *i.e.*, Compostella, in Galicia. *English Gilds*, p. 175. Mentioned 1526.

Gild of St. Michael-on-the-Hill. Founded on Easter Even, 27 March, 1350, for folk of common or middling rank. Feast on the eve and day of Corpus Christi. *Ibid.*, p. 178.

The Great Gild of B.V. Mary, Lincoln. A semi-religious, semi-mercantile foundation (*Venables*, p. 50). To this Ro. de Sutton, merchant, left 5 marcs in 1413. This is probably the Great Gild of Lincoln to which Ro. Huddleston, citizen, gave 3*s.* 4*d.* in 1487. (*Gibbons*, pp. 139, 195.) The gild-hall, which now goes commonly by the name of "John of Gaunt's Stables," was built in the middle of the 12th century, and still stands on the east of the High Street. It belonged to the church of St. Anne (Leland). Dedicated to St. Anne, parish of St. Andrew (*Chantry Certif.*, 1545). See Venables' *Walks through Lincoln*, pp. 32, 50, 51. This "Great Gild" can hardly be the same as the Great Gild of St. Anne, mentioned above, as Ro. Huddleston's Will, 1487, mentions both the *magna gilda Lincoln* and *gilda Sancte Anne*.

Gild of the Fullers of Lincoln. Founded 28th April, the Sunday before Philip and Jacob, 1297. Finds a wax light before the Rood. None to work on Saturday after dinner, nor on holy days. Brethren and Sisters going on pilgrimage to St. Peter and St. Paul (at Rome) to be accompanied as far as the Queen's Cross without the city, and on notice of return to be met there and accompanied to the monastery. Ordinances sealed with seal of the Deanery of Christianity at Lincoln, 5th Sept., 1337. They seem to have chosen a "dean" for their Gild. *Engl. Gilds*, p. 180.

Gild of St. George. Mentioned 1530, 1540.

Gild of St. Luke. For the Painters, Gilders, Stainers, and Alabaster men of Lincoln. Founded 1525.

The Shoemakers' Hall. Put to the northward, 18 Feb., 1549.

Gild of the Tailors of Lincoln. Founded in 1328. Brethren and Sisters to go in procession at Corpus

Christi Feast. To give 1*d.* for pilgrims : ale to the poor (with prayers) on feast days. *Ibid.*, p. 182.

Gild of Tylers or Poyntours of Lincoln (gilda tegulatorum. Founded in 1346. On each day of the feast of Corpus Christi prayers to be said over 3 flagons and 4 or more tankards, and the ale given to the poor. *Ibid.*, p. 184.

The *Weavers' Company.* A trading gild incorporated by Royal Charter. Most of the others were only licensed.

For the later *Company of St. Hugh and our Lady Bell-ringers* (1612), see "Ringers" and (St.) "Hugh's Bells." And for the Minster Brotherhood (12th—16th century), see "*Confraternity.*"

St. Giles (Egidius, abbat, 1 Sept.). At his altar, in 1531, Hugh de Walmesford's chaplain said Mass at 6 a.m. In 1512, H. Langdell was admitted Ravenser chaplain in Chapel of St. Giles. *D.* ii., 64 (1), No. 26. Two of Ri. Ravenser's chantry priests in succession celebrated between 8 and 9. And Ri. Faldingworth's at 10. (*Vicars Choral.*) About 1400 J. Grantham tells us that the chaplain of R. Faldyngworth celebrated "in capella sancti Egidij." (Fo. 42ª.) Also Gilbert Thymbelby, who was a Ravenser chaplain, desired to be buried 1544 at the south end of the altar in St. Giles, though he was actually laid in the Angel Choir. Maddison's *Wills*, pp. 33 (No. 88), 149. (Is there any evidence earlier than Brooke's Guide, 1840, that the chapel where the Taylboys chantry and monuments are was named St. Giles' Chapel?) As

to identification, see the opinion expressed in
" Williamson's Guide," 1890, p. 72.

The Hospital of the Poor of St. Giles, outside
Lincoln. This was made over to the Vicars *cir.*
1275-80. It afforded a home of rest for infirm
Vicars, and supported a chaplain for the souls of
Canon Walter de Welles (1242) and W. de Newport
(*cir.* 1270). *Vicars Choral,* pp. 12, 13, 61. A
"clerk of the hospital" was to be paid a small
sum for the following obits in 1330-40 and 1527;
H. de Lexington, Ri. de Gravesend, H. de Cicestria
and Colswayn, and Simon de Bamburgh. The
ruins of the hospital are on the left side of the
left-hand road (Langworth-gate) going by Eastgate
eastward from the Minster. See *Novum Registrum*
(*in fine*). Statutes, ii., p. 363, *n.* *Cf. ibid.*, 193,
376, 382, 393, 470, 806, *n.*, 839.

"Gloria laus et honor." The hymn in olden
time sung on Palm Sunday morning by seven
boys in a high place, at the second station in the
procession on the south of the church, before going
(at Salisbury) through the cloisters to the west
front. (*Sarum Processionale,* p. 52.) It is the
original of No. 98 in *Hymns Ancient and Modern.*
This antiphon at Lincoln was sung by boys in a
procession on Palm Sunday, either at the mediæval
southern arch which spanned the Bail (until it
was taken down in 1775), or at some other
station where the Cathedral carpenters had hung
a pall, and placed seats decorated with hangings
for the Canons. (*Black Book, i.e., Statutes* i.,

p. 292.) See *Flores Historiarum* (Rolls Series) i., p. 418.

GRADALE. A grayle or music-book for the service of the Mass was kept in the choir-seats; probably one on each side. (*Statutes*, ii., 398.)

LY GRECEFOTE. The bottom of the "Grecian stairs" (Greesen, *i.e.*, steps). (*Statutes*, ii., 395, 396.)

GRATES. The carpenters and the glazier were bound to cover and uncover "grates" in Lent. *Black Book*, p. 291. This was, perhaps, connected with the ceremony of covering the images, as it certainly was with hanging the "Lenten veil" before the high altar. Perhaps the word is a form of "crates," and means the same as herces, or, possibly, lattices in front of cupboards or recesses containing relics. It would be natural to translate it "without fee," but that there is no other "object" to the verbs. Moreover, "grates" is the English equivalent for the French "*grille*." It is interesting to find the term "in the grates" in use in 1681 (Bishop Ken's time) at Wells, probably (says Canon C. M. Church) with reference to the fifteenth century ironwork of Bp. Beckington's chantry chapel.* See Ducange, *Gratus*=une grille.

GROSSETESTE. See "Robert."

GUTHLAC'S ALTAR (ST.). This is mentioned in the list of altars in *Registrum Antiquissimum* between St. Stephen's altar and that of St. John

---

* *The Prebendal Stalls and Misericords in the Cathedral Church of Wells.* (Archæologia Lond., vol. lv., p. 336.)

the Evangelist. I am convinced that this old-fashioned saint had to make way for the *cultus* of St. Anne.

HEARSE. In the Obit-List of 1527 we find—For Bp. W. Smith, "To the Treasurer for wax 15*d.*," "pro erectione le hers, 2*d.*" For T. and Margaret Fitzwilliam, "pro cera circa le hers, 8*d.*," and "pro erectione le hers, 2*d.*" Also, for Dean Flemynge, "ordinanti et preparanti les hers in die obitus, 1*d.*" The "herce" or "hers" was an open-work frame of wood or iron placed round a tomb. It was sometimes wagon-shaped, or arched, at the top (see Rock, *Ch. of Our Fathers*, iii., p. 92) sometimes gabled. It had on the top edge certain perpendicular pricks or spikes for tapers, which gave it something of the appearance of a *harrow* (cf. *ericeus*, a hedgehog), whence its name. Mr. Peacock has given a drawing of a portion of such a hearse which he got in a ruined condition from Snarford Church. (*Engl. Church Furniture*, pp. 26, 126-8.) It has for the upper frieze a thin plate of latten, with the inscription, "Aspice quid prodest transacti temporis euum : Omne quod est nichil est, preter amare Deum." The term thus applied to the catafalque and *chapelle ardente* combined, was originally applied to the triangular stand for the 24 tapers of the mattins service of *Tenebrae* on the "Still Days" in Holy Week, which has the appearance of a transverse section of a catafalque with candles. An iron hearse is attached to one of the Marmion tombs in Tanfield Church, Yorkshire, and one of brass to the effigy of Richard, Earl of Warwick (1439). Those at Lincoln were evidently either temporary structures of wood, &c., or else an iron framework, transported from one chapel to another as occasion served. There is a trace of " a herse of timber to be sett above . . . " in the Commissioners' return of the Cathedral ornaments, to be destroyed or retained, in 1566.* The elaborate hearse of Abbot Islip at Westminster, 16th May, 1532, has been frequently figured (*Vetusta Monumenta*, iv., No. 48 ; Rock's *Ch. of Our Fathers*, ii., 500). One designed by Inigo Jones for King James I. is in Nichols' *Progresses of King James*, iv.—iii., 1049. That for King Charles I., with a cross on the pall, but no lights visible, at least in the scope of the picture, in J. Fuller Russell's *Hierurgia Anglicana*, p. 333, from Sylvanus Morgan's *Sphere of Gentry.* Neither of these retained the gabled form.

St. Hugh's Bells. St. Hugh's tower, the southern of the two western towers, contains a peal of eight. I have given an account of the " Companye of Ringers of Sainte Hughe Bells and our Ladye Bells," which, no doubt, was started as a consequence of the new interest in bell-ringing when Great Tom was re-cast (then in the N.W. tower) in 1610. It is in St. Hugh's tower that there is the Chapel of the ringers, with the list of names,

---

* The list is but a fragment, one half being torn off lengthwise. A careful print of the words and letters which remain is given in *Archæologia* liii. (1892) among *Inventories of Lincoln,* § xi.

1612-1725, partially given in my papers communicated to the Lincoln Architectural Society in
1889-90, *i.e.*, so far as they remain legible. See
Statutes ii., 626-7.

St. Hugh's Altar. The southern apsidal chapel
in the N.E. transept is sometimes called St. Hugh's.
He desired to be buried along by a wall of the
chapel of his patron St. John the Baptist, which
was on the north side of the church. (*Magna Vita*,
V. xvi., VI. xx., pp. 340, 377.) And there his
head was preserved after his translation in 1280.
See below, at pp. 166-7. We read, however, more
than once of an "*altar* of St. Hugh." " [Pers]one
de Paxton ab abbat de Edenbro', 12*li.* de dicta
decima fact' altari beati Hugonis 12*li.* 13*s.* 4*d.*"
(Jordan de Ingham's accounts, 1271.) The Bokyngham chaplain said mass at 6 a.m. at St. Hugh's
altar in 1531. (*Vicars Choral*, p. 41). Was this,
perhaps, in the chapel of St. Hugh's *belfry* at the
west end? We read that chaplains of Bp. Hugh de
Welles' chantry said Mass "*at Peal altar*" at
7 o'clock; likewise that they said a Mass "at St.
Hugh's altar." (*Vicars Choral*, p. 41.) Are the
two identical? According to the plan by J. Coney,
in the modern edition of Dugdale's *Monasticon*,
" St. Hugh's Chapel " is the name of the Bishop's
Consistory Court. Browne Willis (*Survey of Cathedrals*, ii., p. 34), on the authority of Cotton MS.
Tiberius E. 3, places the chantry of Bp. Buckingham,
which was endowed with Lillford Rectory, at St.
Hugh's Chapel. So also Maddison, *Vicars Choral*,

p. 41, from an act of 1531. The chronicle of Louth Park Abbey, p. 16, after mentioning the murder of little St. Hugh, 1 Aug., 1255, says that a few days earlier (15th July) "the altar of St. Hugh was consecrated." See below, "Peal Altar."

ST. HUGH'S TOMB. Behind the centre of the reredos. This was solemnly censed at Evensong and Mass. (*Black Book*, pp. 368, 380, cf. 393-4.) The Treasurer placed a light upon it on the anniversary day of each Bishop of Lincoln, and two on St. Hugh's own day (*ibid.*, 289-90). Offerings were made at it (*ibid.*, 243, 335). *Cf.* Precentor Venables' paper on the *Shrine and Head of St. Hugh*, 1893. See an account of its opening, by E. V., in *Linc. Dioc. Mag.*, Feb., 1887, p. 25. In 1401, P. Dalton, Treasurer, bequeathed 12*d.* each to the two night watchmen at St. Hugh's Tomb. (*Gibbons*, p. 97.)

ST. HUGH'S SHRINE. This stood "on the backe syde of the highe aulter neare unto" (Sanderson adds "north of") "Dalyson's tombe, the place wyll easlye be knowen by the Irons yet fastned in the pavement stones ther." It was removed "to our Jewyll house," by order of Henry VIII., 6th June, 1540, after which the above account was written. In 1641, Ro. Sanderson stated that it was "of beaten gold, and was in length 8ft., and 4ft. broad, as is now to be seen. The irons only now remaining." See Lincoln *Inventories*, by Chr. W., in *Archæologia*, vol. 53, 1892, p. 92. Peck, *Desid. Curiosa*, p. 317. W. Stukeley's *Itiner. Curios.*, tab. xxix.

"FERTUR" OR FERETORY OF ST. HUGH. John Welburn, Treasurer, who died in 1381, gave "one great fertur ('*feretrum*') silver and gilt, with one crose Iles* and one Steple in the mydyll and one crose in the toppe, with 20 pinnacles and an Image of our Lady in one end, and an Image of St. Hugh in the other end, having in length half a yard and one inch; and it is sett in a Table of Wood and a thing in the middle to put in the Sacrament, when it is borne; weighing 17 score ounces and one." This remained till 1548, the other four *feretra* having been plundered. *(Inventories, pp. 14, 44.)*

Keepers of St. Hugh's Altar are mentioned in *Vicars Choral*, pp. 51, 52, A.D. *cir.* 1263-75, 1329. And on p. 50 "Adam de Feretro [Sci Hugonis]" occurs in 1260.

ST. HUGH'S RELICKS. In a 15th century inventory of jewells, &c. (a fragment), we find noted a *tooth* of St. Hugh in a "phylaterium" of crystal standing on four feet with a pinnacle at the top weighing, with the contents, 2 oz. Among tabernacles with relicks, an angel of silver gilt, with two wings spread, standing on six lions, holding in his hands a fertory (now moveable) containing the *finger* of St. Hugh, a little chain silver gilt, 31 oz. A round crystal pyxe ornamented with silver gilt below and above, with *relicks* of St. Hugh and

---

* "One Crose Iles" (1536); "one Crosse Iles" (1548). The somewhat earlier latin inventory unfortunately wants the leaf which would have given us more light as to this phrase. I suppose it means that the reliquary in question was in structure like the model of a church with aisles, &c.

others, 10 oz. In 1536 only the first and third of these remained. In the interval "the *hede* of seint hugh, closed in silver gilt and enamelled" (with 3 old nobles and 2 ducats of gold rivetted in it), "a *toyth* of seint hugh, closed in byrall with silver and gilt," and "*oyle* of seint hugh, in birrall, closed with silver and gilt," besides his mitre, pontifical ring, bede cloth, a book called *Cum animadverterem* (possibly Cato *de moribus*) and several other "relikes, jewels, and othe stuff belonging to St. Hugh head," were delivered to Sir W. Johnson, 27th Nov., 1520. (*Inventories*, pp. 11, 12.)

LITTLE ST. HUGH'S SHRINE. The tomb (with remains of the tabernacle work above it) where lie, lapped in lead, the remains of "young Hew of Lincolne," said to have been slain by a Jewess on a Friday in 1255, and discovered in the house of Jopin the Jew, stands in the ambulatory passage against the outside of the southern wall of the choir, at the back of the *Decani* Stalls, opposite the arcade of the choristers' vestry. (See Chaucer's *Prioresses Tale*, Lives of the Saints, Aug. 27th. Whytford's *Syon Martiloge*, 1st Aug.*) Oblations "parvi Hugonis" are mentioned above under "*apertura.*" The tomb was opened by Dean Kaye and Sir Joseph Banks in 1791, and a body, 3ft. 3in. long, discovered, wrapped in lead. An account by Matthew Paris, *Hist. Angl.*, f. 784. A paper on

---

* Aug. 27th fell on a Friday in 1255. Aug. 1st was Sunday. The date given in the Louth Park Chronicle is 1st Aug. 1255, and the boy is said to have been nine years old.

Little St. Hugh is cited in Wild's *Lincoln*, p. 27, from *Archæologia*. Lethieullier, the writer of it, visiting Lincoln in 1736 was shown a statue of a boy, made of freestone painted, about 20in. high, with *stigmata*, and bleeding wound on the right side. He thought that the shrine given in Stukeley's *Itinerarium Curiosum* belonged to this infant.

IMAGES. Doubtless there was a large number of images of saints in the Minster. The late 15th or early 16th century Treasurer's inventory mentions certain images of precious metal. One "*of Christ*, silver gilt (with a void place in the breast, to hold the Host at the time of the Resurrection)* standing upon six lions. A beryl before and a diadem at the back of the head, a cross in the hand, 37 oz." One "*of Mary*, Mother of God, sitting in a chair, silver and gilt, with jewels in crown, holding a figure of her Son on the right, a sceptre with three pearls in the left, a shield or ouche enclosing the relick of her hairs, 23 oz." The Child held a ball with cross, silver gilt, in His left hand. The inventory of 1536 tells us that this "grett Image" was the gift of Ro. Mason, who was Precentor 1482-93. (*Inventories*, pp. 4, 5, 16.) The latter of these was probably seized as a "supersticious reliquye" when much plunder went to the King's jewel house in 1540; but the image of our Saviour was allowed to remain till 1548 (p. 45), when it was devoted to the repair of the Minster. In 1565-6, "Images—none remaynyng," was the return to the Queen's visitors

---

* "For the Sacrament on Estur Day." *Inventories*, p. 16.

(p. 80). We read in the *computus* of 1420 of the "*Image at the Dean's tomb,*" "Image of *our Lady of Grace,*" "Image of *our Lady on the south of the choir,*" and "Image of *St. Christopher.*" In the accounts for 1399-1400, the last named is described as *new.* In 1537, J. Burton, Burghersh chantry priest, desires to be buried "in the northe yle unto the ymage of St. Christopher." *Maddison,* No. 43, p. 19. Ro. Awbray's will, 1535, speaks of an *Image of our Lady,* apparently on or over the high altar. (See below "Piscinas" No. 1.) In 1433, J. Cotes, Canon, desired to be buried in the chapel *of St. Thomas* "before the image of that saint" (Apostle or Abp. ?). *Gibbons,* p. 158. J. Parkyn, vicar choral, 1 Sept., 1548, desires to be buried "before the *late Image of St. Oswald* of the north syde of the high altare." (*Maddison,* No. 103, p. 38.) In 1537, Ro. Dowffe, vicar, who played the organ for the Lady Mass and Jesus Mass, to be buried "in the north yle before the ymage *of St. Rooke* (St. Roch). *Id.,* No. 44, p. 19. The chapels in which structural brackets (apparently pedestals for images) still remain at Lincoln are as follows: St. Nicholas (N.E. of Angel Choir); St. Blaise (Russell's Chantry), *two*; in Longland's Chantry, several never completed: opposite the Galilee door (St. Thomas's [? of Canterbury] altar); and St. Mary Magdalen's (the Morning Prayer Chapel).

THE IRONS. An altar and chantry, where Katharine Swynford (mother of Henry Beaufort, Bp. of Lincoln), Duchess of Lancaster (d. 10 May,

1403) was commemorated by a Mass at 7 a.m. in 1531. (*Vicars Choral*, p. 41.) It will be remembered that the tomb of her daughter, Joan of Westmoreland (d. 13th Nov., 1440), stood parallel to that of the duchess until it was crowded in at the foot under the same canopy by Bp. W. Fuller, *cir.* 1670. Can room have been found for a minute altar where the second tomb now stands? The panel which her effigy faces may have had a picture or crucifix in it. Possibly the irons may have enclosed a small space outside the presbytery at the south of her monument, so that the celebrant should be unmolested by passers by. Or, again, it is not impossible that there should be a second altar in the choir, though hardly (I think) so far eastward.*

---

* There were two altars in the choir at Ely (as Dr. Stanton tells me), the high altar and the " altar in choir," near which, at the entrance of the present choir, where the original slab still covers them, Bishop Hotham's remains were laid to rest in 1337. The stone canopy over his tomb was removed under one of the arches at the side further eastward in 1771. It is said of his place of burial, " Ipse autem sepultus est in ecclesia sua cathedrali apud Ely, et honorifice collocatus *ad partem orientalem altaris in choro*, versus *magnum altare.*" Wharton *Anglia Sacra*, p. 648, *Liber Eliensis* abridged. In the ecclesiastical province of Rheims, as Mr. Edmund Bishop informs me, an altar in the *chevet*, to the east of the high altar was very common, and the custom spread elsewhere, through the Premonstratensians. But the more remarkable arrangement at Ely (and perhaps at Worcester) was due to a different cause. At Ely the *old* high altar was only one bay eastward of the east line of the transept walls, and the monks' choir was under the lantern. In the middle of the 13th century the building was extended eastward ; a new high altar was dedicated within the added portion (the cathedral choir of modern times) and the former high altar stood in the old place, but became known as "*altare chori.*" It is, I believe, a moot point among antiquarians whether the principal or high altar at Salisbury stood, in 1258, at the eastern transept line beneath the painting of our Lord in Glory, near which is a winch (devised, it is supposed, for the Lenten veil or for the Paschal taper); or whether it stood

St. James' Altar. In the Chapter Acts A. 2. 33, fo. 45ᵇ (Feast of St. Katharine, 25 Nov., 1441), repairs were needed for "windows of the western dove [-cote ?, 'columbe occidentalis'] near the pinnacle, which is mounted by the steps hard by the chapel of St. James." Mr. Maddison suggests that the altar in question may have been in the place where fuel is now kept, and the pinnacle will then be identified as that on the northern turret which is surmounted by a figure with a horn, commonly reported to be a representation of the excellent "Swine-herd of Stow" who (as tradition says) contributed a peck of silver pennies to the minster fabrick. As to the *reputed* position of the Chapel of St. James, see Murray's *Handbook to Cathedrals.* Nothing is said of any Mass celebrated there, in the list of 1531 ; but possibly it was there that one of the Vicars sang Mass between 8 and 9, viz., either for Aveton Chantry, Lacy, Rowell and Luda, or Pollard, or (less probably) for K. Edward II. and Isabella ; for the altars in these instances are not specified. Maddison's *Vicars Choral,* pp. 42-3.

The Jesus Mass. This had an organ accompaniment, cir. 1520, 1536. *Vicars Choral,* pp. 24, 45. Bp. Smyth's will (1514) provided

in something more near to its present position further eastward. The plan dated 1733 (fifty years before James Wyatt was allowed to obliterate almost every trace of the history of Salisbury Cathedral Church), which was reproduced by J. D. Chambers, shows an enclosed space behind the high altar (in the last-named position) somewhat as it was at Lincoln and Peterborough, and at Winchester and elsewhere.

that his chantry priest, with at least one Vicar choral and the Master of the Choristers, together with the boys, should every Friday sing "*Missam de Nomine Jesu, vel de Quinque Vulneribus, cum nota,*" before the crucifix on the south side of the church. (Ro. Churton's Lives of Founders of Brasenose College, p. 516.)*

St. John Baptist's Altar. This altar was being rebuilt and refurnished by St. Hugh at the time of his death, and he had once hoped to dedicate it. By his express desire he was buried along the wall to the south of it. And here his head was kept after the translation of his tomb to the Angel Choir in 1280. At St. John Baptist's Altar was the chantry of King Edward II. and Queen Isabella, and Mr. Maddison has recently observed that in the Chantry Register A. 1. 8. ? fo. 1. the *viscera* of Q. Eleanor were deposited by St. John Baptist's Altar. (Browne Willis, citing Cotton MS. *Tiberius* E. 3, calls the altar where K. Edward II. was commemorated "St. Mary's Altar." *Survey of Cathedrals*, ii., 34.) In J. Grantham's book, *cir.* 1500, I find at fo. 41ᵇ a payment to "a

---

* At *Norwich* the "Jesus Chapel" is an apsidal chapel north east of the presbytery. The organ over the reredos of the high altar did duty for masses in this chapel as well as for choral mass. At *Durham* "Jesus Mass" was sung every Friday at "Jhesus Altar," on the west of the lantern there, opposite the choir door, the Master and the quiristers singing in a loft or gallery to the north. They sang also "Jesus Anthem" in the body of the church after evensong in choir on Friday night, with another anthem, to the tolling of the Galilee bells. *Rites of Durham*, p. 29. Dr. Rock, *(Ch. of Our Fathers*, iii., p. 113 n.)* identifies "Jesus Mass" with that of the Five Wounds. I think it was the Mass of the Most Holy Name.

chaplain celebrating at St. John Baptist's altar for the souls of K. Edward and Isabella his consort." Here, according to Grantham, was a Mass for "H. Lexington, sometime Bishop" (but see next entry). Here, in 1531, were the chantry Masses of W. de Tornaco's and W. de Wynchecumbe's vicars successively between 8 and 9 a.m. (*Maddison,* pp. 42, 43.) The Cotton MS. *Tiberius* E. 3 (cited by Browne Willis, *Cath.* ii., 34), places the chantry of Simon Barton, W. Gare, and W. Thornton at "St. John Baptist's altar." According to the obit list of 1527 (A. 2, 8, fo. 31^b) the chantry of Henry, Duke of Lancaster, "de fabrica beate Marie," paid 12d. to the priest celebrating Mass (on his obit) at the altar of St. John Baptist. In 1383, W. de Belay, citizen of Lincoln, left by will (*Gibbons,* p. 32) torches to the chapel of St. John Baptist, &c. Mass of the Blessed Virgin ("cum nota") with organ accompaniment, was sung here daily "at the first hour" in 1428, 1434, 1436, 1531, &c. (*Ch. Acts,* p. 118^b.) Thus in the Chapter Act, of 24 Apr., 1428, it was ordered " pro novis organis in capella sancti Johannis baptiste vbi missa cotidiana beate Marie virginis cum nota celebratur, et pro emendacione antiquorum organorum in choro maiori, soluend ix. lib." A. 2. 32, fo. 46, cf. fo. 118^b (1436). On difficulties as to the identification of this altar see Venables' *Shrine and Head of St. Hugh,* Maddison, *Vicars Choral,* pp. 31-2.

St. John the Evangelist. The book of J.

Grantham (fo. 42), *cir.* 1500, tells us that the chaplains of Bp. J. de Dalderby's chantry, and those of Sub-dean Henry de Beningworth and his brothers, Sir Robert and Thomas, were here. In 1531, Bp. H. de Lexington's chaplains celebrated at 7 and 9 a.m. respectively, and the Beningworth chaplain (a Vicar) still said Mass here between 8 and 9. (*Vicars Choral*, 41, 42, 43.) Before the altar of St. John Evang. (*cir.* 1260) were laid the corpses of Vicars and junior members of the Church, attended by the choir. (*Black Book*, p. 395.) From the obit list of 1330-40 it appears that Bp. H. de Lexington's chantry paid 12*d.* "to the clerk of the altar of B. John" (*Martilogium*).* The chaplain of H. Lexington's chantry was, in Feb., 1431-2, liable to provide candles for the 'choir' where the daily Mass of our Lady, called *Salve sancta parens*, is celebrated. (*Chapter Acts*, 59ᵇ.)

JUDAS. One of the candles in the herce for *tenebrae* in Holy Week represented the traitor, and is sometimes called the Judas candle, at least by modern writers. The antiphon sung at lauds on Maundy Thursday, when the *last* light was darkened, was "He that betrayed Him had given them a token." (*Brev. Sar.*, dcclxxxii.) But what appears as "a Judace," "the Jewes light" (mentioned with "the pascall post, the sepulcre," and

---

* *Martilogium* is the name given to (A. 2. 3.) a register written in the second quarter of the 14th century by John de Schalby, Canon of Lincoln. See the indexes to the Lincoln *Black Book* (*ed. Cantab.*, 1892), and *Statutes*, part *⁎* (*ibid.*, 1897).

"the maydens lighte," in Peacock's *Church Furniture*, pp. 163-4 *et alibi*, was the forerunner of these modern dummies and save-alls which are sometimes reprehensively painted to counterfeit the true natural wax which, as St. Augustine or some other early writer says, "in substantiam huius lampadis apis mater eduxit." *Processionale*, p. 82. I cannot say whether the name for the wooden save-all was derived from its deceptive character, or from its connexion with the torches in Gethsemane, for Halliwell says that the word is used for the handles or sockets of torches for procession; but the thing is sufficiently explained in the church accounts of St. Mary at Hill, London, 1511. "The Judas of the pascall, *id est* the tymbre that the wax of the pastel is driven upon, weigeth 7 lb." *Ch. Furn.*, p. 163. Rock, *Ch. of Our Fathers*, iv., pp. 244-5. (Canon W. Cooke suggests that the derivation is from *Heb.* vii. 14.) It was put in the upright branch of the paschal candlestick or post, which itself was made of wood, latten, or brass. At Lincoln no judases are noted in the earlier inventories, but in 1566 are "Judaces—iij. of brasse yett remayning." *Inv.* p. 80. Possibly these were bearing-candles for the procession at Mass, or more probably for carrying before the Bishop at pontifical vespers or mattins. See above, "Candlesticks." Also, "now remayning in the old revistrie j alterstone (black), a sepulchre, a (. . . . *word perished*), a crosse for candelles called *Judas crosse*, and other furniture belonging to the same sepulcre, the pascall with the

Images in Fote belonging to the same sepulcre
and a candlestike of wodde." (*id.*, p. 81.) "For
Tymb'r and the making of the crosse that beryth
the Tenebre lyght othur wyze cawlyd the Iudas
light, xviij*d.* It' for pycs' of yron for ye sayd lyght,
iiij*d.* It' for wax for the sayd lyght iij nyghtes,
ij*d.*" (Stanford in the Vale Accounts, 1558-9.)

St. Katharine's Altar. Here chaplains of
the Burghersh chantry said Mass in 1531 at 5 a.m.
and 10; and at 8 o'clock Woolf's chaplain. Here,
too, was Swilingham's chantry. (*Vicars Choral*,
pp. 41, 42; 41. *Muniment*, D. ii., 50, box 2.)
Precentor Venables (in popular books, not citing
his authority) tells us that here Mass was said for
the Brethren and Sisters of the Confraternity of
Lincoln Church. (*Williamson's Guide*, pp. 90,* 121;
Walk through Minster, p. 42.) Browne Willis,
Cath. ii., p. 34, refers to the Cotton MS. *Tiberius*
E. 3, which gives the chantries of Barth. and H.
Burghersh, and Ri. Stretton with W. Woolvey (or
Woolney) at St. Katharine's altar. Stretton had
been prior of St. Katharine's, Lincoln. His chantry
(1334) see *Muniments* D. ii. 51 (box 1); and
chantry register (A. 1. 8.), fo. 4, 6, *et in fine libri.*

St. Katharine's Priory.—This was at the foot
of Cross Cliff Hill to the west of the road south of
Lincoln, but it concerns us here as it is mentioned

---

* I have the authority of the late Precentor (whose loss we feel so deeply,
and that not least in matters relating to the history and antiquities of Lincoln)
for saying that in Williamson's *Guide to Lincoln*, ed. 3, p. 90, line 16,
"St. Catherine" is a mistake for "St. Nicholas."

in the order for reception and enthronization of a Bishop. It was a Gilbertine or Praemonstratensian priory of the foundation of Sempringham. It was founded by Robert de Chesney, A.D. 1148, and was endowed by St. Hugh with the prebend of Canwick, its prior being bound to provide a clerk to follow the choir in the Minster. *Black Book*, pp. 81, 252. The new Bishop spent the night before his installation at the priory and thence walked barefoot to the Cathedral Church, cloth being spread for him and distributed to the poor by his servants after he had passed. *Novum Registrum*, fo. 1ᵇ. Venables' *Walk through Lincoln*, 32, 41.

Kiss of Peace and Loving Brotherhood. After kissing the Altar a new Dean of Lincoln used to be placed in his stall, where he kissed the Bishop and all his Brethren. *Black Book*, p. 280. A Canon on admission kissed first the Dean, or his deputy carrying out the Bishop's installation mandate (*ib.* 274). A Canon likewise, before his departure, kissed the Dean and all his Brethren who had performed the rite of Extreme Unction (*ib.* 295). A layman admitted to " the Brotherhood and Fraternity of this Chapter and this Church of Lincoln" was admitted to the kiss after swearing fidelity (*ib.* 409-10).

As regards similar ceremonies, the little boy (parvus de choro) who came to sprinkle holy water after compline kissed the Dean's hand (*ib.* 370). The two persons who were to cense the altar and tombs, &c., at *Magnificat*, first knelt to say an *Ave*

before the high altar, where carpet was spread at the
upper step, and then kissed the ground. They
likewise kissed the middle of the altar, after censing
it (*ib.* 368). The return to the Commissioners in
1566 says, "paxes—none." And so far as I know
in earlier times there had been at the Minster no
osculatorium or pax *per se.* At High Mass the
Gospeller gave the Priest the Gospel book to kiss,
and the principal Deacon kissed both the "texts,"
and all members of the choir kissed the crucifix
(possibly on the text; *Black Book,* p. 375) while the
Nicene Creed was being recited (*ib.* 379).

LAUNDRESS.—According to the *Black Book,* p.
288, the Treasurer "debet lotrici quatuor s. per
annum." In the Succentor's book of 1527 we
find such entries frequently as "Cissori et lotrici
cuilibet, 3*d.*" At Trinity week, "Lotrici vesti-
mentorum pro septimana preterita, 2*s.* 3*d.*" The
Novum Registrum, part 1, declares that the Chapter
and the Treasurer are to find a laundryman, or
washer-woman, to wash the albes, altar-towels,
towels, or linen. (*Statutes* ii., part 2, p. 303).

LAVATORY. It was the sweeper's duty (1260) to
see that there was a supply of water "in lavatorio
capitarii" for washing hands, and for filling the
chaplains' cruets when they were about to celebrate
anniversary Masses for the dead. The third bell-
ringer was to wait till the Dean (or the Canon in
weekly course) washed his hands after dinner and at
once to begin ringing the first peal for vespers.
(*Black Book,* p. 365.)

LECTERNS.—There were "several in choir and out." These were stripped of their coverings on Maundy Thursday and Good Friday. (*Black Book*, p. 366.) At the lectern in choir the Succentor placed a musick-book, and the 3 canons next in order to him came to sing the Respond at Vespers with the Verse and Gloria Patri (*ib.* 367). Then the cerofers stood by it, having fetched their lighted candles from the high altar for *Magnificat.* The celebrant presently took their place to say the Collect,* the Sacrist and the Canon's Clerk standing on either side. After the Orison, the School Master called some with good voices to sing there ("*organizare*"), or on minor doubles the Succentor deputed some boys for the same purpose (p. 369). At Mattins two of the 2nd form went after the lesson to begin the Respond there (p. 371).

At second Evensong three Deacons sang the verse there (the middle one wearing a silk cope of a different suit from that which his fellows wore (pp. 382-3). Evensong of our Lady was begun there by the Canon in his silk cope, but he put it off and went to his stall with his black choir cope for the Little Chapter and the Versicle before *Magnificat* (p. 385). The 3rd and 6th Responds to the Lessons at Mattins by two Sub-deacons at the pulpit (*margin*) or lectern in choir, the 9th by two seniors at the lectern (p. 387). Before it one who was crossing the choir was to bow before the altar ("*ante*

---

* Only the Collect at Evensong was thus said at the lectern. At the other hours the Orison was said in the stall (p. 385).

altare, in superiori parte chori, *coram* lectrina,"
p. 390).

Ro. Awbray, vicar choral, gave in 1535 "a
carpett to lye upon the banker in the high queare."
(Maddison's *Wills*, p. 11, No. 22.)

A lectern was placed at the head of the dead man
for canons to read the 9 lessons in Vigils of the
Dead, and the Verses were read there by pairs and
the Responds begun, only the last Respond was
sung by three canons (p. 393). At solemn anniversaries of the Dead the lessons were read at the
lectern in choir, but the Verses of the Responds in
the midst of the choir, standing on the stone
inscribed "*cantate hic*" (*Black Book*, p. 395).

In a weird representation of the conversion of St.
Bruno a picture of reading this lesson in choir is
given in 16th century printed Sarum *Horæ* (1529),
at the 4th lesson of Vigils of the Dead.

LINCOLN FARTHINGS.   See *Pentecostals.*

LONGLAND'S CHANTRY.   Below the south door of
the choir, immediately to the west of it.   Bp. John
Longland prepared a chantry chapel, and when he
died (7 May, 1547) his heart was buried at Lincoln
(his *viscera* being interred at Woburn, and his body
at Eton).   But before that date the Commission of
K. Henry VIII. had begun the work which K.
Edward VIth's was soon after to continue in
abolishing chantries.

ST. LUCY'S ALTAR.   In Jordan de Ingham's (or
his successor's) accounts, 1294, "anno octavo," we

find, on the back of an early roll of *Re* and *Ve*, "delivered to Adam Bell, chaplain for the altar of St. Lucye, 13*s*. 4*d*." This is the only mention of this altar which I find.

THE MALANDRIE OR MALANDERY. A hospital of the Holy Innocents founded by Bp. Remigius for the reception of lepers. It stood at the entrance of the South Park. Among J. de Ingham's accounts in 1271 I find:—"Item fratribus hospitalis, Lincoln, 20*d*. Item Leprosis ibidem, 12*d*. Item custodi altaris Beate virginis, 6*s*. 8*d*." The Church of Holy Innocents on the Green had a lepers' chapel of the Blessed Virgin attached to it, but separate from it. Lincoln had another lazar hospital, St. Leonard's, to the north-west; and possibly St. Giles' had originally the same beneficent purpose. (Precentor Venables, second *Walk through Lincoln*, p. 43; first *Walk*, p. 32.) In *Novum Registrum*, part 1, the master "hospitalis beate Marie Magdalene de ly Maladrye extra Lincoln," is mentioned. (*Statutes* ii., part 2, p. 306.)

ST. MARY THE BLESSED VIRGIN. The Minster, or "mother church of Lincoln," is styled in William Rufus' confirmation charter (1090) of the Conqueror's grant of liberties and benefits, "the Church of the Holy Mother of God." And in a charter of K. Henry I. (concerning Biggleswade) A.D. 1132, and in numerous other documents the "church of Blessed Mary of Lincoln." Whether the high altar here was ever (as at Salisbury) entitled the altar of the Assumption I cannot say.

At *Salisbury* the eastern limit of the church was first built, and the principal altar in that part, though destined for the Lady Mass, bore the title of "Holy Trinity (and All Saints)." The retro-choir at *Lincoln* was added 1255-80 (after the new choir of Ely), in readiness for the translation of St. Hugh, and here was the altar of the Blessed Virgin. According to the 4th Injunction of Abp. Courtenay in 1390 the "*missa de die*" was to be celebrated with due honour ("*honeste*") on occasions when the high altar itself was given up to the celebration of a Bishop or a King's obit. The "keeper of St. Mary's Altar" was mentioned, as we have seen just above, in 1271. In 1434 (18th Dec.) Ri. Ingoldesby was "superviser or master of the altar of B. Mary, and her chapel where the Mass of our Lady is sung daily with organ accompaniment," and he was required to provide wax and lights. (*Chapter Acts*, A. 2, 32, fo. 99.) In the 18th century *Chapter Order Book*, 10th Sept., 1771, the northern apsidal chapel in the N.E. transept is called "St. Mary's Chapel"; and Essex frequently styles the same "St. Mary Magdalen's," q.v. (Venables' *Archit. Hist.*, p. ? 28.)

Peter Dalton, Treasurer of Lincoln, gave a pair of silver candlesticks, a blue cope and a green cope, to the Minster. (*Inventories*, pp. 10, 31, 33.) He was buried in the nave (*Desid. Cur.*, p. 312). He died in 1402 *al.* 1405, leaving the position of his burial-place to his dear brother Ri. Wynnewyke and the good will of other my lords his colleagues,* and made bequests to the high altar, the altar of the B.V. Mary ubi celebratur missa *Salue sancta parens*, and to Normanby church. (Gibbons, *Wills*, p. 97.) Browne Willis, *Survey of Cath.* ii. 34, 1742, places at St. Mary's altar the chantries of Dean W. de Thornaco (? Gilb. Humphreyville) and K. Edward II. on the authority of the Cotton MS. *Tiberius* E. 3. (W. of Tournai gave a black cope to the Minster.)

MASS OF OUR LADY. It would seem natural to suppose that this was sung here (as at Salisbury) at the central altar in the *chevet*, due east of the high altar. In Robert Sanderson's time, in 1641, before the troubles, "our Lady's chappel" was the name given to "the middle of the three east chapels." (*Desid. Curios.*, pp. 294-5.) There is the Q. Eleanor monument recently renewed with the old lombardic inscription, "✠ Hic sunt sepulta viscera Alienore quondam regine Anglie vxoris regis Edwardi, filii regis Henrici, cuius anime propitietur Deus: Amen ✠ Pater noster. (See p. 166, "St. John Bapt.") Wherever it was done, the Lady Mass had organ accompaniment, and the celebrant was solemnly assisted by deacon and subdeacon. White was the proper colour for the vestments, but in 1437 the vicar representing the Prebendary of Leicester St. Margaret's in Lincoln Church, at that time a Dean of St. Paul's, complained that

---

* We need some word in English like *confreres* to express the idea of the common brotherhood of canons which was asserted in the days of old by the significant phrase *confrater et concanonicus*.

red was worn. (*Vicars Choral,* pp. 45, 53, 61.) In 1428, 1434, 1436 a Mass of B.V.M. was sung daily at the altar of St. John Bapt., "at the first hour" (*ib.*, p. 32), (cf. "at the hour of prime," *Black Book,* p. 368). About 1330-40 the obit list in Schalby's *Martiloge* (fo. 44) tells us that the chaplain who celebrated Mass of B. Mary "hora prima" had to find 23*s.* 4*d.* to pay for the yearly obit of Simon de Barton. (In 1527 this chantry produced only 18*s.* 4*d.*, unless there is a mistake of *v* for *x.*) He died in 1280, and was buried before the middle altar in the great north transept. At the same altar where the Lady Mass was sung the chaplain of H. de Edenstowe's chantry celebrated at 9 a.m. in 1531. The chantry of W. de Tornaco at the same period was likewise at the altar where the Mass of the B. Virgin was said "prima hora" (*ib.*, 42, 53). Her Mass was to be begun before the bell rang for Prime. (*Black Book,* p. 374.) The order for censing at Evensong in 1260 was for Dean and Precentor together to cense (1) the high altar, (2) tomb of the founder, Remigius, then say *Magnificat* as they made their way [from the nave] to (3) the altar where B. Mary's Mass is celebrated at the hour of prime, (4) tomb of St. Hugh, (5) Dean goes to the altars and tombs on the south side in turn to cense them in order, Precentor meanwhile turning off to the north to do the like. After which (6) they walk together to their places, keeping their own side—*decani* and *cantoris* (*ib.* 368).

COMMEMORATION OF B. MARY. This, as else-where, was a "full service" said every week, except in Advent and Septuagesima; special evensong, mattins with three lessons, and Mass; on Saturday if possible (with 1st evensong on the Friday), or on some other free day. There is evidence of the regular observance of this weekly commemoration in the Rolls of *Re* and *Ve* from 1272, the earliest extant, to the last, 1639-40. When service of B. Mary was said the Treasurer had to provide 3 candles in a bason (pelvi) in choir. (*Black Book*, 290.)

SERVICE OF B. MARY. The Little Office, said hour by hour after the several choir services of the day on all ordinary days, and traced to the 8th century, duly appears at Lincoln. From 1408 or 9 it was ordered that every Vicar on admission should undertake to stay to "mattins of the glorious Virgin, in choir, after mattins of the day," and the Treasurer from much earlier times had been bound to provide two candles in the bason in choir for that service as for ferial mattins. (*Black Book*, pp. 399, 133 *n.*, 290.) The Evensong of our Lady was to be begun at the lectern in choir by the Canon in course after Evensong of the Day, and her Com-pline likewise after Compline for the Day (*ib.* 385). On a few great occasions such as Advent Sunday, Passion and Palm Sundays, and in the three great feasts or weeks of Christmas, Easter, and Whitsun-tide, as on festivals of the B.V.M., the Little Office was not said in choir (*id.* 385).

St. Mary's Tower (the north-west tower). This formerly contained "Great Tom of Lincoln," but the *present* Great Tom (1835) hangs now, with the quarter bells, in the great central tower. Our " Lady bells," a peal of six, bequeathed by Gilbert d'Evyll in 1311, hung in the central tower until they were recklessly melted down when Great Tom (having been cracked in 1828) was re-cast. The company of ringers (1612-1725) whom we have mentioned above (p. 153) went under a double name of " our Blessed Virgin Marie of Lincoln," and " Sainte Hugh Bells and our Ladye Bells in the Cathedral Churche of Lincoln." The Lady bells were rung (2, or, for festal services, 4 of them) by the black-coped choristers for service from the floor of the church : they, *i.e.*, the six bells, " were also chimed in the belfry on Lady Day morning to a chant, which was probably the *Ave Maria, Ora pro nobis*, thus—1st and 3rd ; 1st, 2nd, and 4th ; 1st and 5th ; 1st ; 2nd, and 6th." (Sir C. Anderson's *Pocket Guide to Lincoln*, 1874, p. 93.) When Sanderson speaks of Dean Mackworth being buried S.W. of " our Lady's steeple," he means, no doubt, south-westward of the great central tower, the rood-tower where the Lady Bells were hung. (*Desid. Cur.*, p. 305.)

St. Mary's Gild. This was a trade gild or corporation. I have no evidence that the corporation had a home in the Minster, but it is not *à priori* improbable. See above, pp. 151-2.

St. Mary's Images, &c. In the inventory of

1536 is "a great image of our Lady sitting in a chair, silver and gilt, with 4 poles, 2 of them having arms in the top before; having upon her head a crown, silver and gilt, set with stones and pearls, and one bee with stones and pearls about her neck, and an ouche depending thereby; having in her hand a scepter with one flower set with stones and pearls, and one bird in the top thereof; and her Child sitting upon her knee, with one crown of (*i.e.* on) his head, with a diadem set with pearls and stones, holding a ball with a cross silver and gilt in his left hand, and at either of his feet a scutcheon of arms, with arms: of the gift of Master Mason Chanter" (who died in 1493). This account is similar to that in the earlier inventory, which specifies pearls, diamonds, and other green stones, and says that the moveable "scutum" set with 5 gems and 2 pearls, contained a relic, "Hairs of Blessed Mary." It gives the weight as 23 oz. (*Inventories*, pp. 16, 5.) Figures of St. Mary and St. Hugh ornamented the two ends of the chanter's staff and those of a feretory; and the like appeared in other jewels in the Minster. (*Ibid.*, pp. 14, 21, 19.)

St. Mary Magdalen's Chapel. Here, according to Grantham's book (*cir.* 1500) three vicars celebrated for the soul of Robert and J. de Lacy. (We know that in 1531 one vicar celebrated for J. and Ro. de Lacy, and three for the combined chantry of Lacy, Rowell and Luda, from 8 a.m. successively, and we may conclude that these said mass in that place as in 1490-1510.) Here it is said that Bp. J. Gynewell, who died in 1362, was buried; and in this chapel the chaplains of his chantry said Mass at 6 a.m. and 7 in 1531. (*Vicars Choral*, p. 41.) Remigius having built the Cathedral Church upon the site of the antient parish church of St. Mary Magdalen, the parishioners at first used the nave for their services, and for baptisms, &c. This was found to be inconvenient; and Bp. Oliver Sutton built them a parish church outside the Minster.* About sixty years later Bp. John Gynwell (so Leland says, *Collectanea* i., p. 98, and Godwin *de Præsulibus* follows him) founded a chapel, so that the Penitent Saint might not be altogether neglected in the Cathedral Church; moreover the Bishop was himself buried there. There is everything *à priori* in favour of this statement so far as it concerns the reparation to St. Mary Magdalen's honour, but it has been observed with truth that there are no traces of any chapel added at the date alleged. (1347-62. See Venables' *Architectural Hist. of Lincoln Cath.*, p. 28.) However, the Chapter Act of 1531, cited by Maddison, confirms Leland's statement that there was a chapel of that dedication, and that Bishop Gynewell was there commemorated. I conclude, therefore, that the chapel was of a temporary nature, with, perhaps, wooden screens

---

* At least two rectors of St. Mary Magdalen's parish were buried in the nave of the Minster: one, whose surname was De Branspath, 1376, and J. de Scarle, Sept., some time in the fourteenth century. (*Desid. Curiosa*, p. 310.

clinging to the western pier of the nave, and that the "foundation" consisted mainly in endowing a chaplain, and providing altar, books, ornaments and vestments; and we know from *Inventories* (pp. 14, 44, 64; 25, 50, cf. 65) that he gave a chalice and paten and a red cope to the Minster. The place of his burial at the west of the nave is thus indicated by Sanderson, describing the Minster as he knew it before the Great Rebellion. (*Desid. Cur.*, pp. 305-7.)

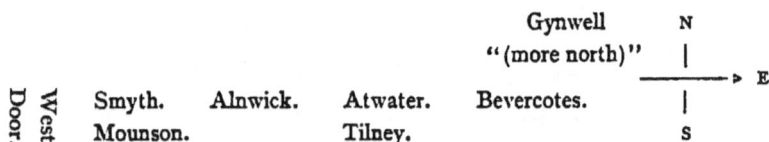

Door.	West				Gynwell "(more north)"	N
		Smyth.	Alnwick.	Atwater.	Bevercotes.	————▸ E
		Mounson.		Tilney.		S

This description brings Bp. Gynewell's tomb near the south partition wall of the morning chapel; and though architectural authorities tell us that this was built before his time (cir. 1230-50, I believe), I think it on the whole the best solution of our difficulties to suppose that his Mass was endowed and established there, and that the chapel had come thence to be known as "Gynewell's," though it was only through the quatrefoils in the screen that his tomb was visible from that altar. In the 18th century the dedications were confused; and when Essex, the architect, speaks of "the chapel of St. Mary Magdalen," he always means the northern apsidal chapel (by many known as "St. John Baptist's") in the N.E. transept. (Venables' *Archit. Hist. of Lincoln Cathedral.*)

"*Mater ora Filium.*" An antiphon of B. Mary,

following *Salve Regina*, &c., in the Sarum Processional, p. 172. Bp. J. Gynewell (who died in August, 1362, and was buried in the N.W. of the nave) gave an endowment from Newbo Abbey for the poor clerks who should sing this anthem. (*Compotus*, 1528.)

MAUNDY. In 1271 we find in an account of petty expenses a charge for slippers for those whose feet were washed at the Maundy. " Item in sotular' die cen' empt' 8s. 4d." In the 15th century, among customary payments, a charge occurs for half-a-dozen or a dozen pairs at 6d. each. K. Henry VII., keeping his first Easter at Lincoln as King, in 1486, washed the feet of 29 poor men in the great hall of the Bishop's Palace. In the Black Book a record of thirteenth century customs tells us that the three cathedral carpenters were required to provide on Maundy Thursday water and vessels for washing the altars and for washing the feet (by Dean and Canons, *Statut.* II. 284), and to warm the water for the latter ceremony " de focali tesaurarii " from the treasurer's fuel (p. 292). On the same day it was customary, at Salisbury, for the Bishop to give a compotation in the Chapter House. Some meal of the kind was provided at Lincoln : for we read (*ibid.*) that the glasier is to find the napkins and cups ("mappas et ciphos "), and that, with the three carpenters and the sacrist and ministers, or servant of the church, he is to have his supper "after the Great Supper." The treasurer himself was to provide towels and wafer cakes (*manutergia*, *nebulas*, the latter being the wheaten "obleys") and wine. (*Ib.* 288.) An account of payments on behalf of the Chapter at a time when the office of treasurer was vacant and in commission (in 1406, as I believe) is preserved. It contains the following items :—" In iz (*i.e.* 1lb.) flour frumenti emp' pro obleys fact' contra diem cene pro le maundy, 2*s.* 6*d.* Et in expens' circa facturam de dict' obleys hoc anno 19½*d.* Et in focali empt' ad idem tempus 2*s.* Et in 6 lagen. vini empt. pro cena Domini (prec' lagen' 12*d.*) 6*s.* Et in 24 lagen. ceruisie emptis pro dicta cena Dñi 3*s.* 8*d.* Et in thak' empt' pro choro per duas vices 16½*d.* Et in frankinsens mixt. empt. pro hoc anno per sacristam, 5*s.*" Hence we see that 6 pitchers of wine and 24 of beer were provided by the Chapter, in ordinary years through the treasurer, for the "potus." On Maundy Thursday and on Good Friday all lecterns (as well as altars) were stripped, "to signify the nakedness" of our Saviour's Body at His Passion. (*Black Book*, p. 366.) Another ceremony on Maundy Thursday, the Reception of Penitents (ejected on Ash Wednesday), was performed by the Dean, if the Bishop were absent. (*Stat.* ii. 284.)

St. Michael's Altar. In 1420 Mass was celebrated here for the souls of Geoffrey Maudlyn and Geoffrey Pollard; also of W. Aveton and W. Hemmyngburgh. And here, in 1531, the chaplain of W. Caux's chantry said Mass at 8 a.m. (*Vicars Choral*, p. 41.) It is not said definitely at this last date where the Vicars were to celebrate for the Avetons (p. 42), or for Geo. Pollard (p. 43), which the poor clerks maintained in lieu of rent; but not improbably it was at the same altar as in the previous century. J. de Grantham mentions (*cir.* 1500) that the chaplain of Dean W. de Lexington celebrated here. (A. 2, fo. 41^b.) Dean Lexington was buried in the great north transept, northward.

MINISTRATIONS. In the Muniment Room (B. ij. 1, 3,) is a list of ministrations due at Lady Day, 1799, and an account of "Vicars' Stalls," Michaelmas, 1800. At Winchester "ministratio" signified the week or term of duty in course taken by one of the chief officers of the church. (Kitchin, *Obedientiary Rolls*, p. 500.) At Lincoln, a canon when celebrating in his own turn of duty is said to be *in propria* (q.v.); but *in cursu*, if taking the turn for a non-resident.

MISSA MATUTINALIS. The "Morning Mass"* was said daily before morning peal (pella matutinalis) and prime, by a chaplain whom it was the Dean's duty to provide. (*Black Book*, p. 373.) In 1245 Roger de Weseham left the Deanery of Lincoln for the bishoprick of Coventry and Lichfield, and 11th

---

* Dr. Rock tells us that in early times (A.D. 950) at Canterbury the high altar stood close up against the east end of the presbytery, and the altar of the Blessed Virgin at the far west, where the priest, looking eastward, faced the people, while in the choir between them was an *altare matutinale* over the grave of St. Dunstan. The *Regularis Concordia*, Monasticon i. p. xxxi., cf. Kitchin's *Obedientiaries Rolls*, p. 177, speaks of "matutinalis missa" (a daily Mass for the King, or for any need); but Rock warns us that in later times "the morrow Mass" came to signify "Mass in black for the Dead." —*Ch. of our Fathers*, i. p. 266*n.*

Feb., 1252, he made over to Henry Lexington, his successor, subsequently Bp. of Lincoln, and to future Deans of Lincoln, certain properties in Wirksworth, Chesterfield, and Quarrendon, charging them to provide a chaplain to celebrate Masses daily "*summo mane*" in the following rotation : Sunday, *de die;* M., T. & W., *pro animabus episcoporum Lincoln. et Lichf. ac decanorum Lincoln.* necnon omnium fidelium *defunctorum;* Th., *de Sancto Spiritu;* Fr., *pro animabus* ut supra ; Sat., *de Beata Virgine.* (Ant. Beek's Book, A. 2. 2. fo. 23[a].) The Morning Mass was a *missa pro itinerantibus.* (*Novum Registrum,* 1440-42, pars i., *Statutes* ii. p. 285.) A Mass was said daily *in aurora diei:* after which chantry priests not being vicars, used to say their Masses continuously, occupying the various side altars up to the time for Mass of B.V. Mary. Then Vicars became free to celebrate from 8 a.m. (Bp. Alnwick's *Novum Registrum,* pars. v., *ibid.* ii., 360-61.) In April, 1531, the Morning Mass was between 5 and 6 a.m., and was celebrated by the priest of the Works Chantry, at the altar of St. George. Simultaneously two other chaplains celebrated a morrow Mass at the altar. (*Vicars Choral,* p. 40.) In the 15th century it had been at the altar of St. Nicholas, but in 1492 was removed to St. Christopher's altar in the nave. (*Ib.,* p. 37.) At Worcester also, and St. Alban's (according to Mackenzie Walcott, *Sacred Archæol.* p. 21), the middle or matin altar stood under a rood beam at the east end of the choir, before the entrance of the presbytery. In some places it may have stood *behind* the high altar.

Missa capitularis (Nov. Reg. lf. 9ª, *Stat.* ii. 305) or *Missa in capitulo* (*Black Book, Stat.* i. pp. 288, 296, 394, cf. *Nov. Reg.* 349), *Missa capituli* (*Black Book*, p. 293). It is now almost universally admitted that this was not celebrated in the Chapter House, where no altar existed, but it was considered to be said " in chapter." (Cf. the phrase " *in conventu* " applied to a community choral service of Canons, &c., out of choir.) It was the opinion of Mr. F. H. Dickinson that this mass was so called from the *capicium* or *chevet*, the eastern limb of the cathedral. (*Missale Sarum*, p. xiii*n*.) Whether there is any connexion between the *chevet* and the word "chapter," as applied to the body of Canons, who under their "principal" head the Bishop, know the Dean as their " numerical " head, I cannot undertake to say. But their private meetings for counsel and correction, followed by the Chapter Mass (a chief part of those devotions which we may call the family prayers of the Society of Brethren) were in existence for some generations before a stately Chapter House (called likewise *capitulum*, as well as *domus capitularis*, after the body who used it) was built for the convenience of the business meetings. When at last, cir. 1250, the Chapter House was built, the capitular body had two homes, the old retired chapel and the no less secluded but more spacious House. Then, after the service of " prime in choir," and the business meeting, corrections, improving reading, and office of *Pretiosa* (see that word), all held in the Chapter House, the meeting adjourned to their united worship (the Chapter Mass) at the altar, where they and their predecessors had celebrated it from the first.

It was the duty of Vicars* (as well as Canons) generally to attend the *missa capitularis* in their chapel (as well as to hear the good book read in Chapter House), and it was reckoned as equivalent to attendance at one of the little hours (just as High Mass was reckoned equivalent to one of the *horæ majores*). At Chapter Mass the altar had two candles. The Precentor nominated one of the Canons to celebrate it, whenever it was to be the Anniversary Mass of a Dean or Canon of Lincoln, departed. The Canon celebrant was attended by Deacon and Subdeacon "revested" (probably in albes and amices). On other days the Priest Vicars

---

* At St. Paul's, London, Chapter Mass was *celebrated* by one of the two Priest Vicars called there *cardinals*. (Registrum Statutorum.)

At Ottery St. Mary's, in 1342, there was a Mass to be said pro copore presenti at the Parochial Altar *in the Nave* " statim post Primam ante incepcionem aliarum horarum *quasi missa capitularis.*" (Grandisson Register, ed. Hingeston-Randolph 1894, pp. 131-2). This was consequent probably upon the alterations then in progress, and may have been a temporary arrangement.

At Durham they went daily into Chapter House between 8 and 9. At 9 a.m. the bell rang for Chapter Mass, which was (at Durham) always "*at the High Altar.*" And he that sung mass had always in his *Memento* souls of all those that had given anything to that church. *Rites of Durham*, p. 82. The Chapter House there has recently been restored as a memorial of Bp. J. B. Lightfoot.

At Wells the " missa in capitulo" was sometimes (perhaps usually) sung at the High Altar, but occasionally elsewhere,—" *alias quam ad maius altare.*" See the Statute *De Thesaurario*, composed, I believe, cir. 1240, and registered in *Liber Ruber* cir. 1310-20. (Reynolds, *Wells Cath.* p. 50.)

celebrated Chapter Mass in rotation, in place of
Canons. It may be conjectured, on the analogy of
other cathedral churches, that whenever a Sunday
Mass, or a *missa de jejunio*, had to give place to the
celebration of some greater festival at the High
Mass, the Mass proper for the Sunday, or the Fast
Day, served for a capitular mass upon some convenient day in the week following. (*Black Book*, pp.
293, 297, 394. See also *Tracts of Clement Maydeston*,
H. Bradshaw Society, 1894, pp. 6, 44, 67, 106, 119,
120, 122, 165*n*, 206-210.) Mr. J. T. Micklethwaite,
than whom none can speak with higher authority in
matters of ecclesiology, writes to me:—"*Missa in
capitulo* was not in any way connected with the
Chapter *House*. The English secular chapter houses
have in no case any preparation for an altar. Nor
have those of the greater regular orders. I will not
be absolutely sure about the Carthusians, because no
English Carthusian Chapter House remains. The
Carthusians do now put an altar in the Chapter
House, and they are a conservative folk; but, nevertheless, I think the custom is modern."

At Salisbury itself H. de la Wyle the Chancellor,
20th Sept., 1326, gave a house "juxta scolas gram-
maticales propinquius ex parte australi ad inuenien-
dum quendam clericum tribus capellanis singulis
diebus *ad altare apostolorum* [St. Peter's altar, at N.E.
extremity of the Lady Chapel, now the site of the
Gorges monument] in ecclesia predicta celebraturis,
et ad duas missas ibidem que celebrantur pro animabus dñi Willelmi de Eboraco quondam Episcopi

Sarum [*ob.* 31 Jan. 1256-7] et Magʳⁱ Radulphi de Eboraco quondam cancellarii ecclesie predicte [ob. 14 Jan. 1308-9], et ad omnes *missas capitulares* que ibidem celebrantur." (Sarum Muniment Room, Press 4 o.) Hence I infer that the Capitulary Mass at *Salisbury* was said in the north choir aisle.

The Capitulary Mass, still existing in the unreformed Churches, is (says Preb. F. C. Hingeston-Randolph) "the community Mass, *i.e.*, the principal Mass of the day (not what we call "High Mass"), at which the community and the members of the choir are all supposed to be present. Wherever there are large communities, the priests, from early morn, go to the several altars, and each says his Mass, one priest only excepted, who has been appointed to say the Capitular Mass, which follows all those others. All who are able to attend have to attend the Capitular Mass, *occupying their stalls.* It is the Mass of the whole community—of the Chapter. Thus, unless any sufficient cause prevents, it is said at the High Altar." (Or else, I would add, in some commodious place, *e.g.*, in the nave or in the retrochoir, where stalls are provided. Chapels thus furnished may be seen on the continent.) "The Chapter *House* has nothing whatever to do with the Chapter *Mass.* There were no altars in Chapter Houses; though sometimes a chapel might be used for a time, *as* a Chapter House, in which case there would be an Altar, but it would have nothing to do with such temporary use of the chapel for the purposes of a Domus Capitularis." The usual time for Chapter Mass, says Mackenzie Walcott, was before 10 a.m. ; but in France the hour is 8 or 9 a.m. It is sung after prime in summer, and after terce in winter. But unfortunately he identifies Chapter Mass, Conventual, Cardinal and High Mass, without distinction. (*Sacred Archæol.* pp. 20, 143.) See what is said by Gavantus and Meratus concerning the two Conventual Masses of the Roman Rite, *Comment in Missal,* I. In Rubric. General. xli. et xliii. ; III. tit. xi. passim.

At St. Paul's, London, in 1339, two altars north and south of the High Altar were consecrated along with it, and were called *capitularia.* Mr. Dickinson said that these were obviously placed there with a view to the celebration of the Missa Capitularis. (*Missale Sarum* preface, pp. vii., viii*n.*) Canon F. C. Hingeston-Randolph has suggested to me that the St. Paul's altars may have been so called merely because the Canons usually said their daily Mass at one or other of them, and could claim preference over other priests in doing so.

The Chapter House in Old St. Paul's stood in the *centre* of the cloisters, an unusual position.

The approximate dates of some of our *Domus Capitulares* are—Chester, cir. 1210, oblong ; Exeter, 1224-44, oblong ; Lichfield, cir. 1240, elongated octagon ; Lincoln, cir. 1250, decagon ; Salisbury, 1280, octagon, on the east side of the (south) cloister, as is common in monasteries ; Wells, cir. 1286-1319, octagon ; Hereford, cir. 1360, octagon. There is evidence in 1240, at Chichester, that a "capitulum"

existed and was *swept*, and in the first part of
the 14th cent. " domus capitularis " there is mentioned : possibly (says Mr. F. G. Bennett) the
chamber over the treasury. In the 18th century the
rectangular chapel of St. Pantaleon, east of the S.
transept was used for Chapter meetings. It is
clear from what is said in the " Black Book " at p.
394 (top), that the *missa in capitulo* at *Lincoln* was
not said at the High Altar. The fact that Vicars as
often as not sang it, is another proof of the same, as
their right to celebrate at the High Altar was denied.
The Chapter House at Canterbury and at Rochester,
as at Bristol and at Gloucester, is an oblong, at York
and Westminster an (irregular) octagon. At Durham
it has a basilican apse, and at Oxford is a square, at
Worcester a circle (within a polygon). There was
formerly a rectangular Chapter House at Winchester,
built cir. 1080-1120.

In a fragment of Lincoln accounts of Jordan de
Yngham, 1271, among " minut' expense," along
with charges for parchment, gum, green wax, &c.,
there are the following curious items :—

" Item in nattis empt' in parvo capitulo. viij. d.

Item in reparacione fenestrarum in Ecclesia propter
ventum, iij. d. ob.

Item in sotular' die cen' empt' viij. s. iiij. d.

Item in puero misso in hosp. xiij. d."

The "*paruum capitulum*" was perhaps so called to
distinguish it from the great Chapter House; but
where was it ?

Missa pro Benefactoribus. By St. Hugh's order in

o

Chapter (cir. 1195-1200) a Mass, as well as a Psalter, was said daily "for benefactors, living and departed." *Black Book*, p. 300. See above, "Benefactors," and cf. *Statut.* ii., 321-2.

Missa pro Defunctis. A Mass of *Requiem* (see Sarum Breviary, ii., 521. *Missale*, p. 860*) was said at the High Altar by the Dean, or principal Canon, for Kings, Bishops, or Deans, once a week. *Stat.* ii. 326.

The Dean, in absence of the Bishop, celebrated also for Kings' and Bishops' *anniversaries. Stat.* ii., 283. The anniversary of a Dean was not kept at the High Altar itself, *ib.* ii., 326 *margin*. Whether any Canon besides a residentiary might celebrate at the High Altar was a disputed point, *ib.* ii., 331 *margin*. When a Canon died, the Dean (or some other of his brethren) said a solemn Mass for his soul at the High Altar on the morrow after the corpse had been brought to the choir of the Minster; after which the burial took place. Before this Mass *pro corpore presenti* the "Commendatio" was said in choir after Prime. The vigils had been kept round the corpse the previous night, the members of the southern part of the quire (*decani*) reciting the Psalter before mattins, and the *cantoris* side after mattins (*ib.* ii., 343). A Mass for Canons departed was said every *day* (except perhaps Maundy Thursday and Good Friday, *ib.* ii., 350 *margin*) with *Placebo* and *Dirige* (*i.e.*, evensong and mattins of the dead) by Priest Vicars in rotation, assisted by two junior Vicars (*nondum presbyterati*). This was *not* at the

High Altar. Special collect was used, if the day happened to be anniversary of the death of one of their number. An office for the dead was likewise said (? once) every week in choir (*ibid.*). See also "Benefactors" and "Works Chantry."

Missa pro animabus Episcoporum Defunctorum. The keeper of St. Peter's Altar (see "*Piscinas,*" no. 11.) said Mass (personally or by deputy) at that Altar for the souls of all Bishops of Lincoln departed. The later MSS. say "daily:" and though this appears to be a mis-reading of the word "*custodie,*" *Stat.* ii., 353, still I find in A. 1. 8. fo. 217, Ri. Marchand on his admission, 26th June, 1484, required to say Mass *daily* at St. Peter's Altar for the souls of Bishops *and Canons.* Besides the ordinary All Souls' Day "animarum commemoratio," on Nov. 2nd, the roll of *Re* and *Ve* 2 F. notes on Tuesday before Easter falling on March 26th, a "*Commemoracio Fidelium,*" and another on Friday, 15th Dec. (? the day before "O Sapientia"), 1475.

Missa de Die. The chief altar service appointed for the day. This was ordinarily said or sung (with deacon and subdeacon) at the High Altar. Sometimes it had to give way, either being transferred to some vacant day near, or being relegated to the subordinate position of a Chapter Mass, or being omitted *pro ea vice;* not, of course, that the High Altar was ever left without some solemn Mass. Archbishop Courteney, after visiting the Dean and Chapter in the time of Bp. Bokyngham in 1390, gave as his 4th Injunction that "when the obit of

Bishops or Kings occur in the church, the Mass of the Day be in no wise omitted; but that it be duly celebrated at the Altar of B. Mary in the said church." (*Statutes* ii., p. 246.)

Missa de Spiritu Sancto. This was the Morning Mass for Thursdays at Lincoln in 1252. Also at the election of a Bishop (cir. 1280) a Mass of the Holy Ghost is celebrated " coram cunctis "; after which follows *Veni Creator* and the orison " Deus qui corda fidelium." They then proceed to elect, and when the result is announced *Te Deum* is sung, and the elect, if present, is led to the High Altar. (*Regist. Antiquiss.* A. 1. 5, fo. 189.)

Missa pro itinerantibus. The daily Morning Mass, founded in 1252 (with other intentions), is said in Bp. Alnwick's draft Registrum (1440) to have this character. (*Stat.* ii., p. 285.)

Missa pro Rege. This is noted for Tuesday after Lady Day (26th March)* in the Roll of *Re* and *Ve* for 1476. Masses *pro rege defuncto* were celebrated at the High Altar.

Missus est Angelus. This is the Gospel (St. Luke i., 26-38) in Sarum use for the Mass *Rorate* appointed for Lady Day, for the (Saturday) commemoration in Advent [It is mentioned twice in the *Black Book* (pp. 385, 388), and in the former instance it is remarkable that Schalby's MS. (known as " Martilogium ") has the variant " *Missus est Gabriel*," which

---

* This was not exactly the date of K. Edward IVth's accession, which was always reckoned 4th March.

is the form as it appears in the use of York*], and for the Mass of the B. Virgin on other week days at other times of the year, and for the proper Mass on the Ember Wednesday in Advent. This was among the days when (at least at Lincoln) an exception was made to the general rules (1) that compline of our Lady follows compline of the day in choir, and (2) that two (not three) bells were rung for the fourth (or last) peal at mattins. (The margin, p. 388, says " at Evensong.")

" MORNING CHAPEL," OR " MORNING PRAYER CHAPEL." The names are commonly given to the north-west Early English chapel in the nave, where a workman's service has been held at 7.40 a.m. for the last 20 years. Hollar's plan, 1672, notes that prayers were said here every morning " hora 6ta." About 1780 the prebendary of St. Botolph's undertook to say them.

Under Q. Elizabeth's Injunctions (1559) it was arranged, at least for Salisbury and Wells, and presumably for all Cathedral Churches, that there should be two daily services in the forenoon. One of these was to be the regular mattins in choir. In Lestrange's day this was at 9 a.m. However, in

---

* In 1416 W. de Waltham, who was Canon of *York* and Beverley, as well as of *Lincoln*, was buried at the last-named, left a breviary of the use of *Sarum* to his clerk. A. Gibbons, *Early Lincoln Wills*, p. 143. In 1389 Ro. de Weston, Rector of Marum, or Mareham, left his " missal of the *new* use of *Sarum* to his clerk if he wishes to be a priest." *Ibid.*, p. 87. In 1403 W. de Wolstanton, Rector of Bondon Magna, gave his portos of *York* use to J. de Scrope. (*Gibbons*, p. 106, cf. 125.) In 1416 J. de Kele, Canon Residentiary of Lincoln, bequeaths missal and portos of Sarum use. *Ib.* 128.

1559 the Chancellor was to provide a lecture in Divinity in English, in a convenient place at least thrice a week at 9 a.m., which all the staff were to attend. So perhaps mattins was at 10. The " Minister " which was " tabled to begin the common prayer in quire " for *one* week was responsible in the week following for an earlier service in the Morning Prayer Chapel. This was to be at 5 a.m. in Summer, but from Sept. to April at 6. It had an order peculiar to itself :—General Confession, Absolution, " the Litanie until this verse, ' *O Lord arise*,' " before which verse a chapter from the New Testament in order was read. After the Lesson the said " verse " was begun, and then " the rest of the Litanie, with all the Suffrages following." (*Sarum Statutes* p. 109, misdated. *Wells Cathedral*, Reynolds, p. clvi.) I infer from this, that in the 16th century the prayer " O God, merciful Father " in the Litany was understood to end " Through Jesus Christ our Lord [*Amen*]." And the verse "O Lord arise. . . Name's sake," was recognised as an antiphon to Ps. xliv. i, and not (as it now commonly is) recited like a respond to the said Collect. In 1597, Whitgift expressed his approbation of a visitation for Canterbury, being desirous " that the Petty Canons, singing men, substitutes, or other the inferior Ministers and servants of the Church, do more daily frequent the first morning service." (Strype's Whitgift, Records no. 38 § 5. from MS. Cotton. Cleop. F. 2.)

Mutatio Chori. The Rev. W. E. Dickson, Precentor of Ely, has recently expressed a wish that the voices of both sides of the choir might be massed together, as they are on the floor of some foreign cathedral churches. It was formerly the custom at Lincoln (as at Salisbury) to group the singers on one side of the choir, for one week *decani*, and the next *cantoris*. On double festivals, however, they always went *decani*, provided that Bishop or Dean were present; but from Christmas to Epiphany inclusive, and again in Easter week and Whitsuntide, the "choir" changed sides on alternate days. Psalms, &c., were sometimes begun in the stalls "*in parte qua chorus est*," and the next from the opposite stalls; for the *Canons* apparently kept their places. *Black Book*, pp. 371, 391. Sarum *Consuetud.* c.xxii. Such was *seemingly* the way.

Mr. Micklethwaite, however, suggests to me that the whole choir did not move, but that the meaning is that the first verse was on one day started *decani*, and on the other *cantoris*. So in the Rule for the Brigittine Sisters of Syon, cap. xxvi., it was directed that "Every other week, the choir shall vary, so that it be on the abbess' side one week, and on the prioress' side another week, beginning evermore the Saturday at evensong." The stall of the abbess was at the entrance of the quire on the right side at the west end, and that of the prioress on the left side. See Blunt's introduction to the *Myrroure of our Ladye*, p. xxxvii.

St. Nicholas' Altar. Here, in 1531, two Can- tilupe Chaplains celebrated Mass between 7 and 8 a.m. *Vicars Choral*, p. 41. The chantry of Thomas and Margaret Fitzwilliam (who died in 1473 and 1463) was here.

Browne Willis, in 1742, on the authority of Cotton MS. Tiberius E. 3, A.D. 1545 (and we may cite also *Chantry Certificate* 33) likewise placed the chantry of Nic. and Joan Cantilupe, and that of T. Fitzwilliam at St. Nicholas' Altar. *Cathedrals* ii., p. 34. Sir N. Cantilupe died in 1355, and his widow, Dame Joan, founded the chantry of St. Nicholas at the E. end of the S. aisle. She built (about 1356) the Cantilupe Chantry House, still standing near the Sub-Deanery, south of the Minster, as a college or hostel for the chaplains and choristers of this chantry. Venables, *Walk through Lincoln Minster*, p. 43.* Leland tells us that the College was corruptly called in his day "*Negem College*," that it was originally constructed for a Master and two or three "Cantuaries," afterwards augmented to seven, and that in the chapel of St. Nicholas lay "a merveylous fair and large Psalter, full in the margin of goodly armes of many noblemen." *Itin.* fo. 49ª. Previously to 1492 Morning Mass had been said at St. Nicholas' altar; then it was removed to St. Christopher's altar in the nave. *Vicars Choral*, p. 37. The Fitzwilliams' monuments are in "the Chaunter's Isle," and so is the burial place of W. Turre, keeper of Cantilupe College 1427. Sanderson, ap. *Desid. Cur.*, p. 297. But the Cantilupes are buried in

---

* The misprint in Williamson's *Guide*, p. 90, line 16, where we should read "St. Nicholas," has been mentioned above. Probably at p. 101, "1336 given as the date of the Chantry House, is a mis-print for 1356.

"William the Conqueror's chapel" adjoining, *ib.* 296.

According to the obit list of 1527 (A. 2. 8, fo. 32ᵇ) the chantry of T. and Margaret Fitzwilliam paid 2*d.* to the clerk of the altar of St. Nicholas.

Non vos relinquam. This anthem was sung at some church in Lincoln in the Ascension Day procession, on which occasion the cathedral carpenters were bound to hang a pall before the said church. *Black Book,* p. 293. It was, in Sarum use, the anthem to the Psalms at first evensong of this feast. *Brev. Sarum,* 1 col. dcccclvii.

Nova festa. In 1480 and other years a payment of 4*s.* 6*d.* to the Treasurer occurs under the head of " *consuetudo solita in ecclesia Lincoln.*" in the *computus* books, as a compensation for wear and tear of bell ropes, and for extra incense in regard of certain " new semidouble feasts, imposed by the Archbishop of Canterbury at his Visitation." In one instance I found the name or initial of the Primate given, but I have lost my memorandum, and have searched in vain to recover the clue at Lincoln.

"O." The anthems sung to *Magnificat* at Evensong on the days before Christmas, " *O Sapientia,*" &c. See *Black Book,* p. 388. Mr. Everard Green has written fully on the subject in *Archæologia* 1886; vol. xlix. p. 219. "Facere O" seems to have applied somehow at St. Swithun's, Winchester, to the Chanter and others on all double feasts (Kitchin's *Consuetudinary,* pp. 18, 28, 41), but perhaps only as a convenient term derived from the December rites.

There was a Whitsuntide " Recreation " called " O, O, O," mentioned in the Wells Chapter Acts, 8th June, 1510.

OBLATIONS. A memorandum (19th Jan., 1322) concerning the falling off of the customary offerings at the tombs of St. Hugh and Ro. Grosseteste may be seen in *Black Book*, pp. 335-8, with some account of the distribution of St. Pelagia's day (8th Oct.). See also Venables, *Tomb and Head of St. Hugh*, and *supra*, p. 108.

" *O Christi pietas.*" The antiphon to *Magnificat* at second Evensong of St. Nicholas on Dec. 5th, on which occasion 100*s.* (or perhaps only 5*s.*) were distributed to the choir. Roll of *Re* and *Ve*.

ORGAN. Playing the organ (" cuilibet cantancium organum, 3*d.*," " trahenti organa, 6*s.* 8*d.*") is mentioned in the *Black Book*, pp. 337-8 A.D. 1322. (The words *organizacio, organizare*, occur pp. 369, 373, apparently of vocal music at the lectern in choir by boys or vicars at the end of evensong and lauds.) Maddison gives a list of organists, keepers, blowers, and players (pulsatores, or *ad lusus organorum*) from 1311 to 1539. (*Vicars*, pp. 80, 81.) He mentions (p. 24) that one of the Vicars received a fee as late as 1536 for playing the organ at the " Jesus Mass." In 1428, April 24th, an order was made for paying £9 for new organs in the chapel of St. John Baptist, where daily Mass of B. Mary is celebrated with music, and for mending the old organs in the greater choir. *Chapter Acts*, A. 2. 32, fo. 46. On Sunday, 16th October, 1446, immediately after the public procession of the day, J. Tiryngton admitted in the "Revestry House" to vicar stall of North Kelsey prebend in the choir, "ad exercicium et custodiam organorum in choro predicto, cum vadijs (wages) in hac parte consuetis." A. 2. 33, fo. 18ᵇ. 10 Sept., 1442, an order for 5 marcs from the fabrick chest was made for new organs in the great choir, to be constructed by one Arnold, "organer" of Norwich, in the best manner possible. On Oct. 14th Robt. Patryngton is commissioned to find with all speed "a scientific man," who has skill to make the new organs in Lincoln choir. A. 2. 33, ff. 51ᵃ, 60ᵇ. The choir organ was formerly placed under one of the arches in the north side of the choir.

ORNAMENTS. A notice of ornaments retained in the Minster in 1553, when Matthew Parker was . Dean, will be found in *Linc. Dio. Mag.*, June, 1889, pp. 92-3.

ST. OSWALD'S IMAGE. This "late Image, of the north syde of the high altare," is mentioned in the will of J. Parkyn, vicar choral, 1 Sept., 1548. Maddison's *Wills*, p. 38, § 103.

PALLS, CARPETS, CURTAINS, and other cloths of linen, woollen or silk, are mentioned in the *Black Book*, pp. 292-3, to be hung up by the carpenters, *e.g.*, at Bail-gate on Palm Sunday, and before a Parish Church on Ascension Day. A veil before the altar in Lent, p. 291. Cloths on lecterns and desks, see above, "Lectern." For a list of silken cloths (panni) for the High altar, "frontletts," etc., see my *Inventories* in *Archæologia*, vol. liii., pp. 36-8, 61-3, 76 A.D. 1536, 1548, 1557.

PASCHAL. The "magnus cereus paschalis," or great taper which stood from Easter Eve to Ascentiontide by the north (or gospel) *ambo* at the choir screen, was made at Lincoln of 3 stone of wax. *Black Book*, p. 291. See Rock, *Ch. of our Fathers*, i., 212, iv., 98. The "pascall poste" remained till 1566. (*Inventories*, p. 80.) The Treasurer had to find a paschal taper, the weight of wax in it being 3lbs., as the draft *Novum Registrum* says, p. 303, but the marginal correction was "2 stone" ("*duas petras*"), and all thereto belonging, such as colours, flowers, cords, &c. It was probably decorated with date and ornaments. It was objected that these items fell under the obligation of the servants of the Fabrick. The Treasurer provided also a candle weighing 1lb., to be carried on the pole ("*hasta paschalis*") for the "new fire" on Easter Even. See Sarum *Processionale*, pp. 76, 80 (woodcuts).

ST. PAUL'S CHAPEL AND ALTAR. I do not know on what evidence or authority it is said that the northern apsidal chapel in S.E. transept (or, indeed, any other at Lincoln) had this dedication. It is so called in *Williamson's Guide to Lincoln*, p. 86, and in the map contained in several of the late Precentor's useful little works. In the map in the new *Monasticon*, 1846, facing vi. p. 1266, it figures as "Lady Joan Cantalupe's Chapel." I should be grateful for documentary authority for either of these identifications. I find that St. *Peter's* altar is styled, in *Registrum Antiquissimum*, "the altar of the Apostles St. Peter and St. Paul," and this makes it seem less likely that there was any altar of St. Paul individually.

A tooth of St. Paul was among the relicks at Lincoln.

PAUPERES CLERICI. The Poor Clerks were a college or community of twelve men not in priest's orders. (*Statutes* ii., 361-2, 407, 411.) From their number the Dean appointed "keepers of the altares" to assist the celebrants. They had buildings (*mansum*) by benefaction from Geof. Pollard, with a charge to provide a light in a silver basin, and his obit mass in the cathedral church. (*Nov. Reg.* v.) They had statutes of their own, revised in 1526, whereof a fragment is extant. See *Statutes* ii., pp. 559-563. Did they cease to be Poor Clerks, and take Holy Orders, when appointed to a Keepership? The Keeper of St. Peter's altar at all events was, I believe, in priest's orders.

PEAL ALTAR. The "morning peal" (*pella matutinalis*) was rung in, or under, the south-west belfry, midway between the mattin chime (*signum matutinale*) and the hour of prime. *Black Book*, p. 373, and *margin* "De Pella—pele altar." *Novum Registrum* pars 5. *Statutes*, ii., p. 361. Here in 1531 the chaplain of Bp. Hugh de Welles' chantry said Mass at 7 a.m. Maddison's *Vicars Choral*, p. 41.

We have an instance at Wells in St. Cross altar

(the N. side) of a chapel under a western belfry in
1305. (C. M. Church, *Wells History*, p. 420.)

The obit list of 1527 (A. 2. 8, fo. 31ᵇ) has a note
that " Magister sive custos cantarie volgariter nun-
cupate *peel awter* debet solvere predictum obitum
[Hugonis Wells episcopi]."

At the Visitation of 1437 a complaint was laid
that the musick books in choir, in Lady Chapel,
and " in capella *le pele*" were not consonant. Also
that the vestments belonging to " *le pele altare* "
were torn and shabby, and that John Bellringer
kept a dog " in cubili juxta altare de *pele*."
(*Stat.* ii., pp. 404, 407.)

The obit of T. Alford, in the list of 1527 (fo. 31ᵇ)
pays ("clerico altaris *le peel*, 2*d.*"). T. Alford,
preb. of Carlton Pagnel cum Thurleby, who died
in 1485, was, according to Sanderson (*Des. Cur.*,
p. 315), buried somewhere in the nave. See also
Bp. Alnwick's Visitation, *Statutes*, ii., 404, 407.

We read of another and more solemn Mass for
the soul of Hugh de Welles, sung by a Vicar, with
Deacon and Sub-deacon, between 8 and 9 (p. 43), at
St. Hugh's altar, where a chaplain of Bokyngham
Chantry also celebrated at 6 a.m. (p. 41). Were
" St. Hugh's Altar" and " Pele Altar" the same?
I am inclined to think not. At all events, there
was an altar of St. Hugh in a part of the Minster
far removed from *Le Pele;* but St. Hugh's *bells*
were here. Hence the S.W. chapel also took his
name.

PENITENTIARY. The sacrist at Lincoln was appointed to hear confessions within Minster Yard. It was mentioned in 1437 that the chaplains had got into the way of resorting to confessors of their own choice. The Bishop was asked to appoint a suitable person. *Statutes*, ii., 404, 342 (*Nov. Reg.* iv.).

PENTECOSTALS. In the *Black Book* (p. 307) there is a letter of St. Hugh, repeated by his successor William of Blois, charging chaplains in every parish in the Diocese to induce all householders to bring a worthy oblation at Whitsuntide to a common centre, " to the remission of their sins, and for a sign of obedience and recognition of their mother of Lincoln." In 1348 Bp. Gynewell issued his commission to the provost to deal with those who unrighteously withheld pentecostal oblations. (*Ib.*, 361-2.) The offerings were divided at the yearly *apertura summi altaris*, the Treasurer, among others, usually receiving thence a compensation for certain official expenses. (*Ib.*, 401.)

In May, 1444, there was a commission appointed to levy " le smoke ffardyngis alias dict' Lincoln̄ farthinges," in Leicestershire, for expenses of the prebendal church and belfry of Leicester St. Margaret. The pentecostal oblations took the form here, as in Salisbury Diocese, of a *chimney-tax* ordinarily payable to the Mother Church at the Pentecostal Procession.

PELLIFORUM. The "Peltry" or Skin-market. St. Peter's " ad Pelliforum " and St. Edmund's "juxta Minores " (the Franciscans' House) are

churches mentioned at Bp. Alnwick's Visitation.
(*Statutes*, ii., 293.) The skin market "occupied
part of the site of the present Butter Market."
(Venables' *Walk*, p. 27.)

St. Peter's Altar. Before this altar the Sub-
Dean, W. Bramford (or "Bramfeld," see Screding-
ton Grants), was murdered by a subdeacon vicar
25th Sept., 1205, not long after its erection.
(*Waverley Annals, Worcester Annals.*) The keeper
of this altar sang mass daily, himself or by deputy,
for the souls of all Bishops [and Canons] of Lincoln
departed. He was also usually appointed to the
office of *auditor causarum* to the Chapter. It was
his duty to recite the invitatory, and to read the
lessons at Mattins of the Glorious Virgin Mary on
feasts of nine lessons. See *Black Book*, pp. 121*n*,
246, 253, 276, 325-330, 347, 352-60. Several
keepers of this altar were buried in the south-east
transept, viz. T. Waltham, 1453, Ro. Newton cir.
1508, and W. Hill, 1556; so also was Ri. Stafford,
clerk of St. Peter's altar, 1414.

The obit lists of 1330-40, 1527, note payments to
the keeper of St. Peter's altar, not only from the
chantries, &c., of Bishops Sutton, Buckingham,
Gynwell, Russell and Smith, but also from K.
Edward III., Henry, Duke of Lancaster, A. Bramp-
ton, T. de Perrariis, N. Wymbysh, T. Alford,
Gilbert and Gillian d'Umfravill, Ri. Whitewell,
J. Crosby, T. and Marg. Fitzwilliam. And Dean
Fleming and Treasurer Welborne's obits included
payments to the clerk of St. Peter's altar. See also

the Chapter Act of 1290 in Schalby's book, pp. 7ª, 32ª, *Statut.* ii., pp. 169, 353. Why was it that in 1432, 24th Aug., J. Duffield, keeper of St. Peter's altar, applied for leave to make a door through the wall near the chantry of Richard [Fleming], late Bishop, seeing that Bp. Fleming's chantry was on the north side of the angel choir? (*Chapter Acts*, A. 2, 32, fo. 65.) Perhaps his lodging was in Eastgate or somewhere north of the Minster, and he therefore required a short cut through the church.

ST. PETER'S RELICKS. The beard and chasuble of St. Peter are mentioned.

PILLIUS, OR PILEUS, a cap. The celebrant at the high altar put down his cap at *Gloria in excelsis*, and it was handed to a boy (as the Canon reading a lesson in the choir at Westminster hands his cap to the verger). The boy had a fee or *pour boire* ("vinum" : *Black Book*, p. 377) of 1½*d.* It occurs only occasionally in the Succentor's collection of documents in 1527, viz. for Lady Day and Trinity Sunday, St. John Bapt., the Assumption, and Feast of Relicks.

PISCINAS AND AUMBRIES. The *Black Book* mentions at High Mass, after reading the epistle in the pulpit, the principal subdeacon, with his secondary subdeacon (the third remaining at the altar) going before him with the closed book on (ex) the left hand of the choir. At the choir door a thurifer relieves them of the book (which is thus available for the principal deacon, who is to read the Gospel), and they go into the vestry, where the sacrist or his clerk is ready to give them the chalice with the corporas-cloth and bread. The secondary subdeacon then cleanses the chalice from any spot, hands it to his principal, who carries it with a special napkin (*sudario quodam*, perhaps of striped silk like those at Westminster, and answering to the modern *velum subdiaconale*), and the other carries the corporas-cloth with a special napkin, and they walk together to the high altar. After kneeling at the upper step to say an *Ave*, they conjointly place the chalice on the altar. Presently the principal subdeacon carries the chalice to the priest (who has been saying his prayers in his *sedile* after reading the epistle to himself with his remaining attendants at the altar). The secondary subdeacon follows with the cruets (*phiolas*) with wine and water. The priest (still at the *sedile*) pours in first wine then water, only such a quantity that the mixture may preserve the quality and colour of wine. Then he shall carry the chalice behind the altar in some convenient and decent place. The secondary deacon was then to unfold the corporas-cloth upon the altar aforesaid. (*Black Book*, pp. 377-8.) After the Nicene Creed the Priest censes the chalice and corporas-cloth. After *Sanctus* the principal deacon, attended by the two other deacons, finds the paten with its special napkin and hands it (" with the offertory veil," *Sarum*) to the subdeacon, who holds it (" gives it to the acolyte to hold," *Sarum*) till the Lord's Prayer. Then the deacon takes it, gives it to the Priest (" kissing his hand," *Sarum*) after the prayer, "Deliver us, O Lord, we beseech Thee, from all evils, past," etc. When the sacrament is finished, let the secondary deacon fold the corporas-cloth, and the secondary subdeacon cleanse the chalice. After *Ite missa est* the priest shall give the chalice to the principal subdeacon, and the corporal to the secondary subdeacon, who hold napkins in their hands for the purpose. All go to the vestry, the deacons leading on one side, and the subdeacons on the other.

One point noticeable in the *Sarum* rule for the same ceremonies is the lack of any direction for the chalice after the mixture being carried from the sedilia to a fitting place *behind the altar*. Probably the structure of the " room " beneath the tabernacle at Lincoln (see above, " *Beam* ") was specially adapted for this purpose. Then, in the Sarum account, it is said that " the elements were brought into the church after the introit, and put in the place assigned for them." A credence, or table of proposition is not expressly named. The chalice was brought in, during the Epistle, and taken to the place of administration,* and the corporals spread on the altar by the acolyte [arrayed in alb and silken mantle]. The epistle over, the subdeacon, after washing his hands, made ready the bread and wine, with the aid of the acolyte, in the place of administration. Up to this point the Consuetudinary (*cap.*

---

* Dr. Wickham Legg takes "*loco ipsius administracionis*" to be " simply the place of preparation, be it [at the south end of the] altar, or at the credence."

92) is our authority; but the Missal adds that the subdeacon makes ready the bread, wine, and water, after the grail and other liturgical formulæ have been said privately by the priest, the water being first blessed by the priest, apparently while he is in the *sedilia.** So far as I can find, Mr. C. H. Pearson's statement that cruets and pix with the bread, and likewise basins with water and a towel were placed "on the shelf over the Piscina,"† rests upon a mere conjecture. At least the Osmund Register, to which he refers us, makes no mention of a piscina, but says simply, "ad locum ubi panis, vinum, et aqua ad eukaristie ministracionem disponuntur;" and, afterwards, "calice in loco debito reposito," and "in loco ipsius administracionis." (*Cap.* 92.)

The arrangement of Piscinas and Aumbries‡ for the cleansing and conservation of the holy vessels was, at Salisbury, very simple.

(I.) AT SALISBURY.

In the retro-choir (or Lady Chapel, as it is called at Salisbury) the "Salve" altar of our Lady's Mass at the extreme east, was dedicated 28th Sept., 1225, to the *Holy Trinity and All Hallows.* This easternmost altar is flanked, or rather attended in the rear,

---

* *Preparation and Oblation of the Gifts,* by J. Wickham Legg, St. Paul's Eccl. Soc., Vol. III., p. 73.

† *Sarum Missal in English,* Ed. 1868, p. 52.

‡ The antiquated "aumbry," or "ambry" (which survives as a north country provincial word) is a form of *armarium, armariorum,* the closet, or place where implements (*arma*) are stored.

by two altars, *St. Peter and Apostles* on the north,
and *St. Stephen and Martyrs* on the south, both
dedicated on the same occasion as the Trinity and
All Saints altar. Here there are two aumbries in
the wall on the extreme north (by St. Peter's), and
two piscinas in the extreme southern wall corresponding (by St. Stephen's).

Before Wyatt's alterations there were, most probably, wings, or return walls, south and north of these
altars respectively, and these may have contained a
double piscina for the northern altar, and one or
more aumbries for that in the opposite aisle. As
regards the two transepts, in the eastern transept,
the shorter of the two, there were four altars, two on
each side, *St. Katharine's and St. Martin's* on the
north, and *St. Mary Magdalen's and St. Nicholas* on
the south. The northern pair have two aumbries
(with remains of original wooden doors in the
northernmost wall) and two shallow recesses with
shelves in the return wall southward. The more
easterly recess has a piscina to this day below its
stone shelf. In like manner in the S.E. transept, the
celebrant at St. Margaret's altar had a double
aumbry immediately to his right hand, and his
neighbour at St. Nicholas' altar had a double piscina
to his left.

Further south, opening off the last-named transept
is the *vestibulum*, an octagonal sacristy with a treasure-
chamber above it. In the N.W. side of the octagon
are three large aumbries still in use. In its western
side (now hidden by a press, as Mr. Freemantle

has shewn me)* is a recess two feet square and one and a half feet deep. It is natural to suppose that the sacristy at Salisbury once contained an altar and a piscina or drain, but of this I have no proof.

At the intersection of the short eastern transept with the nave, there was, as some antiquaries think, in old times the site of the High Altar, dedicated Sept. 29th (or 30th), 1258, in honour of the mystery of the Assumption, beneath the painting of our Lord in glory.† As regards the rinsing of the chalice at the High Mass, my present opinion is that this was done partly in one of the basins (*pelves*) brought thither by the acolyte. (In the other basin no doubt the celebrant washed his fingers ; and this I take to be the *raison d'etre* of a double piscina at the side altars.) And the ablutions, so far as they were performed in the basins, would probably be ultimately poured away in the Sacristy.‡ For the disposal of such things is no public ceremony of the Church, nor does it belong to the duty of the principal celebrant to do it, when another is ready to do it reverently. (See *Observations on Ritual Conformity*,

---

* My thanks are due to Mr. Freemantle for giving me the benefit of his stores of knowledge relating to Salisbury Cathedral.

† The position of the High Altar at Salisbury was discussed by G. G. Scott in a paper re-issued by his son, Gilbert Scott, in *The Sacristy*, 1881, iii. 249. Also in *Wilts Archæol. Magazine* XVII., pp. 136-47, by Succentor Armfield, and in XIX., pp. 336-7, by Canon Rich Jones, who repeated his remarks in *Osmund Register*, I., p. XXXII.

‡ Here, as elsewhere, Wyatt made alterations and obliterated landmarks. An ancient lavatory, which is said to have once stood near the vestry, is now in the " Morning Chapel," in the place of St. Katharine's altar, which I have, provisionally, called " St. Martin's."

by J. D. Chambers, late Recorder of Sarum, 1881.)

In the great (or western) transept at Salisbury there were six altars; the altar of St. Thomas of Canterbury the martyr, that of St. Edmund of Canterbury the Confessor (formerly Treasurer of Sarum), and the Relicks Altar of St. John the Baptist—all in the N.W. transept. To the left (or north) of St. Thomas's Altar some traces of a double aumbry (filled up by Wyatt) can be discerned, but all traces of the piscinas are, I believe, removed. The S.W. transept was occupied by altars of St. Margaret, St. Lawrence and St. Michael; and to the south of the last named, the two piscinas remain.

Touching other chapels at Salisbury, the Hungerford Chapel, annexed to the N.E. end on the left hand of the *Salve* Chapel in 1464), has been removed (in 1789); so has been the Beauchamp chapel, annexed, in 1482, northward of the retrochoir. Of these each may have had its own altar piscina and aumbry, for such was a common arrangement in the 15th century.* The iron chapel (a second Hungerford chantry, cir. 1429) has been removed (1778) from a N.E. bay of the nave to flank the choir or presbytery on the south, while the Audley chapel of 1520 still stands on the

---

* The stone ornaments of the entrances to the Beauchamp and Hungerford chapels were worked into the east wall of the Lady Chapel, right and left of the *Salve* altar reredos, by Wyatt, now replaced by an oaken triptych, behind which an original painted mediæval consecration cross may be seen, corresponding in design to the stone crosses mentioned.

opposite verge—its original position. An altar of
St. Osmund, erected about 1456, east of the High
Altar, a separate altar of All Saints, an *altare quod
vocatur* Jesian (*i.e.*, "our Lady in Gesem," or
"Gesina," *i.e.*, in presepio" or "in expectatione
partus"), frequented by "the wymmen that ben
in our Lady bondis" (*Bidding the Bedes*, 1483,
H. O. Coxe, p. 34. Cf. Rock *Ch. of our Fathers*,
iii. 269, *n.*), which the Right Wor. A. R. Malden,
F.S.A., now (1896) Mayor of Salisbury, has kindly
pointed out to me among records of the Visitation
by Bp. Beauchamp in 1461,—a morning altar and
altar of the Holy Ghost, have left no traces of
their site. The Fabrick Altar of the Holy Rood
probably once stood in the loft, or "*pulpitum*"
where the Epistle and Gospel were chanted over
the west door of the choir.* Altars of St. Andrew,
and of SS. Mary, Denys and Laurence, and
St. George, and the "*altare parochiale*," probably
stood against partition screens in the nave at
Salisbury.

But it is time now to pass to Lincoln.

(II.) Lincoln Altars, &c.

The position of the various altars in Lincoln
Minster is not so readily ascertained, but the
arrangement of *piscinas*, though different from that
of Salisbury, is fairly plain.

---

* Wyatt removed the old stone screen, or two pieces of it, each measuring
13ft. 3 by 7ft. 9), to the so-called "Morning Chapel," and embedded the stone
doorway of the Beauchamp chapel between them.

1. The dedication title of the *High Altar* at Lincoln, where the "Great" (or High) Mass was sung, ordinarily about 10 o'clock a.m., is unknown to me, but it is easy to conjecture that it was of (the Most Holy Trinity) *Blessed Mary* (and All Hallows). I have given reasons above, when discussing Salisbury, for supposing that there was no piscina at the High Altar. Robert Awbray, Dean Fleming's chantry priest in 1535, left "to the High Altar of our Lady of Lincoln" (is this the dedication title, or merely indicatory of the whole Minster?) "a crosse of golde to be nayld upon the Altare besyde the Image of our Lady to the honour of her." Maddison, *Lincoln Wills*, No. 22, p. 11.

2. The *Irons*. The tombs of Katharine Swinford and her daughter Joan, Countess of Westmoreland, formerly stood side by side, "sideing the choir" (*Sanderson*, 1641); not endlong together, as when Hollar sketched his plan, cir. 1672. There was, I suppose, a space at the foot of them eastward (it is still enclosed with an iron grate or railings on the south) sufficient for a small altar, where the Duchess of Lancaster's chantry priest might celebrate. Having no room to spare, and being at no great distance from the revestry, this altar, very possibly had no piscina attached to it. The present canopy to these tombs is not original.

K. Swinford's mass at "le Irons" occurs in the time tables of 1506-7, and 1531. *Statutes* ii. p. cclxiv.

Crossing the sanctuary, and going out by the

north door of the choir, or presbytery, as was done in washing the altars at Salisbury, we proceed to the N.E. transept, which contains two chapels.

3. The "little chapel" (*Sanderson*), called by *Browne Willis* "Canon Thomas' chapel," (possibly from J. Thomas, who died Prebendary of Asgarby in 1412: unless indeed "Thomas" be merely a misprint for *Thornaco*) from the authority of an anonymous account in 1771, is said in Brooke's *Guide* (1840) to have been "founded by Canon W. de Thornaco" [Archd. of Lincoln, Dean 1223, suspended 1239, buried at Louth Park 1258] and dedicated to St. Hugh." The Louth Park Chronicle (p. 16) speaks of an altar of St. Hugh dedicated 15th July, 1255. The next sentence following refers, no doubt, to Louth, but the previous one certainly relates to Lincoln, and I think we may be justified in identifying the smaller of two apsidal chapels in the north-east transept at Lincoln as the chapel of St. Hugh, which at one time contained an altar of St. Hugh. Here there is a double piscina to the S.E., and a double aumbry in the N.E. wall.

4. The northern apsidal "large chapel" (*Sanderson*) is, no doubt, the new chapel "on the north side," where Sir Hugh was arranging to amplify the altar of *St. John Baptist*, his patron, when he was on his death bed, in Nov. 1200, and beside which, according to his desire, his remains were originally laid. This chapel, as our learned Lincoln antiquary the late Precentor Edmund Venables has

explained, was enlarged by a rectangular addition eastward (removed by Essex in 1772); but in 1280 the body of St. Hugh was removed to a place rather to the north of the centre of the new Angel Choir, which was still known in 1641 as "Our Lady's Chapel" (in 1672, "*Capella Beatae Mariae*," see No. 7 below).*

Browne Willis in 1742, following the Cotton MS. Tib. E. 3, and the other contemporary chantry certificate (cir. 1545), places the Barton, Gare, and Thornton chantry "at St. John the Baptist's altar" (where mass of the B. Virgin was daily sung), and W. Thornaco's chantry, and that of K. Edward II. (and Isabella) at "B. Mary's altar"; and H. Edwinstowe's chantry "in the *chapel* of B. Mary within the church," or, as the time-tables of 1506 and 1531 express it, "at the altar where the Lady Mass is sung." And the table of 1531 implies that the "Thornaco" chantry was at the Lady Mass altar, which (as we see from the case of Salisbury) was not of necessity dedicated under the *title* of the B.V. Mary. See further under No. 7 below.

Now there is a difficulty about these chapels, the "Chapel of St. John Baptist" and the "Chapel of our Lady."

In the 18th century the northern one (No. 4) is frequently called "St. Mary's" (sometimes St. "Mary Magdalen's," possibly with intent to get

---

* So also it is said in Brooke's *Guide* (1840), that this northern apsidal large chapel was "dedicated to the Blessed Virgin." This statement may, I think, be traced to Hollar's plan of 1672.

over the difficulty of having two Lady Chapels so
near together), while in the 15th century we constantly read of "the Chapel of St. John Bapt.,
where the mass of B.V. Mary is said 'hora
prima.'" The best suggestion which I can make
(a mere conjecture) is, that some time or other
after St. Hugh's body was translated in 1280, the
letter of his request, that he might lie near St.
John the Baptist's altar, was carried out, by the
simple expedient of interchanging the names and
dedications of the larger apsidal altar and that at
the extreme east. So the *altar* of St. John Baptist
was in the east central Lady Chapel, where the
mass *Salve* of our Lady was sung. Apart from
the natural desire of the chapter to comply with
the great Saint's last wishes, while they strove at
the same time to give him greater honour, another
slight argument in favour of my suggestion has
occurred to me. Though "the mass of our Lady
at the altar of St. John Bapt. at the 1st hour" is
a description not uncommonly used, we also find
it in another form,—"the altar where the mass of
the B. Mary is celebrated daily at the first hour,"—
as if to avoid some confusion which might arise
if the dedication-title of the altar were named. If
there had been no danger of confusion, how much
simpler it would have been to say plainly "at St.
John Baptist's altar," instead of employing either
of the circumlocutions which are invariably used.

In the chantry certificate 33 we read of "Eden-
stow chauntrie in *capella* beate Marie" (7e),*

* See *Statutes* (1897, Cambridge Press) part II. p. cclvii, whence the
meaning of these references will be plain.

"Barton, Gare, et Thornton chaunterie ad *altare* Sti. Johannis Baptiste" (7*h*), and "Cantaria vocata Thornaco chauntrie, ad *altare* beate Marie" (8), where also was that of K. Edward II. (10).

"The Chaplain of the Chantry of H. de Eden-stowe between 9 and 10 o'clock, at the altar where mass of the B. Virgin is daily said." 1531.

The vicar celebrating, between 8 and 9 o'clock, for the chantry "for W. de Thornaco, at the altar where the mass of the Virgin is said *prima hora.*" (Ibid.)

There was probably a piscina and aumbry here, before the twofold alteration in the wall of this chapel was made.

I cannot say why Simon Barton's chantry was placed here, rather than in the great north-west transept where he was buried. Perhaps the altars in the last-named had not been set up in 1280 when he died.

5. *Holy Trinity Chapel.* Bp. Richard Fleming's chapel annexed about 1431 to the north side of the Angel Choir. A piscina is constructed in the south wall. The Fleming Chantry was at the "Trinity Altar" according to the list or time-table of masses in 1531. Maddison's *Vicars Choral*, pp. 41, 42. But it does not occur so early as that of 1506. It is called the chantry of *Robert* Fleming (dean in 1452-83) "in capella S. et Individue Trinitatis" in the chantry list of 1545. There was more than one chaplain here. Colynson's and Chedworth's

chaplain also said masses at the altar of Holy
Trinity. Ibid, 42. Bp. J. Chedworth was buried
in the north aisle just outside the door of Fleming's
chapel in 1471.

⁎ It will be well here to insert the earliest list
of altars of Lincoln. I saw it for the first time
when I was at Lincoln in November, 1895; and
I now think it may modify some of the conjectures
which I have made in the earlier pages of this
book, as on the other hand it certainly supports
some of the suppositions which I laid down.
A scribe in the *Registrum Antiquissimum* (begun cir.
1210-15, but rubricated by the hand of the rubri-
cator of the Black Book, cir. 1338, according to
Mr. Bradshaw), after remarking that before Bp.
Sutton's time the chapel of St. Mary Magdalen
consisted of an altar in the Minster, but had been
removed into the "atrium," or yard, for the peace
of the choir and security of the church, as well as
to facilitate the performances of occasional offices
for the parishioners, &c., &c., proceeds to note
that the reader would find (what now at least is
unfortunately not extant) at the end of this
volume or register, under the title " De Altaribus
et Altaristis," full information "concerning the
other altars [beside St. Mary Magdalen's] in the
church," that is to say, Saints (*a*) Michael, (*b*)
Andrew, (*c*) Denys, (*d*) Hugh, (*e*) Katharine, (*f*)
John Baptist, (*g*) Nicholas, (*h*) the Apostles Peter
and Paul, (*i*) Stephen, (*k*) Gu[th]lac, (*l*) John the
Evangelist, (*m*) Thomas the Martyr, and (*n*) Giles.

Thus *e*, *f*, *g* are clearly the three altars in the retro-choir or Angel Choir; *a*, *b*, *c* are in the great north aisle; *d*, in the N.E. transept, its altar dedicated in 1255. (The other apsidal chapel may have had no altar in it since the Translation of St. Hugh. It had at one time been a chapel of St. John Baptist.) *h* (and possibly *i*), apsidal chapel (or chapels) in S.E. transept; *k*, an altar with an East Anglian dedication (St. Guthlac, of Croyland, Abbat) of which all further trace, I believe, has perished. I can only surmise that it *may* have been near Little St. Hugh's shrine, or else in the revestry; or again (as I think the most probable supposition), one of the altars in the great south aisle may originally have had this dedication, which, at a later date, was exchanged for another title. In which case:—*k*, *l*, *m* would be the three altars in the great south aisle; and *n*, an altar in the nave, perhaps at the south-west, or else it may have been in the S.W. transept, *i.e.* in addition to the three others which appear to have been in that part of the Church.

To resume our circuit of the church :—

6-8. At the east end of the Minster are three chapels. In the centre " our Lady's Chapel," as Sanderson called it (No. 7 below). To the north of this,—

6. " Borough's," *i.e.*, Burghersh Chapel with *altar of St. Katharine.* Here were the Burghersh and W. Wolff's chantries. *Vicars Choral*, pp. 41, 42. Browne Willis, in 1742, following the authority

of Chantry Certificates of 1545, places here the
"Stretton and Woolvey's" chantries, besides that
of the Burghershes.   The tomb of Bp. Henry
Burghersh (Dec., 1340), and his father, Robert
Lord B., forms the southern boundary of this
chapel ; and the bishop's elder brother Bartholomew,
one of the first Knights of the Garter, lies on the
other side, where in the 17th century the tomb of
Leo de Welles, 1461, is marked.   It is called the
"Buckingham chauntrie" for two chaplains at
the altar of "*St. Hugh and St. Katharine*," in
Chantry Certificate, 33, 7*b*. Cf. No. 3 above.

The old Chantry Register (ff. 3, 169, 175) places
the Chantry of William Fitz-Ulf, priest of St.
Swithun's, "in altari S. Katerine."   The same
appears as the chantry of " W. Wolfe " in the
time-tables of 1507, 1531, and the certificates of
1545.   But the last-named mention that Ri. Stretton's chantry was amalgamated with it.   Ri.
Stretton was prior of St. Katharine's, 1334.   The
supplement to the Chantry Book, f. 392, assigns
masses for J. Bukyngham Bp. (1362-97; d. 10 Mar.,
1398) "in capella S. Katerine," and here, as we
saw above (No. 3), one at least of his masses was
celebrated in 1545.   Another supplement or appendix added to the original portion of the old
book of Lincoln Chantries (Chantry Reg. f. 334)
places in the same chapel the masses of Barth.
and Rob. Burghersh, "ubi corpus bone memorie
H. de Burghersch quiescit."   And those masses
are said to be at St. Katharine's *altar* in the time-

tables of 1507 and 1531 and the certificate of 1545.
Here, I think, are traces of a piscina in the floor,
near the east wall.   This appears to have been
fitted with a stone basin, and a pierced shaft or
pipe.

7. The Rev. John Kaye, jun., who has bestowed
diligent attention upon the architecture of the
Minster, writes:—" It is probable that there were
two chantry chapels occupying the space under the
great east window, separated by a partition wall.
That on the north side founded by K. Edward I.,
in memory of his wife Eleanor, whose *viscera* were
interred here."

Here are clear traces of a piscina in the floor,
against the east wall, toward the southern end of the
bay.   In favour of Mr. Kaye's suggestion, it may
be alleged that St. Hugh's shrine was most probably
not in the centre, but on one side, towards the north.

It seems, however, to me most natural to place in
the centre of the space beneath the window the altar
" where a daily *mass* of the Blessed Virgin was sung
before the shrine of St. Hugh," although the altar
need not have been dedicated by her title.   At
Salisbury, where (as at Lincoln) the whole church
was to be known as St. Mary's, her name, or rather
one of the mysteries commonly associated therewith,
was reserved for the high altar, but the daily mass
of the Virgin was always from the first celebrated
at the extreme east, in what was then called the
" *Salve*" (and now the " Lady") *Chapel*, but at an

altar which had quite a different dedication (Holy Trinity and All Hallows). And the like may be so far true of Lincoln, that the Blessed Virgin's mass was sung at an altar which did not from the first, or generally, bear her name in its special dedication. See what I have said above, at No. 4, in favour of supposing that, when St. Hugh's remains had been translated in 1280, the title of the *altar* was made "*St. John Baptist's.*" It is clearly called so in the Chantry Register, where it is said that the *viscera Alienore regine* (1290) were deposited "before the altar of St. John Baptist." These remains are placed in Hollar's plan (1672) on the north part of this central chantry bay or chapel. Her effigy, lately executed in gilt bronze by the munificence of the late Mr. Joseph Rusten from Dugdale's drawing and the monument in Westminster Abbey, is now on the other side beneath the central window.

On the other hand, we find in the records of a visitation, held by Bp. Alnwick's Commissary in 1437, a complaint brought by W. Shipton, a vicar, concerning the "sub-deacon and deacon, ministers of B. Mary's altar at the daily mass of our Lady." *Statutes* ii., p. 394.

It was a foregone conclusion that the altar of the "Lady *Mass*" should, sooner or later, come to be known as "St. *Mary's Altar.*"

8. "William the Conqueror's Chapel" (*Sanderson*) with the Cantilupe and Fitzwilliam Chantries. Here was the altar of St. Nicholas, at which the chantries

of Nicholas and Joan Cantilupe (his widow, who died
in 1358) were placed. See supplement in Chantry
Book, ff. 323, 375. Two Cantilupe masses were
celebrated here at the altar (1507), or chapel (1531),
of St. Nicholas. So also the Chantry Certificates
of 1545. In Hollar's map (1672) the tombs of Lord
N. de Cantilupe (cir. 1355) and Robert Wymbysh,
subdean of Lincoln and prior of Nocton (1478),
"*alias* Darcy Ab.," are shown in the northern verge
of this chantry. The old Chantry Register itself
(ff. 2, 20, 224) places the chantry of Peter de
Hungaria, canon, at St. Nicholas' altar; and Browne
Willis (*Survey* ii., p. 34), in 1742, mentions that T.
Fitzwilliam's obit had been kept here.

Here are traces of a piscina, probably supported
originally by a pillar. There is a bracket (as if for
an image) on the east wall toward the southern
extremity, about 8 feet above the floor. In *chancels*
the patron's image, according to Dr. Rock, was
placed to the north, and that of B. V. Mary to the
south.

9. *Altar of St. Blaise*, in the chantry chapel of
Bp. John Russell (1495), annexed to the south side
of the Angel Choir. See the obit list of 1527. In
the Chantry Certificates of 1545 is mentioned "the
chantry of J. Russell and obit of K. Edward IV.
(who died 9 Apr., 1483), *in capella S. Blasii.*

Here is a single piscina constructed in the south
wall. There are two brackets, or pedestals for
images in the east wall, right and left of the altar,
about 5 feet from the floor.

10. Bishop J. Longland's chapel, annexed about 1547. It is doubtful whether there was ever an altar dedicated here or a title affixed, chantries having been abolished, or made over to K. Henry VIII. in 1545 (37 H. viii., c. 4), and to Edward VI. in 1547. Several writers, such as Wild and Mackenzie Walcott, give the dedication as St. Catharine's, but state no authority. On the screen is the inscription, "*Longa Terra Mensuram eius* (Arms of K. Henry VIII.) *Dominus Dedit.*" The Bishop's heart alone was buried here; his body at Eton. There is a piscina in the south wall; several brackets unfinished are in the west wall.

11. We come now to an apsidal chapel, the nearest in the south-east transept. This has a double aumbry in the N.E. face, and a double piscina in the S.E. It is at present used as the Lay Clerks' vestry. John Coney's map, cir. 1830, in the modern edition of Dugdale's *Monasticon,* calls this "Lady Joan Cantelupe's chantry." Brooke's Guide, cir. 1844, goes further, and says, "founded . . . . by Joan Cantelupe, and dedicated to *St. Paul.*" I believe this statement may be traced to an anonymous writer of 1771, on whom Wild largely depended. However, I have not found any notice of any altar in honour of St. Paul in the Minster (apart from St. Peter). The Apostles Peter and Paul are combined together in the Register at Lincoln, as elsewhere. Bishop Henry Lexington (d. 1258) was buried just outside the screen of this chapel

according to Hollar's plan. Unless the authority for making No. 12 the altar of St. Peter be found to be overwhelming, I should prefer to describe No. 11 as the *altare apostolorum*, viz., St. Peter and St. Paul.

12. Another apsidal chapel, with a *single* aumbry N.E., and a double piscina S.E., arranged much as in No. 11. Here, according to common tradition, was the tomb of B. Robert (*i.e.* Bp. Grosseteste). J. Coney, cir. 1830, places here " Bishop de Well's Chapel," which Brooke's *Guide* (p. x.), a few years later, expresses more precisely* as "founded by Bp. Welles, and dedicated to *St. Peter.*" The altar of St. Peter was one of the most important. Here mass was sung daily for Bishops of Lincoln departed. Some keepers and clerks of St. Peter's altar were certainly buried in the adjoining transept. The altar of St. Peter, or its keeper, is frequently named in the Black Book. I am inclined to think that one of the two apsidal chapels was St. Peter and St. Paul's, and the other (and if I am not mistaken this was not No. 11 but No. 12) was St. Stephen's, which is mentioned next in order after St. Peter and St. Paul's altar in *Registrum Antiquissimum.*

After studying the time-tables of *missae currentes* (to adopt a term from Salisbury) which our Dean and Chapter issued for the guidance of Chantry

---

* The tomb of Hugh de Welles is placed in Hollar's plan due south of Fleming's in the east end of the north choir aisle. Fragments of the canopy of Robert Grosseteste's sepulchre have been preserved, and in the opinion of Edmund Venables are sufficient to justify a restoration. *Lincoln Cathedral,* p. 60. (Ibister & Co., 1898.)

Chaplains in 1507 and 1531, and for a knowledge
of which I have to thank Mr. Maddison, I cannot
help remarking that nothing is there said about
any use to be made of this *Altare B. Petri* by any
of the *chaplains*. We know, moreover, of no case
of any *Vicar* celebrating there any of those
numerous chantry masses or obits, about which the
Chantry Book gives so many particulars. We
know, however, that the keeper of St. Peter's altar
undertook as his principal duty to say mass
("daily," some MSS. say) "at the said altar of
St. Peter for the souls of all Bishops departed,"
and that he was in priest's orders, and that some
keepers and clerks of this altar were buried in one
part or another of this transept in the 15th and 16th
centuries, as also were some of the most honoured
Bishops of Lincoln in the 13th century — Ro.
Grosseteste (1253), H. Lexington (1258), and Ri.
Gravesend (1279). I am well aware that the altar
itself stands in a somewhat obscure apse, in the
S.E. transept (now used for the men's vestry), but
it is the counterpart of the place in the N.E.
transept, which was most sacred in St. Hugh's
eyes (the altar of St. John Bapt.), and I see not
how to escape the conclusion that here the Chapter
Mass was celebrated. If so, the congregation,
gathered to this homely service of the Lincoln
Minster family, would take their places just where
we stand at the present day for prayer, before and
after Divine Service in choir. We find that
Chapter Mass was sometimes, if not always, sung

at Salisbury at an altar of the same dedication (St. Peter and Apostles) in a somewhat similar and not much more convenient place, but, as here, in one of the oldest (and oldest fashioned) corners of the Church, which fact at Salisbury is somewhat in favour of this conclusion for Lincoln.

This may help also to account for the curious term *" lavatorium capitarii,"* and the changing of copes *" in capitario"* (Black Book, pp. 365, 369, 382), the revestry and the lavatory being both of them near at hand. In the old Chantry Register (lf. 4, 6; cf. 33, 217) we read of *cantaria pro animabus episcoporum defunctorum ad altare S. Petri.*

13. The Revestry Altar. This was, no doubt, used for putting out ornaments and vestments to be ready for use. The silver-gilt cross stood upon it (in its socket) when not in use for processions. Also two great tabernacles with images of ivory and the Story of the Passion (*Lincoln Inventories*, pp. 4, 7). Possibly holy water was blessed here *privatim in vestibulo* on certain days. (See *Processionale Sarum*, ed. 1882, pp. 59, 3.) Near the altar here those who were not well enough to go into the choir might say their Divine service in the vestry. (*Nov. Reg.*, p. 355.) There are several aumbries and recesses, but under the present wainscots and shelves it is impossible to see whether any of them was originally a piscina, as seems likely to have been the case.

14. The Lavatory, with fire-place and antient

conduit, possibly the successor of the old "*lava-torium capitarii*" mentioned in the Black Book, p. 365, in a late 14th century MS. of the Custom Book of 1270.   There is a fire-place here, but I do not see any reason to suppose that there was also an altar.

15–17. Passing the shrine of Little St. Hugh, 1255, and turning into the great south transept we reach three chapels, divided one from another by low arcaded walls :—

15. "*Capella Fundatoris,*" sive "*pro benefactori-bus.*" Possibly St. Guthlac's or St. Edward's Chapel of the Works.   The title of the northernmost of the chapels in the south-west transept is wrapped in obscurity.

Hollar's plan (1672) calls the N. chapel in S. aisle " *Capella Fundatoris.*"*   This, perhaps, was the ground on which a writer, in 1771, followed by Wild, Walcott, and others, calls that the chapel of "St. Edward the Martyr and Remigius."   J. Coney's map (cir. 1830) calls this "Henry Duke of Lancaster's Chantry"; and Brooke's *Guide* (cir. 1844) thus far following Wild's authority of 1771, adds " dedicated to St. Edward the Martyr." Precentor Venables says (in Murray's Hand Book) —what seems to me, *à priori*, unlikely†—that the

---

* In Schalby's day William the Conqueror was ranked as our "Fundator,' Remigius our " Stabilitor."

† I mean that I think it unlikely that a chapel or altar dedicated in honour of St. Anne should have borne that title so early and then have been displaced by an altar of St. Edward.   I should *à priori* have expected the inverse order.

altar of St. Anne was changed to the title of St. Edward (the Martyr), and was founded by Henry Duke of Lancaster and Earl of Lincoln, for four priests, whose effigies (as well as the inscription "*Orate pro benefactoribus istius Ecclesie,*") are carved over the entrance. The priests of this chantry had (cir. 1320) a house (formerly the Chancellor's) west of the Deanery, and near the Treasurer's. It was pulled down in 1828. It should be observed that the title of St. Anne's altar is found in 1390 and 1531, and the title of St. Edward (for which the late Precentor could not recollect his authority), I suppose, dropped out of use. There is no altar of St. Anne (nor of St. Edward) in the list in the *Registrum Antiquissimum* early in the 14th century, but an *altare Sancti Gu[th]laci* is placed in order between St. Stephen's and that of St. John the Evangelist. Possibly a somewhat old-fashioned East Anglian dedication had to make way for the title of St. Edward, which may well have been popular in the 14th century.

An impetus to the *cultus* of St. Anne was given in 1383 when Abp. Courteney received a bull from Pope Urban VI. on the subject of a festival in her honour; but, as we shall see presently under No. 17, the altar or chapel of St. Anne must be placed at the other end of this S.W. transept. It is a fact well known to archæologists that in the earliest times a "chantry" was not considered to be a *locality*, such as a chapel or an altar, but it implied merely the *foundation* of a mass for souls which was capable, in many instances, of being said on one day at one altar, and the next day at another, although the founders of chantries did, no doubt, oftentimes express their preference for a particular altar, and in particular instances (especially in the 15th and 16th centuries) they would make provision for a new structural chapel with an altar enclosed within it.

And in some instances the title of some specific chapel is expressly named in the deed or "ordination" regulating the duties of the priest or priests employed to fulfil the engagements of such and such a chantry, and we come in common parlance to speak of the Hungerford Chantry when we ought more strictly to say "the Hungerford Chapel," or the Chapel constructed or assigned for the chantry mass founded by Lord Hungerford or for the repose of his soul. In the case of the "Works" or "Fabrick Chantry," at Lincoln, I think it not impossible that at the date when the inscription "Orate pro benefactoribus istius ecclesie" was carved upon the screen of No. 15 it was designed that chaplains of the Works Chantry should say mass there regularly to fulfil their obligations to celebrate on behalf of living and departed benefactors to the fabrick of Lincoln Minster (according to the endowment founded by Henry Duke of Lancaster, or by Treasurer J. de Welborne, who died in 1381, or some other). But if that may have been the case in the 14th century, we must bear in mind that at all events the arrangement was otherwise in the 16th century. In 1506-7 three priests of the Works

Chantry were directed to celebrate mass, the first at the altar of St. George, the second at the altar of St. Anne, and the third likewise at the altar of St. Anne. Mr. Maddison has now proved that the altar of St. Anne was not at No. 15 but No. 17. It may then be suggested that the altar of St. George was at No. 15 in 1506 and 1531. In that case the former of two suggestions made by me in a note on p. 182 above, and printed before we had learnt about the true position of St. Anne's chapel, appears to have been approximately correct.

16. The central chapel in the great south transept is called in Hollar's plan (1672) "Consistorium Decani et Capituli." In J. Coney's map (cir. 1830) it is called " Bp." [Henry] " Lexington's Chapel "; but in Brooke's *Guide* (cir. 1844) it is said to have been "founded by Dean Lexington and dedicated to St. Andrew." "Dean Lexington" would most naturally mean *William* L., who died in 1272. But Wild's anonymous authority of 1771 says "*Bishop* [Henry] Lexington, when Dean" (1245-54). Mackenzie Walcott (whom the late Precentor assisted in 1866) evidently felt some misgivings. He says, "St. Andrew, or St. John Baptist, with an arcaded wall (now the Dean's Consistory Court), founded by Bishop Lexington." *Lincoln Memorials*, p. 45. It is not near the tomb of either of the Lexingtons.* Bp. H. L.'s chantry was at the altar of St. John in 1531. But it was St. John *the Evangelist.*

---

* Hollar places Bp. H. de Lexinton's tomb (1258) in the south-east transept.

An *altar of St. John the Evangelist*, where exequies of Vicars Choral were celebrated, is one of the very few which are mentioned by name in the Black Book (p. 395). It is named in wills of 1390 and 1433. The tomb and shrine of John de Dalderby (1319) stood opposite the south-west corner of this central chapel, and cir. 1485 John de Grantham places John de Dalderby's mass "at St. John's altar." In 1531 the Henry Lexington and Beningworth Chantries were so placed.

The "altar of St. John the Evangelist" is named next that of St. Anne in the will of Ri. de Beverley in 1390. So when the Guide Books call the centre chapel "St. Andrew's (or St. John's)," I should certainly add "more probably the *latter*." And the list in *Registrum Antiquissimum* suggests the same conclusion. Moreover, after I had written my opinion to this effect, I received a note from Mr. Maddison, telling me that the circumstance of W. Shipton, priest vicar, being buried here, in this centre chapel (No. 16), and his will (proved in 1465) desiring that he should be buried "*coram altari S. Johannis evangeliste*" establishes it past a doubt.

The old Chantry Register places "in altari Beati Johannis Evangeliste" the chantries of (*a*) J. de Dalderby, Bp. 1300-1320, lf. 1, 6, 12, 150; (*b*) W. Ruffus, or Ruphus, de Roveston, physicus, or medicus; lf. 3, 33, 212; and (*c*) H. de Benyngworth, sub-dean 1294-1318, who "chose his sepulture before (coram) this altar," lf. 2, 22, 24, 80, 274. There were two chaplains of the Beningworth chantry celebrating at this altar according to the time-tables of 1506 and 1531. And these tables mention also another pair of chaplains celebrating there, and that of 1531 tells us that it was for the soul of H. Lexington, Bp. 1254-8.

17. *Chapel of St. Anne.* "The south chapel in the cross Ile" (Sanderson) is rightly called "Canon Tailboys Chantry." W. Tailboys, preb. of All •Saints and Nassington, resigned the precentory at the accession of K. Edward VI., but did not die until 1572. Gilbert Lord Talboys, of Angos and Kyme, died about 1540. But the chapel appears to have been associated with the earlier Lords of Kyme; for in Hollar's plan "*Capella et Tumulus Humphreyvelli*" is marked here. Gilbert d'Umfravill of Kyme, Earl of Angos, and Gillian, his wife, died cir. 1308; and Gilbert and Maud cir. 1381. Sir G. Taylboys, Knt., has a monument here. ? 1514. He gave a corporas case, embroidered with his arms, to the minster.

This S.W. chapel is said in Brooke's *Guide*, "Description," &c., p. 4, to have been dedicated to *St. Giles.* A celebration by Hugh de Walmesford's chaplain at *St. Giles' altar* is mentioned in the Chantry Book Supplement, lf. 339, and at the visitation of 1437 (*Stat.* ii., pp. 405-6). Walmesford's mass (1344) was at St. Giles' altar also in 1507 and 1531, as were, "in *capella* S. Egidii," those of Ri. Ravenser (1386) and Ri. de Faldingworth, *i.e.*, Richard, *rector of* Faldingworth, son of Herbert de Neuport, cir. 1253.

The Faldingworth chantry in St. Giles' chapel is mentioned likewise in the old Chantry Register, lf. 3, 108.

But I cannot at present tell on what authority Brooke names the southernmost chapel after St. Giles, though it is perfectly plain that an altar and a chapel in honour of St. Giles was established *in some part or other* of the Minster as early as circa 1335 and as late as 1530. On the other hand, as we shall see presently, the title of St. *Anne's* Chapel for the south end of the great south transept rests on 16th century evidence.

On the other hand, the early 14th century list of altars in *Registr. Antiquiss.* places the altar of St. Thomas (Becket) the Martyr next after that of St. John the Evangelist; and this, if we suppose the list to proceed in orderly sequence, should lead us to place the altar of S. Thomas either at No. 17, or else at No. 15. Perhaps there were four altars in this aisle. One of them may have been under the circular window known as the "Bishop's Eye."

The altar of St. Giles, if we rely upon the order in which the altars are named in the documents, must have been either here, or, (just possibly) accommodated in the Consistory Court Chapel, No. 20, which, I believe, was dedicated to St. Sebastian. A glance at the records of Wells or York will show that altars with double dedication were then not uncommon. Mr. Logsdail assures me that he has heard on good authority that the Tailboys family dedicated their chantry altar to St. Giles. I dare say that some of my readers can give me 'chapter and verse' for this belief, in accordance with which I have placed the altar of St. Giles here at No. 17, rather than at No. 20, or elsewhere. [Thus I wrote in 1896. But I confess that I might very possibly have written otherwise had I then known for a certainty what I seem once barely to have, for a moment, surmised, namely that No. 17 was called the chapel of St. Anne. This appears clearly to have been the case, for the Rev. Arthur Roland Maddison, M.A., F.S.A., now (January 1898) prebendary of All Saints, Thorngate, in reading a will, dated in the year 1556, has recently discovered the fact that a testator expressed a wish that he might have a place for his grave assigned him opposite "the quere of the Chapel of St. Anne, now called Umphreville's, at the south end of the cross yle by the great steple." It was called "Umphreville's" because of the Talboys monument with the Umfraville arms on it, the Talboys being representatives of the great Umfraville family.]

Here is a double piscina as in No. 15. Above the altar space in the middle of the E. wall of this chapel is a bracket for an image, 7 or 8 feet above the floor, thus facing the Galilee door.

18. Under the lantern in the Rood Tower was the *altar of Holy Rood*, or *St. Cross*, below the "Crucifix, Mary, and John." This may have been either against the choir screen on one side of the entrance, as there were altars at Wells, Exeter, and many

other places, or (as I think far more probable in the case of an altar "before the rood") upon the "jube" or choir screen, which was ascended by steps on either side for the ceremony of chanting the Epistle and Gospel at High Mass. Such, I understand from Mr. Edmund Bishop, was the arrangement of the altar at St. Albans; and Dr. Rock mentions altars on rood screens, and on other elevated positions, as not uncommon.

Matthew Paris mentions that Remigius the Founder was buried before the altar of St. Cross.

19. Hollar's plan (1672) marks (as Mr. Kaye tells me) Dean Macworth's tomb (d. 1451) to the west of the south-western pier of the lantern or rood-tower. And Mr. Maddison has found a record of the presentation of a chaplain for the Macworth Chantry " in capella sancti *Georgii*," 9th July, 1457. If this was near Macworth's grave, we must suppose that there was once an altar here so far screened (by some structure now removed) that it could be called a chapel. No altar of St. George is mentioned in the old Chantry Register; but, doubtless, the *cultus* of this saint received an *impetus* after the institution of the Most Noble Order in 1344; and Abp. Chicheley's injunction in 1414 points to a general recognition of his patronage in merry England. It occurs to me to enquire on a mere conjecture, whether the now nameless " Dean's Chapel " (No. 28) may not have been called St. George's in the 15th and 16th centuries. In the

time-tables of 1507, 1531, we read that the "first,"
or "morrow mass," was celebrated *at St. George's*
altar, by one of the Works chantry priests, and
another mass later in the day by the chaplain of
Treasurer Crosby's chantry.   Crosby died in 1477.
The date of his will is given by Hardy; but I infer,
from Mr. Gibbons' book, that wills are not found
in the Bishop's registry between 1472-80.   Crosby
was buried in the Minster, but the place of his tomb
is unrecorded.

19*a.* It is *possible* that there may have been a
"Jhesus altar" by Macworth's tomb at the south-
east of the nave, as there was a mass of the Most
Holy Name of Jesus, or else of the Five Wounds,
to be recited *cum nota* on Fridays, with choristers
singing before the crucifix on the south side of the
church, according to the provisions of the will of
Bp. W. Smyth in 1514.   However, I think it rather
more likely that the reference there is, not to the
great rood, mentioned just above at No. 18, but
to some other crucifix on the south *west* pier of the
nave, near the burial place of Bp. Smyth.

20. *Altar of St. Sebastian.*   Attached to the
south-west end of the nave is an Early English
Chapel annexed in 1250.   Since 1609 this has been
assigned as a Consistory Court for the Bishop, and
for the Archdeacon of Lincoln's Visitations.   J.
Coney's map, cir. 1830, calls it "St. Hugh's
chapel" (possibly because of St. Hugh's bells in

R

the steeple), and Brooke's *Guide*, cir. 1844, says more explicitly "dedicated to the Holy Trinity and the Blessed Virgin by St. Hugh." But I think he has carelessly copied from Wild's statement (1819) that it was founded by "Bp. Hugh," possibly meaning Hugh de Welles. This statement may, perhaps, have given rise to two other inaccurate statements, that it was "St. Hugh's Chapel," and that it was "Trinity Chapel." There can be no doubt that the real Trinity Chapel is Bp. Fleming's, No. 5 above, though many others may have *shared* this as a general dedication (="to the glory of God"). Our architectural authorities date the consistory chapel as subsequent to the time of St. Hugh: they now place it, I believe, later than Hugh de Welles also. In Bp. W. Smyth's will (proved in 1514) *St. Sebastian's Chapel* is said to be on the south side of the cathedral church, and near the place which this Bishop (founder of Brasenose College) designed for his own burial. He was buried at the west end of the nave, rather to the south side, not very far from the door of this chapel, and near the great west door. A fragment of his tombstone is now in the cloisters. A marble tablet was erected in modern times to his memory near to the place of his burial by members of the College which he founded. In the S.W. chapel there is a double piscina. It is noticeable that though the chapel (known in modern times as the consistory) is an old structure, we do not find the title of any chapel or altar of *S. Sebastian* until after the death

of Bishop Smyth. Thus it is named as an altar in
1531, but not in the corresponding time-table of
1507. But the *chapel* (or altar) of St. *Giles* is
named both in early and late records: the chantry
of Ric. de Faldingworth "in capella S. Egidii,"
Old Chantry Register, lf. 3, 108 (and similarly at
the altar of St. Giles in 1531), that of Hugh de
Walmisford, at the "altare B. Egidii," in the
supplement to the same register, lf. 339, and in
1507, 1531. The chaplains for Ric. Ravenser have
this altar likewise assigned to them in 1507, 1531.
I conclude, therefore, that the consistory court may
have been always known as the chapel of St. Giles,
and that an altar of St. Sebastian was added within
it, or in an adjoining part of the nave, early in the
16th century. It is, however, right to add that
most writers* place St. Giles' altar at No. 17, and
at St. Sebastian's Chapel his mass was celebrated
in 1531. From analogy, and relying on the list in
Registr. Antiquiss., I should have been rather
inclined to place here the *altare sci. Egidii*, so that the
last altar in the list (that of St. Giles) might balance
the (*quondam*) altar of St. Mary Magdalen (No. 23)
with which, starting from the N.W. corner of the
nave, the list began. Here in the Consistory Court,
at the S.W. corner of the nave, there is a double
piscina (without any intervening shaft), not in the

---

* [Since Canon A. R. Maddison's happy identification of the Talboys
Chapel (No. 17) as being certainly dedicated in honour of St. Anne, some at
least of the writers to whom I have referred in the text might not improbably
be inclined to reconsider the question.]

eastern, but in the southern wall. The basins are
filled with convex blocks of stone, evidently very old.

21. St. Hugh's, or the Ringer's Chapel, under
the S.W. tower. Here, I suppose, was "*le pele*,"
or *Peal Altar*, where the mattin bell was rung, and
where one of the two chantries of Bishop Hugh de
Welles (1235) had its place at least in 1531. Pele
Chapel had its own vestments and music books;
and in Bishop Alnwick's time one of the bellringers
kept a dog lying near the altar. In the 17th and
18th centuries lists of the "Masters and Company
of Ringers of St. Hugh's and our Lady Bells"
were painted on the walls. The pinnacle of the
turret supports an effigy of St. Hugh. "*Le pele*"
was mentioned at Bishop Alnwick's Visitation in
1437, *Statutes* ii., 404, 407. There is no trace of
any piscina or aumbry here.

22. St. Mary's Tower. The "North Tower,
formerly Great Tom's Tower" (*Brooke*). The
turret is surmounted by the figure of the "Swineheard of Stow." It seems not improbable, as Mr.
Maddison observes, that this may be the chapel
of St. James "near the stairs leading to the western
tower," mentioned at No. 35 below.

23. The Morning Chapel, or Morning Prayer
Chapel (opposite St. Sebastian's, or the Consistory
Court). Here, as Hollar's plan tells us, after the
Restoration, "Morning Prayers were said at 6

o'clock." This custom was continued until about 1790; the prebendary of St. Botolph's for some time previously performed the duty. On a recommendation from my Father, at his visitation in 1873, the Dean and Chapter once more revived the custom of providing what has now been for twenty years the "Workmen's Service" at 7.40 on weekdays. This was frequently undertaken by the late Archbishop of Canterbury when Chancellor. We may identify this chapel with that of *St. Mary Magdalen*, mentioned in 1506-7, 1531, and in the account of Bp. J. Gynwell's will, cir. 1363. Also, more explicitly in the Chantry Register as "capella B. Marie Magdalene, ad caput occidentale ecclesie, ex parte boriali, ubi celebari consuevit missa de B. Virgine hora prima pro animabus Roberti de Lascy, Ricardi de Rowell, et Hervici de Luda."

Though the walls of the building cannot really have been built so late as Bp. Gynwell's day (1347-63), yet there may be so much of truth in Leland's statement as to justify our supposing that the said bishop endowed and furnished a chantry there. His burial place, in the nave, is just south of the pillar, which ranges with the eastern wall of the chapel whereof we are speaking. There is a large aumbry there, and an old double piscina in the east wall. These are respectively north and south of the altar space. There is also a single piscina (perhaps Norman in workmanship) in the floor just below the equally plain double one in the wall. Overhead, 9 feet from the floor, is the bracket for an image ; below which is a painting (not very antient) of a dove. And here I will propound to any who can answer it, a question by the way: When the Bishop of Lincoln held a Synod in the Church, did they say the Mass of the Holy Ghost at the rood altar, or at a temporary or portable altar, or where? The place for the sitting of the synod was left to official discretion. (*Black Book*, Stat. i., p. 293.)

24. *The altar of St. Christopher (in the nave).* This is mentioned in the will of J. Cotes, prebendary of Thorngate, 1433 (*Gibbons*, p. 158). St. Christopher's *Gild*, in 1392 and 1416 (*ibid.* pp. 86, 128). In the computus of the year 1408-9 we find among receipts 29*s.* 8*d.* " de oblacionibus factis ad *nouam* ymaginem Sancti Xpoferi hoc anno." (In 1408-9 the receipts " de apertura stipitis sci Xpofori " amounted to 16*s.* 8*d.*) And again in J. Burton's will, 1537, we read of "the north aisle (leading) to St. Christopher." St. Christopher's stock (*stipes*) and his image have been mentioned above (see pages 109, 163). I suppose his altar to have been on the N. side, either against the choir-screen, or corresponding with the (southern) no. 19 in the bay of the nave next the central lantern, and thus hard by the tomb of the founder Remigius. The mass of T. Alford's chantry was said at St. Christopher's altar in 1531, and we know that Alford was buried in the nave in 1485. In 1492 the " morning mass " was ordered to be said at St. Christopher's, instead of at the altar of St. Nicholas. (*Vicars*

Choral, p. 37.) In 1535 Robt. Awbray, Fleming-chantry priest, desired to be buried "besyde Sainte Christofer's altare, at west ende of Sir Robert Pecoke's grave." Maddison, *Wills*, No. 22, p. 11.

25-27. We come now to the great north transept with three chapels. I would suggest that these contained the altars of St. Michael, St. Andrew, and St. Denys; and the order in the early 14th century list makes it highly probable that these were in one group, St. Andrew's being in the middle.

25. St. *Denys'* altar (Sancti Dionysii). The chantry in the N. transept, at the end nearest to the choir, is called "Bp. Buckingham's chantry" in J. Coney's map, cir. 1830. But there are objections to this. Browne Willis (*Survey Cath.* ii., 34) places the Buckingham chantry at " St. Hugh's altar," on the authority of Cotton MS. *Tiberius* E. 3, a chantry return of 1545. So also the order of 1531, *Vicars Choral*, p. 41. On the other hand it was, says Brooke's *Guide* (1840), following his anony-mous authority of 1771, "founded by Bp. Bucking-ham [d. at Canterbury 1398], and dedicated to St. James the Apostle." And so say Walcott's *Memorials* and Murray's *Guide*. But the late Pre-centor Venables says, " St. Thomas the Apostle," Williamson's *Guide*, p. 73 ("Thomas," perhaps, was merely a misprint for "James." There certainly was an altar of St. Dionis, or Denys; for a chaplain saying mass for the dead there is

mentioned in a deed of 20th April, 1221, in the Chantry Register, lf. 181ᵃ, and W. Fitz Fulk's chantry there is mentioned, *ibid*, 2ᵃ, 19ᵇ, 184. Dean W. Lexington's chantry was served there in 1420 (with Widington and Hiche's); but in 1500 W. de Lexington's chantry mass was at St. Andrew's altar (*Grantham's Book*), and in the Chantry Book itself (*cir.* 1330) at St. Michael's altar.

26. *St. Andrew's* altar. The middle chapel in the great N. transept is called "Canon Sutton and Woolvey's" in J. Coney's map, cir. 1830. "The chantry of Canon Richard Sutton and W. Woolvey's, and dedicated to St. Denis," says Brooke's *Guide*, following the authority of 1771, on whom Wild relied. This Richard Sutton is unknown to our annals. (?) Richard Stretton. Dean W. de Lexington was buried before the northernmost chapel (No. 27), nearer the Dean's door; but the *computus* of 1420 mentions a payment "*pro animabus Joh. Wydyngton, W. Lexington et Nich' Hicche ad altare sancti Dionisij*," which I take to be No. 25.

At the *altar of St. Andrew*, which I incline to place here at No. 26, in the middle of the three (and *Registrum Antiquissimum* bears me out) was the chantry of W. Aveton. The old Chantry Register (lf. 1, 6, 16, 251 ; cf. 332) takes notice of the chantry of Nicholas de Hiche, subdean, "in altari S. Andree, vbi requiescit corpus [eiusdem]." And in the additions to the same book we find the chantries of Walter Stanreth, treasurer (lf. 357), and of Henry

Beck, lord of Normanby with Ric. de Whitewell and other friends (lf. 374), "at the altar of St. Andrew the Apostle." A mass here is noted in the time-table of 1506-7, but the person commemorated, as frequently happens in that list, is not specified. The Aveton and Pollard chantries appear sometimes, but not, I believe, invariably, at St. Andrew's altar.

27. The altar of *St. Michael.* The most northerly chapel in the great N. transept is called in Coney's map "Fitzwilliam's chantry": Brooke's *Guide* says, "founded by Thomas Fitzwilliam, and dedicated to St. Nicholas":—It is, however, far removed from the tombs of that family, and the title is, perhaps, a misnomer. Murray's handbook calls the chapel "St. Nicholas or Michael"; and the latter (as I gather from the *Registr. Antiq.*) is correct. Precentor Venables inclined to St. Nicholas, perhaps on the authority of Wild and 1771. But that title is undoubtedly pre-occupied by No. 8, the Cantilupe Chantry altar, which is, moreover, near the Fitz-william tombs. In Hollar's plan (1672) the tombs of Deans W. Lexington and J. Shepey are placed near the screen of this chapel. There are traces of a piscina here in the floor near the N.E. corner. Ric. de Beverley's will in 1390 mentions the altar of St. Michael in close juxtaposition with those of St. Andrew and St. Denys, just as the *Registrum Anti-quissimum* had done. At St. Michael's altar in 1531 was the mass of W. Caux. No mention, however, is made of this in the corresponding time-table of

1507. The old Chantry-register places the chantry of W. Lexington (Dean 1263-72) "ad altare S. Michaelis," lf. 3, 32.

28. On the western side of that shorter northern transept in which we began our circuit, outside the choir, there is a large chapel which at one time had an upper floor or loft, and which still contains *apothecae* or recesses for the drugs of the minster-dispensary, if not for the stores of cloth (*pannus*) which was (or ought to have been) distributed to the poor. In Coney's map this is the "chapel built by Bishop Saint Hugh." Precentor Venables gave it the name by which it is best known, "the Dean's Chapel, said to have been the Pharmacy." It is hard by the Deanery, and in or near it several Deans of Lincoln have been buried. I have never heard any saint's name assigned to it as a title, but it does not follow of necessity that it never had one.* There is here a single piscina (fluted) in the floor; but, as Mr. Logsdail suggests, it is not impossible that it may have been a drain or sink intended for use in the Dispenser's craft. Mr. Micklethwaite however is of opinion that these floor sinks were to be used for a purpose mentioned in the *Rationale* of Durandus (lib. iv. cap. 30 § 20), namely for pouring out a few drops from the crewets "to clear the

---

* On p. 143 I have made a suggestion that the title of St. George might perhaps have been assigned to 'The Dean's Chapel.' But on further consideration I am inclined rather to place St. George's altar on the south side, and possibly at No. 15.

spouts of dust before 'making' the chalice." *The Ornaments of the Rubric,* Alcuin Club Tracts, No. 1. p. 41, *n.* (Longmans, 1897.)

29. The "*camera communis*" was never, so far as I am aware, a chapel. There was a "Clerk of the Chamber," and also a "Clerk Writer of the Chamber" (*Black Book,* p. 398); but the exact nature of the business there, or by them transacted I have yet to learn.

30. *Domus capitularis.* I mention the Chapter House here, merely for the purpose of repeating my conviction that the *capitularis missa,* or *missa in capitulo,* was never celebrated in that building. " The Chapter Mass " (see p. 188) existed some generations before any " domus capitularis " was built at Lincoln, and it is at least possible that the two (missa capitularis and domus capitularis) have no *direct* connexion even in their names; for it seems reasonable to connect the term either with "*capicium*" (*chevet*), the eastern part of a great church, or else with " *capitarium.*" Chapter Masses are sometimes celebrated in the nave of a great church, sometimes (*e.g.* at Durham) at the choir altar, sometimes more privately in the retro-choir. At Salisbury they were, if I rightly read the evidence, in the N.E. corner of the Church. As to Lincoln, I hazard the conjecture that the special mass mentioned in the old Chantry Register (lf. 4[b]) as celebrated in the important, though somewhat

diminutive, apsidal chapel of St. Peter in the S.E. transept was the Chapter Mass. Cf. *Black Book*, pp. 293-4, 289, 297, 394 ; *Chantry Register*, lf. 4, 6, 33, 217. In most of these the distinction of Chapter Mass from Mass at high altar is expressed.

There still remain a few titles of altars at Lincoln, for which I can at present assign no certain site.

31. *An Altar of St. Lucy* is mentioned in Jordan de Ingham's *computus*, 1294 :—" 13*s*. 4*d*. delivered to Adam Bell, chaplain, for the altar of St. Lucye."

32. The " altar of St. Edward," mentioned by the late Precentor Venables as formerly attached to the altar of (?) St. Anne. See Nos. 15, 17, above.

33. *The Altar of St. George.* See Nos. 19, 28 above. Morning Mass here at 5 a.m. in 1531 (the " first mass " in 1507) celebrated by one of the priests of the Fabrick or Works Chantry (cf. No. 15). J. Crosby's chaplain also celebrated here at 6 o'clock. Crosby was treasurer 1448-77. In 1507 one Sir Matthew Blackborn also was directed to say mass here between 9 and 10 a.m. Mr. Maddison finds a presentation to the Mackworth chantry (9th July, 1457) " in *capella* sancti Georgii."

On p. 143 I have suggested that the chapel which contained the altar of St. George may have been the one which is now known as " the Dean's Chapel," No. 28. Further consideration, however, while these pages are in the press, leads me to return to my earlier supposition that St. George's altar was in or near the Chapel of Benefactors, No. 15.

34. *The Altar of St. Stephen.* Ro. Aubray, Dean Fleming's chantry priest, in 1535, gave "to St. Stephen's altare a vestment of bawdkyn." (Maddison, *Wills*, No. 22, p. 11.) Here was celebrated the mass of T. Whitwell's chantry in 1507 and 1531. It was founded for the souls of Ric. Whitwell, K. Edward III., Simon de Islip, J. de Welborne, treasurer, Lady Joan de Cantilupe, and many others (see supplement to chantry register lf. 368). Whitewell, preb. of Empingham, died about 1352. See Muniments D. ii. 51 (3). His chantry was connected with that of Robert Chesterfield (who had also a chantry at St. Nicholas altar in St. *Swithin's* parish church, Lincoln, whence the chaplain had a dispensation, in 1423, to celebrate elsewhere, because the altar was dark, Chapter Acts, A 2, 32, fo. 23^b). In the *Registrum Antiquissimum*, St. Stephen's altar is mentioned next after that of St. Peter and St. Paul (see above, No. 12), and may possibly have been, like that, one of the apsidal chapels in the S.E. transept. I have already expressed my opinion (p. 229) that No. 11 (the more northerly of the two apsidal chapels in the S.E. transept) was the Chapel of St. Peter and St. Paul the Apostles, and that the other chapel in that transept, the one facing the entrance to the Canon's Vestry, contained the altar of St. Stephen.

35. *The Altar of St. James.* I do not remember to have seen any statement about any *mass* assigned to St. James' altar; but repairs of the window " at the west *columba* (?) by the pinnacle, which is mounted by steps near the chapel of St. James," were ordered in chapter on the feast of St. Katharine, 25th Nov., 1441. (A. 2, 33, fo. 45^b.) It seems impossible that this can have been the southern altar in the N.W. transept, the site which some have assigned to an altar of St. James. But it may very probably have been in the ante chapel to St. Mary Magdalene's Morning Prayer Chapel, under St. Mary's Western Tower. See 22 above. This is now a coke cellar. The " pinaculum " there will be (as Mr. Maddison observes) that which has the " Swineheard of Stow " for its finial.

36. *The Altar of St. Thomas* " the Apostle." (?) In 1536 W. Baytman, an " old " vicar, desired to be buried within the chapel of St. Thomas (Maddison's *Wills*, No. 42); but whether apostle or martyr we have not been told. I have not as yet traced a chapel of St. Thomas the *apostle* except in Williamson's *Guide*, p. 73. I may here mention that the late Precentor, shortly before his lamented death, assured me that he had never personally investigated the localization of the chapels and altars, but simply repeated what other topographical writers had said as to the name of each.

37. *The Altar of St. Guthlac,* mentioned in *Registrum Antiquissimum,* between St. Stephen's and that of St. John the Evangelist. See above, No. 15.

38. *The Altar of St. Thomas* (Becket) *the Martyr.* The chantry mass of a Gilbert of Kent (de Kancia), a vicar's chantry, was celebrated here between 8 and 9 a.m. in 1531. *Vicars Choral,* p. 43. In the old Chantry Register the altar of B. Thomas the Martyr is mentioned as the place for the chantry of W. Thorenton, Canon, and of W. de la Gare, Archdeacon of Lincoln, with whom was associated Ric. Stretton. (lf. 2, 22, 119-141.) Subsequently the Thornton and Gare chantry was united with that of Symon Barker at St. John Bapt. altar. (Chantry Certificates 1545.) At St. Thomas' altar was also the vicar's chantry mass for Gilbert Kent (de Kancia) cir. 1240-45, according to the register, lf. 3, 205, and the time tables of 1507, 1531. Here, likewise, was the chantry mass of W. Thornton and W. de la Gare cir. 1500. (*Grantham's Book.*) An "altar of St. Thomas" (with no further specification) is mentioned in the wills of Ric. de Beverley (1390), and J. Cotes (1433). In both of these (as also in *Reg. Antiquiss.*) the altar of St. Thomas is named next after that of St. John the Evangelist, which is thought to be that in the north transept opposite the shrine of John de Dalderby. There was an image of St. Thomas by his altar. (Gibbons, *Wills,* p. 158, cf. p. 33.)

[*Brackets for Lamps or Images.*]

The chapels in which structural brackets (for images or lamps) are now extant are these:—St. Nicholas (No. 8, N.E. of Angel Choir); St. Blaise (No. 9, Bishop Russell's chantry), two; in Longland's chapel (No. 10), several bases never completed; and St. Mary Magdalene's, the Morning Chapel (No. 23). The only other bracket extant is in No. 17, opposite the Galilee door, where some writers would place the altar of St. Giles, but which I rather inclined to identify with that of *St. Thomas the Martyr* until Prebendary Maddison brought to my knowledge a notice, dated 1556, which speaks of the quire (or 'quere') of the chapel of St. Anne, now called Umphraville's, at the south end of the cross aisle by the great steeple, and which accordingly precludes our assigning any *other* altar (be it St. Thomas' as I supposed, or St. Giles' as others have alleged) to the position directly opposite the Galilee door. It is, of course, possible that the title of St. Thomas of Canterbury might be for a period discredited and suppressed, but not for a sufficient length of time to account for the difficulties which meet us.

A brief alphabetical reference to the sections of this long article, headed *Piscinas*, &c., 209-255, or at least to that portion which relates to altars and chapels at Lincoln (pp. 216 foll.), may be found convenient.

Altare summum, 1.

Anne, 17; cf. 15.

Andree, 26; cf. 25-27, 16.

Blasii, 9.

"Benefactors'," *see* 15.

"Borough's (*i.e.* Burg-
hersh) Chapel," *see* 6.

"Buckingham's Chan-
try," 25.

"Cantelupe's," *see* 11.

Capitulum, Capitarium,
etc., *see* 12 and 30.

"Consistorium Decani
et Capituli," 16.

Consistory Court, 20.

Christophori, 24.

Crucis, 18.

Decani, 28.

Dionysii, 25; cf. 27.

Edwardi, 32; cf. 15.

Egidii (? 17), 20.

Fabrice, cf. 15.

"Fitzwilliam's," 27.

"Fundatoris," "Ca-
pella," *see* 15.

Georgii, 15; cf. 19, 28,
33.

Giles *v.* Egidii.

Guthlaci (?), 15, 37.

Hugonis, 21; cf. 3, 6,
20.

"Humphreyville" (Um-
fravill) Chapel, 17.

"Irons," 2.

Jacobi (James), (?) 22;
cf. 25.

Jesus Mass, 19[b].

Johannis Bapt., 4; cf. 7.

Johannis Evang., 16.

Katharine, 6, *see also* 10.

"Large Chapel," *see* 4.

"Little Chapel," *see* 3.

"Lexington's Chapel,"
see 16.

Longland's Chantry, 10.

Lucie, cf. 31.

Marie, B. Virg. (our
Lady's), 7; cf. 4, and
1.

Mary's Tower, 22.

Mary Magdalene, 23.
(*See also* 4.)

"Morning Prayer
Chapel," 23.

Michaelis, 27; cf. 25-27.

Nicholai, 8 ; cf. 27.

Pauli (?), 11.
"Peel Altar," 21.
Petri, 11 (*al.* 12).
Pharmacy, 28.

Remigius (?), *see* 15.
Revestiarii, 13.
"Rood," *vide* Crucis.
"Ringers," *see* "Peel."
"Russell's Chapel," *see*
9.

Sebastiani, 20.
Stephani, 34; cf. 12.
"Sutton and Wool-
vey's," 26.

Tailboys' Chantry, *see*
17.

"Thomas' Chapel," *see*
3.
Thome Apostoli, 25,
36 (?).
Thome Martyris, 17
(37).
Trinitatis, 5; cf. 20.

"Welles' Chapel," *see*
12.
"William the Con-
queror's Chapel," *see*
8.
"Works," cf. Fabrice.

No Altars in—

14. Lavatorium.
29. Camera Communis.
30. Domus Capitularis.

Pıx. The vessel in which the consecrated and
reserved Host was hung over the altar, in later times
under a canopy. Sometimes the pyx or vessel, was
in the form of a dove, or a pelican, sometimes a cup,
sometimes a palm tree with pendent head, as may be
seen in the north of France at the present day. It
was suspended by a chain, or pulley, over the high
altar. This string snapped ominously one Candlemas, while K. Stephen was offering his taper at

Lincoln, where Bp. Alexander was officiating. (*Roger Hoveden*, fo. 278.) In the Lincoln Inventory of 1548 (*Inv.*, p. 63) is noted " the great Cupp that did hang over the high altar with three knops and other pieces, all guilt, weighing 53 oz."

"Præciosa." The verse " Right dear in the sight of the Lord : *R.* Is the death of His Saints," was part of the Chapter Office in connexion with the service of prime, which secular cathedral churches and some collegiate chapters observed in common with the monastic orders. Before the Mass of the Blessed Virgin was concluded the bells rang for " prima in chorum," otherwise " great prime." (*Black Book*, pp. 373-4.) After which the bell went for " prime out of choir," all going to take their places round the Chapter House. The thurifer in his surplice mounted a pulpit and read a lesson, *i.e.*, the section of the Martirology which related to the holy persons to be commemorated on the day following. If there were any obits or anniversaries of benefactors or other local personages recited, a priest behind the reader said, " May their souls, and all Christian souls departed, by the mercy of God, rest in peace." The choir answered " Amen." *De profundis* was said for the anniversaries, except on double feasts. Also the collect *Absolve, quæsumus.* Then followed " *Preciosa*," and pardon was asked for offences, and, if it were a Sunday or holy day, the thurifer recited from the wax-covered board (*tabula*) a list of readers and singers, and the duties assigned to them by Chancellor, or Vice-Chancellor, and

Precentor or Succentor. A Deacon in his surplice read another lesson. Some say that this was the Little Chapter (*capitulum*), and thence derive the term *in capitulo*, or *capitularis*. But I am convinced that this other lesson was a moral or devotional reading from some book of sermons, or the like. At Salisbury it was invariably taken from the writings of Hamo Halberstatensis, a pupil of Alcuin, except during the octaves of the Assumption and Nativity of the B. Virgin, when other *lectiones ad Primam in capitulo* are provided in the Sarum Breviary (iii., pp. 696-730, 780-829). See *Tracts of Clem. Maydeston*, p. 41. "Preciosa" is mentioned in the margin of the *Black Book*, p. 382, and in *Novum Registrum*, part 3, near the beginning. At Sarum at least the Psalm *Levavi oculos* was said, with certain prayers and collects, "after reading the board."* See Brev. ii., pp. 54, 56, cf. i., p. dcclxxxiv., as to Maundy Thursday Prime in Chapter. It appears from Lincoln documents that the correction of offences and the recitation of a section of the Custom Book relating to the divine service of the ensuing week belonged, in the 14th century, to the Saturday meeting in "capitulo chori," and that the Chapter business and correction followed "Preciosa" immediately.

PROCESSIONS. On 21st June, 1438, the Chapter received letters from Bp. Alnwick enjoining pro-

---

* 'The Board' *i.e.*, '*tabula*,' the 'wax brede' on which was written and posted-up the list of officiants for the week or for the following day.

cessions in the city and in the Minster on Wednesdays and Fridays, and granting indulgence of 40
days. Chapter Acts A. 2, 32, fo. 129. In the next
volume of Acts a slip bound in at fo. 28-9, with
others of 1440-42, directs chaplains to attend all
masses, evensong on Sundays and double feasts,
and *specially processions*. We have, so far as I am
aware, no Lincoln *processionale* extant, but the *Black
Book*, p. 290, shews that there were the usual processions at Evensong on the three days of Christmas,
in which deacons, boys, and priests respectively took
the leading part (in honour of St. Stephen, etc.);
on Palm Sunday also there was a procession outside
the Church, as well as on St. Mark's and on Rogation
Days, *id*. 285, 292. The Whitsuntide processions
of parishioners to the Mother Church (p. 307), while
the orders of processions on Sundays and holy days
is given 375-95. Processions of honour (venerationis
causa) are just mentioned, p. 273, in the case of a
new Bishop, and I have edited a specimen relating
to the reception of Bp. Longland in 1522, in the
third fasciculus of *Statutes*, pp. 556-8. A brief
account of the procession for Oliver Sutton's funeral
in 1299 will be found in *Statutes* II., p. cxxii.

PROCESSIONAL STONES. Circular stones let into
the pavement of the nave, to mark the positions to
be occupied by members of the cathedral staff in the
procession, were visible at Lincoln until they were
recklessly destroyed when the nave was re-paved in
1782. Similar stones are visible in Carter's plan of

Wells Cathedral, taken in 1798, and now preserved by the Soc. of Antiquaries. In Mr. Reynolds' print thereof, 11 + 11 stones are shown parallel to the 4 + 4 western columns of the nave. Canon Church's restored plan (1894) for the 13th century represents a larger number of such stones,

viz., $1 + \begin{Bmatrix} 1 + 27 \\ 1 + 27 \end{Bmatrix}$ + Bp., *i.e.*, 58 stones in all,

occupying the entire length of the nave. A more perfect specimen is given in Mr. J. Arthur Reeve's noble *Monograph on the Abbey of S. Mary of Fountains* (folio, 1892), p. 15 and plate 1. There two rows of 25 stones, with one for the cross-bearer in front, and one for the Abbat to bring up the rear, or 52 in all, occupy six bays out of the 10 or 11 in the nave. (The choir at Fountains encroaches upon the eastern bay of the nave.) At Lincoln Bp. Alnwick desired to be buried at the W. end of the nave, in the place which he occupied in the procession on the north side by the third pillar. It was one of the complaints laid against Dean Mackworth that he would not walk in line behind the Canon in the last rank. The place of Alnwick's burial, as marked on Hollar's plan, in 1672, is slightly to the south-west of the central point of an imaginary line, bisecting the Consistory Court and the Morning Prayer Chapel. This would just leave the actual round stone on which the Bishop's feet used to rest untouched for use by his successors.

"PROPRIA" (*sc.* hebdomada, *seu* septimana).

Each prebendary had to take his choice between living away from Lincoln, so as to serve his prebendal church in person, or going through the form necessary to take his place as one of the Residentiary Canons. In the former case he paid a Vicar-choral to attend for him, both in choir and likewise in processions, but no vicar could do his duty at the high altar or in executing principal part of the offices in choir as canon in a weekly duty (*hebdomadarius*). In the latter case, about the time of the audit in September, at a Chapter meeting, he made a formal " protestation of greater residence " (declaring his determination to reside for two-thirds of the next few years, after which a "minor residence" of *one*-third would discharge his obligation. A house or " lodgings " in Lincoln was assigned to him, and he invited his *confratres* " to eat bread " there on such a day. Then, besides attending Chapter meetings, and reading an occasional lesson, or singing a verse or the like in choir, when "intabulated" by the Chancellor or the Precentor, he had to take a week's duty from time to time as Canon of the week. This might devolve upon him in two ways. The theory was that every prebendary took his week's duty in rotation (only giving place to the Bishop or Dean at Christmas or other principal feasts). If the prebendary whose week it is happens to be one who has " protested residence," and who is consequently living in the Close, or " Minister Yard," he takes it naturally, and it is styled " his own " (" *propria* "). But if the week belongs by right to a *non*-resident, then one or other of the Residentiaries *in rotation* undertakes it, *loco absentis*, and is said to celebrate "in course ("*in cursu* "). It is hardly necessary to add that he meanwhile pays a country vicar to serve his prebendal church. See also J. F. Wickenden's paper *On the Choir Stalls of Lincoln Cathedral*, from Architectural Journal (? 1879). *Linc. Dio. Mag.* April—June, 1888, pp. 188, 204, 220; May, June, 1890, pp. 73, 96; May, 1891, p. 69.

PROVOST.   "Praepositus." A Canon chosen yearly to act as bursar of the "common chamber." *Nov. Reg.*, *Stat.* ii., 354. At one time there had been a "Præpositus ad Communitatem" and a "Præpositus ad Fabricam ecclesiæ," but in the 15th century the two offices were amalgamated. *Stat.* iii., 406. There is also a Provost of the Vicars.

THE PSALTER. The recitation of the entire psalter and litany by the Canons can be traced at Lincoln to the time of St. Hugh. See *the Black Book*, pp. 274-5, 296, 300, 408. Cp. *Novum Registrum*, part 2. The "Beneficia Ecclesiæ Lincoln" are carefully recited by Grosseteste, and summed in the documents printed by Dimock in Appendix F to Giraldus Cambrensis vii. as granted by St. Hugh and his contemporaries and successors, pp. 217-19. Thirty-three masses weekly in the Church of Lincoln itself are mentioned in these documents. W. of Blois, St. Hugh's successor, directed the like number of masses there for the

brethren and sisters of the Lincoln Fraternity.
Besides the aforesaid there were 8,400 masses and
8,550 psalters of " religious " persons not in priest's
orders. The total of the Paters and Ave Maries
" nemo scit nisi solus Deus." And in Grosseteste's
time the psalters of the "religious" men available
for the Lincoln brotherhood were 40,000 and 16,330
" psalteria." On the Daily Psalter of the Canons
at Wells see Canon Church's *Early History of Wells*,
pp. 20, 340-42, and his monograph on this subject.
It is an institution likewise at Salisbury, and at St.
Paul's, and has been in part introduced recently at
Truro and Southwell.

PULPITUM. The lectern where lessons were read
at mattins (the suitable " responds " being chanted
at the lectern).* *Black Book*, p. 371. The Epistle
at high mass was read "in pulpito " ; likewise the
Gospel " in magno pulpito," pp. 377, 379 margin.
No doubt this was an *ambon* on the rood loft or choir
screen. Sometimes three sang in the great pulpit
in copes of two suits, the senior being vested in his
own suit between the others of a second pattern. A
canon reading in the pulpit was attended by a vicar,
or clerk, in black choir habit, when not in a silk
cope. (*Liber Niger*, *Statutes* I. p. 382.) The
Treasurer had to provide the candle (*minutam
candelam*) in choir, in "*pulpitum*," and elsewhere
when it was necessary. (*Ibid*, p. 291.)

---

* " *Ad lectrinam in choro,*" the *lector* or reader himself having gone " *in
pulpitum.*"

PUNISHMENTS. In the 13th and 14th centuries it
was the custom that canons who had been dis-
obedient, or were found guilty of some other open
offence, should be degraded from their stalls, and
placed either at the choir door behind the Dean, or
at the end of the boy's row, to do penance according
to the magnitude of their fault. (*Martilo.*, fo. 12.)
Likewise, in December, 1434, W. Burn, a vicar
choral in minor orders, is set to stand in his surplice
on the step before the high altar all the time of high
mass for three Sundays, reading upon the Psalms of
David, with head uncovered, and holding a burning
candle of half a pound. (*Chapter Acts*, A. 2, 32, fo.
99[b].) In 1309 it was agreed that there should be a
meeting every Saturday "in capitulo chori," when
the section of the custom-book which detailed the
services for the next week was to be read publickly,
and any offences noted in the past week were to be
corrected. This was in accordance with monastic
customs. Schalby adds that the correction took
place on Saturdays after *Praeciosa*.

"QUERECOPES." *Cappae de choro.* This term
occurs in an indenture in Norman French, dated 7th
Sept., 1377, in which Gilbert Dumframville (Umfravill or Humphreyville), earl of Angos and lord of
Kyme (who had a chantry in the great south
transept), gives certain vestments of cloth of gold,
with his own arms embroidered as orphreys upon
most of them, to "Herrye de Quaplade, prior, and
the Austin Convent of St. Mary's, Kyme, in

Lincolnshire," on condition that if they were sold or alienated a fine should be paid to the Minster, ("au Dean et Chapitre, ou Chapitale, de esglise cathedrale de Nicole "). The vestments were to be used at Noel, Pasch, Ascension, Pentecost, Trinity, de Corpore Christi, Nat. Jo. Bapt., "les cink' festes de Nostre Dame, la fest de tous seyntes," SS. Peter and Paul, Thomas of Canterbury, S. Cudberd, S. John de Beverlee, and other principal feasts, and on the four yearly commemorations of the donor and "Maude sa compaigne" and his relatives "et de tous cristiens." They consisted of a chasuble of cloth of gold, with the arms of the Earl of Angos dumframvill and Kyme for orphreys, a priest's albe, amice, stole, and phanon (*i.e.*, maniple), with two albes, tunicles, amices and one stole for subdeacon and deacon respectively; "troys quere copes de dit drape ouesque (avec) les orfrayes des dits armes, trois amice ouesque les parures de dit drape," a corporas case, and corporas cloth therein, two towels (probably to lie on the altar), "dount lun ad une fronter de veluet blue enbrode de dites armes," —all "dune suyte" (*unius sectæ*). The blue velvet frontal no doubt was arranged like what we should call a frontlet, but was attached to one of the linen cloths, of which there were usually three thicknesses on an altar table. (*Muniments*, D. ij., 62, iii.)

QUIRISTER. This form of the word "chorister" is now retained only perhaps at Winchester College. It occurs, however, at Lincoln in "a note of (35)

double feasts for three Quiresters for one yeare,"
A.D. 1623. (C.V. 6, in the Muniment Room.) At
Salisbury the boys in the foundation were called
"*canonici pueri*" al. "pueri," Osmund Register
(ed. Jones, Rolls Series), i., p. 22*n*.

"RE ET VE." A Clerk of re(cedendi) et ve-
(niendi) was employed to keep an account or
roll of the presence or absence of Canons in the
Close, and to mark them, so that allowances for
residence might be correctly paid. The earliest roll
which I have seen belongs to the year 1278-1279,
and the latest to 1641-42, so it is evident that they
were carried on until Cathedral Chapters were for
that time abolished. In 1888 I communicated to
Archæologia (London) a copy of a '*Booke to direct the
Roles of* Re *and* Ve,' for the year 1635-36, with some
account of one for the year 1639-40. More recently
(1897) I have edited a fifteenth century *Rotulus de
Re et Ve* in *Statutes* fasc. iii. pp. 812-823 (Cambridge,
University Press), prefixing some account of the
remains of the series of these rolls in general, *ibid.*,
pp. 800-810.

RELICKS. The mass of Relicks of Blessed Robert
Grosseteste, Bp., was said *in aurora* on St. Pelagia's
Day, 6th October. *Black Book*, p. 337. The
following relicks were said, in a record dated
October, 1501, to have been deposited in what
is called a *mamellus* under St. Hugh's belfry
(the S.W. tower) :—Relicks of St. Bartholomew,

SS. Marcellus and Marcellinus, martyrs, a bone of St. Stephen, of St. Hugh, and St. James; a bone of the finger of St. Thomas, and a stone from Mount Sinai. (S. Peck, *Desiderata Curiosa*, p. 318, 4to, 1779.)

In inventories of the late 15th and 16th centuries we find at Lincoln, besides St. Hugh's head, a bone of St. Laurence, the beard and chasuble of St. Peter; a part of a tooth of St. Paul, one of St. Cecily, of St. Hugh, and of St. Christopher; also one of his bones. Relicks of St. Edmund, Abp., Anastasia, Eustace, Agnes, Vincent, Gregory, Clement, Bernard, Stephen (several), Holy Innocents, Thomas the Martyr, Machabeus, Alexius, Valeria, Cesarius, Sebastian, Erkenwald, White (Candida, V.), Remigius of Lincoln. A finger of St. Hugh, one of St. Katharine, part of the head (and certain bones) of St. John Baptist, hairs of the B. Virgin, a head with bones of St. Ursula's companions, the jaw of Thomas Cantilupe, Bp.' of Hereford, a joint (*junctura*) of St. Sebastian, of Margaret, and of George, besides part of his breastplate and his collar-bone. Some links of the chain wherewith St. Katharine bound the fiend, along with a portion of the Holy Sepulchre, and of the Table from the Upper Room at Jerusalem, several portions of the Holy Cross, besides a part of St. Andrew's. The schedules of four other reliquaries are mentioned but not transcribed, while no less than 18 others are noted in general terms as "unknown," or of "divers saincts." One of these items was :—" j. cista alta et rotunda, panno serico cum ymaginibus cooperta,

continens reliquias lauandas in Festo Reliquiarum."
Apparently, therefore, only a specimen was taken
for the ceremony of washing the Relicks.* The four
servants of the Church were required to find water,
vessels and other requisites for the washing of the
Relicks. *Black Book*, p. 293.

The " Feast of Relicks " at Lincoln was on July
14th. (It was at Westminster on the 16th of that
month, and at Salisbury—after several alterations—
on the Sunday after the 7th.) Precentor Featley,
after the Restoration, gives "*A note to know Relique
Sunday. The 2nd Sunday after the feast of St.
Peter and St. Paul is Relique Sunday.*"

In the rule for processions in the *Black Book*, p.
375, between the thurifers and the second sub-
deacon come " three little clerks in surplices,
bearing relicks."

REMIGIUS, first Bishop of Lincoln, called in the
antient lists of Obits " Remigius episcopus, *Lincol
ecclesiæ Stabilitor.*" (Statutes ii., p. ccxxxviii.)

His tomb, which was in the north-east of the nave,
where its reputed covering has been replaced in
recent years, was to be solemnly censed according
to the ceremonial contained in the *Black Book*, p. 368.

" REQUIEM." A mass of the dead (with Deacon

---

* For the Inventories from which this list of Relicks is gleaned see my com-
munication to the Society of Antiquaries in 1892, entitled " Inventories of
Plate, Vestments, &c., belonging to the Cathedral Church of the Blessed
Mary of Lincoln," in *Archæologia*, Vol. liii.

and Subdeacon assisting. *Statutes* iii., 410). See above "*Missa pro Defunctis*," p. 194.

"RESURREXI." This Easter Mass (*Missale Sarum*, pp. 359, 381) was ordered for Thursday after Easter Week (and some other days) in Rolls of *Re et Ve.* See *Statutes* fasc. iii. p. 815.

REVESTRY. See "Vestry."

B. ROBERT. Application was made to Rome for the canonization or beatification of Robert Grosseteste (Bishop of Lincoln, 1235-53) in 1301, but without success. He is, however, constantly called "beatus" in Lincoln documents. The obit of J. de Dalderby (in whose case the same process had a like result in 1328) paid 4*d.* to the keepers of the fertory [? and] of Saint Hugh's head, and the tomb of Blessed Robert. List in Schalby's *Martiloge* inserted cir. 1330-40, fo. 44[b]. See below, the article on "Tombs," and cf. *Black Book*, 335-7.

ROOD TOWER. The central tower in which the modern "Great Tom" now hangs, but formerly the six small "Lady Bells." Hence it was, perhaps, that Sanderson (or Dugdale)* uses the confusing term "our Lady's steeple" in speaking (as it is

---

* Peck's *Desiderata Curiosa* ii., 304, where mention is made of the altar tomb of the famous Dean "Henricus" (surely it ought to be "Johannes") Mackworth "by the great south west pillar of our Lady's steeple." However, I am not quite certain that this, the ordinary interpretation, held by Lincoln

thought) of this great tower, which is now sometimes also called (corruptly) the "Broad Tower." Dr. Rock distinguishes the "perch" ("*pertica*") which occupied a place in many churches, corresponding to the choir screen, from the solid "beam" ("*trabs*," behind the altar), of which we have spoken at p. 110, under letter "B." The "perch" was a thin metal rod, or a broad lath, depending from the roof by a rope to about 12 ft. from the pavement, at some distance to the west of the high altar, and on this the rood was placed in some instances. But at Lincoln, as in other great churches, there was a *pulpitum* containing the two ambones, the one for chanting the Epistle on the south, the other, for the Gospel, to the north, having the entrance to the choir below them and between. Above this structure probably a rood-beam was supported with the crucifix upon it, and St. Mary and St. John on either side. No doubt the Altar of Holy Cross, if not actually raised upon the middle of the pulpit stage (or rood loft) as at Canterbury, was somewhere near it on the floor of the lantern. (Cf. Dr. Rock, *Ch. of our Fathers*, iv., 211.)

At Lincoln, a Rood Altar, near which the founder Remigius was buried, is mentioned by Matthew Paris. Is there any evidence that such an *altar* existed in the later church?

---

topographers, and elsewhere adopted in this book, bidding us look for Mackworth's tomb near the central tower, may not need to be re-considered. May not Sanderson have meant by "our Lady's steeple" the N.W. tower? In his notes elsewhere (*Desid. Cur.* ii., p. 308) the central tower, or Rood Tower, is called "the lanthorn."

In the *Metrical Life of St. Hugh* six lines describe the crucifix at Lincoln, and a golden tablet or bas-relief (*tabula*) of the life of Christ at the entrance of the choir :

> Introitumque chori Majestas aurea pingit :
> Et proprie propria crucifixus imagine Christus
> Exprimitur, viteque sue progessus ad unguem
> Insinuatur ibi. Nec solum crux vel Imago,
> Immo columpnarum sex, lignorumque duorum
> Ampla superficies, obrizo fulgurat auro.

The two *ligna* may have been horizontal beams, the upper one supporting the crucifix, the lower one (forming the lintel of the choir entrance, and possibly the western support of the *pulpitum*) being raised on six columns, with the entrance in the midst.

"RORATE." This mass of the Blessed Virgin daily in Advent, as on Lady Day (see *Missale Sarum*, 761, 726), is ordered for the last Monday in Advent in Lincoln Rolls of *Re et Ve.* See *Statutes* iii. p. 823.

RUSHES. The *Black Book* (p. 286) requires the Treasurer to find, among other things, "naviculas in choro et coram altaribus, et capitulo stramen vel iunctum (*i.e.*, juncum) in festis duplicibus." This passage was put on record about 1214; "naviculas" is subsequently glossed "nattulas," *Stat.* ii. p. 160.

"SALVE." This mass of the Blessed Virgin ("*Salve sancta parens*," *Missale Sarum*, p. 779) is

ordered for her weekly "full service" of commemoration in choir on Saturdays, and for daily use in
the Lady Chapel from the Purification to Advent,
in Sarum use, and we know that it was specially
noted as for use at Lincoln on the Wednesday after
Lady Day according to a Roll of *Re* and *Ve*, and in
ordinary weeks on Saturdays.   It was counted there
likewise as a " daily mass of St. Mary."   At Salisbury it gave its name to the chapel at the extreme
east " ' *Salve* ' Chapel; "* and at Lincoln in like
manner we read in 1401 of a bequest to " the altar
of the B.V.M. ubi celebratur missa *Salve sancta
parens.*" (Gibbons, *Wills*, p. 97.)   Feb. 23rd, 1432,
W. Stevenot, and three other singers at this daily
mass of our Lady, claimed 2s. from J. Walpole and
Laurence Bagshot, chaplains of Bp. H. Lexington's
chantry as arrears on account of light burning
" in choro ubi dicta missa celebratur," meaning
(presumably) not the " high choir," but the " angel
choir." *Lincoln Chapter Acts.*

SCALA.   Ducange mentions that the *ladder* was
one of the symbols of " higher justice " in France.
It was erected by authorities possessing the " power

---

* At Salisbury the Daily Lady Mass was instituted by Bp. R. Poore in
1225. There was a certain "singing at *Salve*," or " *Salve de Jhesu,*" on
Fridays in Lent at the parish Church of St. Edmund, in Salisbury, mentioned
in the accounts of 1477 and 1557. Whether it was the name of a mass or of a
special devotion, such as an antiphon, in that instance, I do not feel certain.
Men from the Salisbury Cathedral choir, apparently, came to help on such
occasions. and were regaled afterwards with figs, bread, and drink. *Accounts
of St. Edmund's Parish*, Salisbury (Wilts Record Soc.) pp. xii., 103, 249, 268.

of the sword" for criminals convicted of serious offences (bigamy, perjury, witchcraft, or blasphemy) to mount, so as to make their infamy and punishment visible to all beholders. Similarly, when Bishop Alnwick gave orders to denounce those who rescued the incorrigible sorcerer, T. Holditch, from justice, in 1442, it was to be at mass time in Boston Church, "*sub scala constituta,*" "cruce erecta, pulsatis campanis, candelis accensis et demum in eorum vituperium in terram projectis, extinctis, pedibusque calcatis." (*Statutes* iii., 498-9.)

SCHOOLMASTER. By the Lateran Council in 1179 it was decreed that a Schoolmaster should be appointed in every Cathedral Church. This was repeated in the Lateran decrees of 1215, cap. ii. The Constitutions ascribed by Spelman (ii., p. 157) to Bp. Poore, of Salisbury, in 1217, order that he should have a "competens beneficium" to enable him to instruct four scholars in grammar. At Lincoln "magister scholarum" is mentioned in the *Black Book*, p. 276, next after the canons (and before the sacrist, succentor, provost and celebrant at St. Peter's altar) as sharing in a distribution of wine. A Master of the Choir boys is mentioned in Bishop Gravesend's order. The order concerning distributions of oblations in 1321-2 (*ibid.*, p. 336) assigns 5*s.* "Magistro Scholarum grammaticalium," but only 12*d.* "Magistro Scholarum cantus." The Sacrist also was to have 5*s.*, "because he works harder than the rest." On p. 338 the Master of the Grammar

School appears, however, in the same category as the " scoparius " or sweeper! The " Master of the Song Schools" is mentioned incidentally also on p. 369 respecting some special singing at festal evensong.

SCUERARIAM, "scilicet claustrum " (the cloister). *Statutes* fasc. iii. p. 388.

THE SEARCHERS' CHAMBER. In the " Dean's Aisle" north of the choir, towards the cloister door, and " north of the Lady Wray's monument is [*i.e.*, in 1641] a chamber of timber, where the searchers of the church used to lie; under which, every night, they had an allowance of bread and beer; at the shutting of the church doors the custom was, to toll the greatest of our Lady's bells fourty tolls; and, after, to go to that place and eat and drink; and then to walk round and search the church." (Account by Sanderson and Dugdale, Peck's *Desid. Curiosa*, p. 305. Cf. "Scrutatio ecclesie," *Black Book*, p. 386.) The place indicated was within sight of St. John Baptist's Chapel, where St. Hugh's head was kept, and not far from his shrine; so, possibly, this had once been the rendezvous of the two "custodes Sancti Hugonis in nocte vigilantes." His head, set with gems, had been stolen in 1364, but was marvellously recovered and re-set by the munificence of Treasurer Welborne. The Treasurer had to find 14 candles apiece for lay-sacrist, the watchmen (vigil), and the lighter of the candles "ad scruta-

ciones ecclesie faciendas." *Nov. Reg.*, part 1.
(Or half that quantity in summer.) See below
" Watchers."

St. Sebastian's Chapel. In Bp. W. Smyth's
will (proved 30th Jan., 1514) this chapel is said to
be on the south side of the cathedral church, and
near to the place which he designed for his burial.
This was at the west of Bp. W. Alnwick's tomb,
which was rather to the south side of the nave, near
the second pillar from the west end, and where that
prelate had been wont to stand when the procession
halted. This was near St. Sebastian's chapel.
According to the testator's wish daily mass in Bp.
Smyth's memory was said by the chaplain of his
chantry at 8 a.m. in 1531. *Vicars Choral*, p. 41.
See Ra. Churton's *Founders of Brasenose*, pp.
355-360, 512, 514.

Sempstress. The "*custuraria,*" or "*custuaria*"
(couturière), received 3*s.* per annum from the
Treasurer. *Black Book*, p. 288. *Nov. Reg.*, part 1.
We find in 1527 payments, " Sutori sive cissori (*i.e.*,
scissori) pannorum lineorum pro tota septimana
preterita, 2*s.* 3*d.* *Stat.* ii. p. ccxxviii.; iii. 303.

Easter Sepulchre. As at Durham, this was a
recess prepared on the north side of the high altar
for the dramatic rites of Holy Week and Easter.
At *Durham* the crucifix which had been placed on a
cushion at the lowest " greeces " or steps in the

choir for the ceremony of Creeping to the Cross, after the singing of " the Passion " on Good Friday, was subsequently laid in the sepulchre, together with another Image of Christ, in the breast of which, as in a monstrance, the Presanctified Sacrament was exposed, with two tapers which were kept burning till Easter Day. Between 3 and 4 a.m. on Easter morning two seniors censed the Sepulchre. They took out the Figure of the Risen Christ, with the Cross in Its hand, and the crystal Breast exposing the Host. They elevated the Image upon a cushion, singing the antiphon " *Christus resurgens*," placed it upon the high altar, censed it, carried it round the church under a canopy, in procession, and replaced it on the altar until Ascension Day. (*Rites of Durham*, pp. 10, 11.)

Likewise at *Lincoln* an "Image (silver gilt, with a berrall) void in the breast, for the Sacrament for Easter Day," is noted in inventories of 1536, 1548. It represented our Lord with a cross in His hand, and weighed 37 oz. See *Inventories* (in *Archæologia*, Vol. liii.) pp. 16, 45. I infer from the marginal notes that this Image of our Saviour was taken out of the charge of the Treasury, in 1536, or soon afterwards, and that its value was assigned to the repair fund for Lincoln Minster about the year 1548.

The Easter Sepulchre is (says Precentor Venables) "of the best Decorated period." The Roman guards sleeping are represented here in stone as in the sepulchres at Heckington, Hawton, and

Pattrington - on - Humber. (*Murray's Guide to Eastern Cathedrals*, p. 367.) Mr. Peacock mentions also Bottesford, Northwold, Holcombe, Burnell, Southport and Woodleigh (*Engl. Ch. Furniture*, 1866, p. 28) as having sepulchres, and gives a drawing of that at Navenby in Lincolnshire (at p. 140).

There was at Lincoln a " Hospital of St. Sepulchre in the Quire." *Vicars Choral*, pp. 63, 64. A " Gild of the Resurrection " also is mentioned by Miss Toulmin Smith as existing in 1374. As recently as March, 1566, there were " now remayning in the olde revestrie one alterstone (black), a sepulcre, a [brass] crosse for candelles called Judas crosse, and other Furniture belonging to the same sepulcre, the pascall with the Images in Fote belonging to the same sepulcre and a candlestike of wodde." From the fragment in the Bishop's Registry in Alnwick's Tower—see *Lincoln Inventories*, p. 81.

Of eight altar cloths three were sold by the Dean and Chapter ; the other five remained " with one precious cloth to laye upon the altare, and one for the sepulcre wrought with Images."

SERMONS. The *Black Book*, pp. 284-5, states it to be a part of the duty of the Chancellor to find canons or other responsible persons (*viros autenticos*) to preach to the people on all Sundays ; in Chapter on the three first days of Christmas, the Epiphany, three days of Easter, the Assumption and Nativity [of B.M.], All Saints' Day, and St. Hugh's.

Likewise on Ash Wednesday and five days when there are stations and processions outside the Minster, viz., Palm Sunday, the Greater Litany (*i.e.*, St. Mark's Day), and three Rogation Days.

The *Novum Registrum*, Part I., required the Chancellor to ask the Dean's approval of his nominee whenever the sermon was to be preached "choro presente." The Sermon-Sundays were limited to the four Sundays in Advent, and the Sundays from Septuagesima to Easter inclusive. There was to be a sermon also for Ash Wednesday. The Chancellor was to preach in person on Easter Day and Christmas Day in Latin "in capitulo," but on Palm Sunday and on the Assumption in English. The Dean was required to "feed the preacher" on Ash Wednesday and Palm Sunday, the celebrant was to do so on the other Sundays, and the Chancellor whenever else any one was found "able and willing" to preach. These particulars, as to the 15th century custom, appear to have been furnished to Bishop Alnwick by Chancellor Partrich himself. The Bishop added that the Chancellor or his Vice-Chancellor was to give a month's notice to the Priors of the Friars Mendicants of Lincoln to arrange sermons in their churches on St. Mark's Day and Rogation Days, if there were to be stations held there. (*Statutes*, fasc. iii. p. 301.) After the Restoration Bp. Sanderson revised the preaching turns (*dies assignati*) for the Canons. (*Ibid.*, pp. 630-635.)

SERTA. We read of garlands of roses worn by Canons and others at St. Paul's, *e.g.*, on the commemoration of St. Paul, 30th June, 1405, being the occasion of Roger Walden's inthronization. Wharton *De Episcopis Lond.*, 150. (Rock, *Church of our Fathers*, ii., pp. 72-77 notes). But the "garlondes" which appear in Lincoln Inventories (p. 36) A.D. 1536, were of silver or silver gilt, and were set with precious stones and pearls. They were nine in number, the greater number being broken. It is possible that they may have been placed on the heads of images. But in 1401 Treasurer P. Dalton in his will (*Gibbons*, p. 97) gives "to the gild of Corpus Christi in Lincoln, whereof I am a brother, my *sertum*, which I have been wont to wear in the solemnity of that gild; and forasmuch as Master Geoffrey Lesthropp, sometime Canon of Lincoln, (preb. of Heydour, died in 1380) hath provided a like garland for the graceman of the gild, I will and direct that the said garland which I have be kept for the use of the Mayor of Lincoln, a brother of the gild."

SEYNEY. For this word the Lincoln writers in the 14th and 15th centuries could find no Latin noun or verb equivalent; so they wrote, "*de le seyneis*" [A. 2, 3, lf. 30^b], and "*potest* seyney" [A. 2, 7]. This expressed a furlough in the Canon's residence of two-thirds of the year, a sort of concession to human weakness like the "exeat" or the "half-term holiday" in the school terms of our day.

It was an absence from Friday to Monday, which might be taken once a fortnight without breaking canonical residence. (Apart from this, a Canon might be absent two consecutive nights in any week.)

SHIP. A *navicula,* or *acerra,* to hold incense for use in the censers. In 1536 and 1548 there was a silver-gilt ship "with two coverings" (probably like a basket with two flaps), having "a spoon with a cross in the head," weighing together 33¼ oz. There were also seven pair of censers silver-gilt. In 1557 there were only "2 pare of sensers copper and gylte." Item one shippe of copper. (*Lincoln Inventories,* pp. 20, 46, 72.) However, in 1548 the Sacrist had omitted two pair from his inventory (*id.* p. 63). In the 15th century there had been 9 censers and 3 ships (*id.* pp. 10, 11).

SHRINES. There were until 1540 "twoe shrynes in the sayd Cath. churche, the one of pure gold, called St. Hughe's Shryne, standing on the backe syde of the highe aulter near unto Dalyson's tombe; the place wyll easlye be knowen by the Irons yet fastned in the pavement stones ther.

"The other, called St. John of Dalderby his shryne, was of pure silver, standing in the south ende of the greate crosse Ile, not farre from the dore wher the Gallyley Courte is used to be kepte." (*Endorsement in the Inventory of* 1536.)

Sanderson adds that St. Hugh's shrine was to the north of Dallison's tomb (in other words, in the centre of the Angel Choir), and that it measured 8 feet by 4. (Peck, *Desid. Curiosa*, p. 317.)

SMOKE FARTHINGS, or "Lincoln Farthings." See above, p. 207, "*Pentecostals*."

SPICES. (*Species*, epices.) Something of the nature of dessert was served in the Canon's dining hall on certain occasions not named. Then, after dinner, the order of the service was (1) wine, (2) ale, (3) wine and ale. On other occasions it was (1) ale, (2) wine, (3) ale. (*Black Book*, p. 381. And see my note, *ibid.* p. 75, for the custom at St. Paul's, London, which throws some light upon this usage.)

STALLS. The terms "gradus superior," "secunda forma," and "in stallis," occur in the *Black Book*, p. 394. On the upper step or rank sat the Canons, and probably the vicars in priest's order, or the substitutes of absent prebendaries; on the south side the Dean occupying the west extremity, and the Chancellor the eastern end next the Bishop's throne. The Precentor and the Treasurer, in like manner, were placed at the west and east ends of the northern seats. The carved stalls were given by Treasurer Welbourn, cir. 1350-80. That Vicars of absent Canons ought to occupy the choir stalls of their "masters" was stated at Bishop Alnwick's Visitation in 1437. See *Statutes* ii., p. 409; cf. "vicarii stallorum suorum," *ibid.* p. 377. The phrase "occupans stallum" is also found as applied to the Vicar of a Prebendary. Of course they did not take the place in Chapter House, being Vicars *choral* (not capitular). As to the terms *prima* and *secunda forma*, if I rightly interpret the lists and the statements given on the one hand in Mr. Maddison's *Vicars Choral*, pp. 5, 58, 64, 70, 71, and, on the other, such accounts of Sarum customs as, *e.g.*, Osmund Register, i., p. 22 (cap. xii.), Rich. Jones' *Fasti*, p. 197, it must be inferred that Lincoln and Salisbury differed in their usage as to the relative dignity of "first" and "second" in just the same manner as there is a diversity of usage as regards the relative order of the forms or classes in certain of our boys' schools at the present day. As a rule 1st *class* is higher than 2nd, but 4th *form* is lower than 5th. But I cannot properly verify this point.

At *Truro* certainly in modern practice, and in accordance with the provisions of the Draft Statutes prepared by the late Abp. of Canterbury when he was Bishop of that See, "the second form" is next in dignity below the Canon's Stalls. Thus in cap. 7 we read that "if the Vice-Chancellor of Truro be not a Canon he shall have his stall in the second form," and in c. 18 (5), Priest-Vicars, deputies of the dignitaries, diocesan inspector, and officers approved by the Bishop and Chapter, as also by Vicars. "Such spare stalls of the second form as are not needed of the choir may be allowed to students being graduates, or to prebendaries of Endellion Collegiate Church in choral habit."

At *Lincoln* the senior or old vicars were in Priest's Orders and occupied the " *First* Form " (next below the stalls of the Canons which were " in superiori gradu "). In their number were included the chief Chantry Chaplains, the Succentor, Vice-Chancellor, and Sacrist, occasionally as in 1310, 1407, certain penitentiary *confessores chori*, as well as the Provost of the Senior Vicars. Although the Canons in what at Lincoln was called (I believe) the Canons' Stalls, as Mr. Wickenden tells us, are and were 62 in all, the row below them is only 48 (in 1879), and previously only 46; if I do not misunderstand, the occupants of the *second* Form were "young Vicars" in Deacon's, Sub-deacon's, or Acolyte's order; these also had their own *praepositus*, the Provost of the Junior Vicars. Among them were thurifers, and cerofers also to carry the bearing candles or standard tapers placed on the altar steps after the procession at mass. And the chorister boys *pueri* or *parvi de choro* were with them, probably in the " second " form " *in area.*" Possibly also the minor chantry priests, clerks and poor clerks.

At *Salisbury* all the Priest Vicars, and some few even of the Deacons, sat in the uppermost stalls or seat with the Canons. Perhaps, in *very early* times, before the stalls with canopies were constructed, the seat was not exactly subdivided into separate stalls, and the Canons, etc., who were in church, not improbably closed up their ranks so as to leave no gap.

At *Hereford* there was a "third form." *Statutes* ii., pp. 67, 72, 79, 83. The order of prebendal stalls at Lincoln at various periods may be seen in the *Black Book*, pp. 301-7 ; in *Novum Registrum*, part I., and in J. F. Wickenden's paper in *Archæol. Journal*, cir. 1879. See also the papers by Mr. A. Curtois on *Secular Foundations*, Linc. Dioc. Mag., vi., pp. 72-3, 88-9, cf. p. 96 ; vol. vii., 69 (? E.V.) ; viii., 71-74, 85-88, and by other writers, iii., 188, 204-5 ; iv., 220, 221.

STAPLE PLACE. In the parish of St. Swithin, at Lincoln. See *Statutes* iii., p. 408.

STATIONS. It was in accordance with primitive custom that on certain solemn days the Clergy met in the Mother Church, and went together in procession to a special service in one or other of the city churches. Scudamore *Notitia Eucharistica*, pp. 205-6*nn*. Smith and Cheetham, *Dict. Chr. Antiq.*, art. "Statio," §§ 1, 3. Mention is made in the *Black Book*, pp. 284-5, of sermons at Lincoln "at the place of the Station on Ash Wednesday, Palm Sunday and the Greater Litany (St. Mark's Day), and the three Rogation Days, when there are solemn processions outside the Minster." And Chancellor Partrich informed Bp. Alnwick, cir. 1442, that on St. Mark's Day and Rogation Days "the stations of the processions" were not unfrequently in the churches of the Mendicant Friars in Lincoln. *Statutes* iii., p. 301.

STAVES. " Rector staves with silver plaites, two yet remaining," are inventoried in the Commissioners' Return from the Minster in March, 1566. In 1536 there had been 2 pair of wooden staves or batons for rulers of the choir, 2 pair of silver ones, and one (probably for the Precentor's use) given by Chanter Prowett, cir. 1470. The vergers' silver maces are what now remain. In the Sarum *Processionale*, 1882, the woodcuts of 1502 and 1508 shew (at p. 76) the places of two pairs of rulers of the choir by a rough sketch of four tau-headed staves. Similarly the place of the Sacrist, leading the procession to turn by their left hand, is indicated in the drawing at p. 104 by the representation of a plain verge, just like a short conductor's baton, without ornament.

ST. STEPHEN'S ALTAR. Here T. Whitwell's chaplain said mass at 9 o'clock in 1531. *Vicars Choral*, p. 43. The chantry of *Richard* Whitwell, preb. of Empingham, is noted in Muniments D. ij. 51 (3). Licence of Mortmain to found the chantry of Whitwell in the Cathedral, 3 July, 1371, *ibid.* " Richard Whitewell " appears in the obit list, and he is said to have founded a chantry for the souls of Rob. Chesterfield and others, cir. 1355, D. ij., 5 (3).

SWEEPERS. It was the duty of the three carpenters who were among the " servants of the church," *Black Book*, p. 292, either to sweep the Minster themselves, or else to employ three others (who were probably of the class styled "*garciones*" in documents belonging to Lincoln and other churches) in Passiontide, and they were to have ½*d*. apiece each day *pour boire*. Besides these three, there was a *scoparius* who had to clean up the dirt and rubbish every evening when the doors were locked, and who had to see that there was water in the lavatory, and to act as a supernumerary bell ringer (*id.* p. 365). The "*scoparius*" received 10*s*. yearly from the oblations at Grosseteste's tomb, but nothing from John de Dalderby's (*id.*, p. 337-8).

SYNODUS. One yearly synod was to be held at Michaelmas, another on the morrow of Trinity Sunday. *Black Book*, p. 293. The carpenters were to place the seats for a synod when Bishop, Archdeacon, or official presided, in whatever part of the church was considered best (*ibid.*).

TABERNACLES. In the late fifteenth Century inventory there are nine " tabernacles with relicks " entered, two of them being described as standing on the altar in the vestry. In 1536 and 1548 there were only six, apparently, remaining. In 1553 (May 18th) there were but five, and the entries were struck out of the list. The fragmentary commissioners' certificate of March, 1566, has the two following entries, in part torn away:—" Item a tabernacle of wodde in the [*a word lost*] Item four boxes for relicks remay[neth]. (See my *Lincoln Inventories*, pp. 4, 15, 44, 64, 81.)

Respecting the tabernacle for the Sacrament of the Altar we have this reference from Sanderson and Dugdale's account of Lincoln monuments in 1641. "In the east part [of the Minster choir] stood the altar. A door into the room there at each end. Upon the room stood the Tabernacle. Below, many closets in the wall." S. Peck, *Desiderata Curiosa*, ed. 1779, p. 300.

TABULA. (*a*) the "board," or 'wax-brede'; a tablet smeared or coated with green wax, on which the names and duties *pro cantu et lectura* were entered. See under the word '*Praeciosa*,' p. 259, above, and cf. *Black Book*, pp. 283, 285, 371, 381, 383, 391, 393. *Statutes* ii., pp. 142, 159; iii., 219.

In later times the lists were written on some other writing material at Exeter (and probably in other places also). See the extracts in Rock's *Church of our Fathers*, iv. 127-130, Rev. H. E Reynolds' Abstracts of Exeter Chapter Acts, pp. 73-5, and my *Tracts of Clement Maydestone*, p. 235*n*.

(*b*) A tablet recording the title and date of the dedication of an altar. Bp. W. of Blois directed the erection of such tablets in his constitutions for the Diocese of Lincoln in 1229. (Wilkins' *Concilia*, i., 624), following a similar direction of the Council of Celchyth, A.D. 816, cap. 2. See Rock's *Church of our Fathers*, i. 228-9*n*, where specimens of such *tabulae* are cited. Compare likewise the inscription which Leland transcribed in the time of King Henry VIII., not perhaps with absolute accuracy, from the Lady Chapel at Salisbury. It has, however, the character rather of a personal memorial to a famous bishop than of a dedication tablet.*

The "tabula" belonging to a church at Clee in Lincolnshire recording a dedication by St. Hugh in 1192 is cited in Peck's *Desiderata Curiosa*, p. 321 (though the place is not there named), and in the late Archd. G. G. Perry's *Life of St. Hugh*, p. 364.

TAILOR. See "*Cissor*" (p. 131).

TENEBRAE. This ceremony of Mattins on three nights of Holy Week is described in the *Concordia Regularis* of Æthelwold. See Dean Kitchin's *Compotus Rolls of the Obedientiaries of St. Swithun's, Winchester*, 1892, p. 184. Nothing is said there of a *Judas* candle (see above, p. 168), and the number, 24, is explained as bearing an allusion to the hours of the day, the *tenebrae* service being thrice repeated to signify that the Light of the

---

* Orate pro anima Ricardi Poure quondam Sarum episcopi qui ecclesiam hanc inchoari fecit in quodam fundo ubi nunc fundata est, ex antiquo nomine Miryfelde, in honorem beate virginis Marie iij. cal. Maij in festo sancti Vitalis martyris anno Domini Mccxviiij. [29, ? 28, Apr. 1219], regnante tunc rege Ricardo post conquestum primo. Fiutque ecclesia hec in edificando per spatium xl. annorum, temporibus trium regum, videlicet antedicti Ricardi, Johannis et Henrici tercij. Et consummata viij. cal. April anno Domini Mcc. lx°. [25 Mar., 1260]. Iste Richardus episcopus fundavit missam beate Marie virginis [29 Sept., 1225] solenniter in hac capella quotidie celebrandam, et appropriauit rectoriam de Laverstoke ad sustentacionem eiusdem misse   Qui quidem Richardus episcopus postea translatus fuit ad episcopatum Dunelmen: fundauitque monasterium apud Tarraunt in comitatu Dorset: vbi natus nomine Richardus Poure: ibique cor eius, corpus uero apud Dureham, humatum est.   Et obijt xv. die April Anno Domini M[ccxxxvij.]."
See Leland *Itin.* iii. p. 92, fo. 62=p. 77.

World was for three days hidden. At Lincoln the Treasurer found 25 little candles, 24 weighing one pound. *Novum Registrum*, part 1, *Statutes* iii. p. 303. The Sarum Breviary rubrick speaks of 24 candles, representing 12 Apostles and 12 Prophets whom the Jews persecuted. Cf. Beleth *Rationale*, cap. 101. The York Breviary mentions one larger candle in the midst "according to our use." According to Beleth the midmost candle represented our Lord Himself. When the *tenebrae* office was over, the Sacrist struck his book or desk as a signal. In some French churches others who were present joined the Sacrist in this *strepitus*, which was explained as symbolising the revolution of Nature at the Passion. (St. Matt. xxvii. 51 ; St. Luke xxiii. 48.) Dr. Rock thought that the ceremony of *Tenebrae* had its origin here in England. Its abandonment helped (it is said) to wreck the Quignonian rite. The candles (according to Beleth, *D. Officii Explic.*, s. *Rationale*, cap. 101) are extinguished with the figure of a hand made of wax.

TEXTS. The ancient books of the Gospels— (*evangeliaria*, or, perhaps, we ought to distinguish them as *evangelistaria*) often containing only one of the four Gospels as a volume by itself, the portions appointed for various masses being merely marked in the margin where they occurred in their biblical order—were kept as ornaments of the altar, in bindings of precious metals jewelled and decorated. They were carried in procession to the altar (compare the "Lesser Entrance" in the Greek rite) and were used not only for reading the missal lections, but occasionally for the taking of solemn oaths, as at one time also was the drawing of the Passion introduced in the initial T of *Te igitur* in the Canon of the Mass.

In some places the ornamental plaque or cover designed for such a book, even without any pages of the sacred text, served as a pax-brede or *osculatorium* for ministering the kiss of charity. Such a *tabula osculatoria* often had a *ligula* or strap, to hold it by, behind. See Dr. J. W. Legg's *Westminster Inventory of* 1388, pp. 41, 42, in *Archæologia*, 1889. There remained at Lincoln in 1548 *textus evangeliorum* " after Matthew" (two examples), and " Mark" and " John," besides three texts for "Lenten and yᵉ passion." *Lincoln Inventories*, pp. 47-8. See also the *Black Book*, pp. 131, 215, 274, 276, 375, 379.

ST. THOMAS THE MARTYR. The altar of St. Thomas (Abp. Becket) the martyr is mentioned in *Registr. Antiquiss.*, cir. 1330. Here, according to J. Grantham's book (cir. 1490-1500, fo. 42) a chaplain celebrated for W. de Thornton and W. de la Gare. Here also in 1531 Gilbert de Cancia (Kent) was commemorated by a priest-vicar celebrating at his chantry between 8 and 9 a.m. *Vicars Choral*, p. 43. *Statutes*, ii. pp. lxxn., cclxii-cclxvi.

The Gare chantry was founded by W. de Thornton in 1311 (Muniments, D. ij., 51), but I believe it was at the altar of St. John Baptist. See *Chantry Register* (A. 1, 8), fo. 2. Richard de Beverley, canon, in 1390, gave a bequest to this altar; and J. Cotes, canon, in 1433 desired leave to be buried there, before the Image of St. Thomas, and to have masses sung there with collects according to the use of Sarum. See Gibbons' *Early Lincoln Wills*, pp. 33, 158.

In Murray's *Guide to (Eastern) Cathedrals*, the chapel of St. Thomas at Lincoln—which contains (by the way) " a large decorated bracket against the wall," — is marked as being the chapel at the extreme south of the great transept, and it has been described (by the late Precentor Edmund Venables) as " of St. Giles (or St. Thomas)," p. 350. In the same volume the southernmost chapel in the great north transept is marked as the " chapel of St. James " (merely a misprint, I presume, for *Thomas*) in the plan; but it is described at p. 351 as dedicated to " St. Thomas the Apostle." So also in *William-son's Guide*, p. 73. I have not as yet found any documentary evidence of the existence of any altar or chapel of St. Thomas the *Apostle*, at Lincoln. To assign the southernmost place in the great south transept to an altar of St. Thomas (the Abp. and Martyr) agrees very well with the order in which altars are mentioned in *Registrum Antiquissimum*, but it has been found (by Mr. Maddison) that, at least in the sixteenth century, this chapel at the extreme end of the great south transept was Saint Anne's.

THRONE. "Stallum episcopi" is mentioned in the *Black Book*, pp. 273-4; "sedes cathedralis," *ibid.*, p. 273. It had a white napkin spread on the desk or "form" in front of it (*ibid.*, p. 366).

"Ordo *stallandi* episcopum" is the term used for enthronization of a Bishop about 1522.

TOMBS OF BISHOPS ("*Tumbae episcoporum*"). We learn from the account of the Treasurer's duties entered in the *Black Book* (pp. 289, 290), *Statutes* iii., p. 408, and elsewhere, that it was the Lincoln custom to keep two lighted candles (of $1\frac{1}{3}$ lb. of wax) set up during service-time upon a bishop's tomb when his Anniversary-day or obit came round, and a single candle on the Tomb of every other bishop buried in the Minster. At *Magnificat* in festal even-song the Dean and the Precentor censed the high Altar, then the Tomb of Saint Remigius the founder, ('*stabilitor*' he is somewhere called),* the Altar where the Lady Mass is said at the first hour, and the tomb of St. Hugh. Then the Dean censed Altars and Tombs on the south, and the Chanter those on the north (p. 368, cp. p. 394).† After the creed at high mass the priest censed chalice and corporas, two deacons censed the priest, then the high altar round about, and afterwards 'the tombs of the saints' (p. 380). In the list of *Vicars Choral* Mr. Maddison (p. 50) notes "Philippus, *de tumba*" and 'Adam, *de*

---

* Viz. in the Obit List written in the great Latin Bible at Lincoln, cir. A.D. 1185.

† Bp. Simon of Ghent's and Bp. Roger de Mortival's tombs were censed at Salisbury. See W. H. Frere's *Sarum Customs*, lii. 23-24.

feretro.' The latter no doubt is keeper of St. Hugh's feretory or shrine. Mr. Maddison says that Adam was keeper of Bp. Grosseteste's Tomb, but this is incompatible with the date 1200-1250 which he gives on the preceding page. Was there a keeper of the Tomb of *Remigius?* No doubt a few years later Grosseteste died and was buried and a *custos tumbe beati Roberti* was appointed. There were oblations of the faithful made at his tomb and at the tomb and relicks of St. Hugh. See above 'St. *Hugh'* and 'B. *Robert'*; and cf. *Black Book* pp. 122, 335-8, as to the falling off of the offerings, in 1322.

TORCHAE. Large tapers (originally of *twisted* wax, 'intorticia') 'ad corporis Christi leuacionem.' *Statutes* ii., p. 403.

TREASURY. In 1412 Eliz. Darcy left £200 to be kept in some secret place in the Minster, and to be distributed to chaplains annually for masses. There is a treasury chamber beneath the canons' vestry, and likewise a strong chamber above the north-west chapel in the nave, accessible only by a ladder. Loans were sometimes effected from the offerings at the Tombs, or from the treasure-chests, *cistae*. W. Gaske 'keeper of the Red Chest' *(ciste Rubie)* gave to the Minster a black cope, having in the back a representation of Souls rising to their 'Doom.' This chest was apparently for the Works.

TRINITY. Holy Trinity Chapel. Here in 1531 Bishop Richard Fleming's chaplains celebrated at 7 and 8 a.m., and the chaplains of the chantry of J. Colynson and J. Chedworth at 9 o'clock. *Vicars Choral*, p. 42. Of Bp. Chedworth's tomb, Leland says : ' J. Chedworth, sepultus occidentali parte ecclesie, prope Sutton ' (*Itin.* ed. 1744, ii. p. 3, fo. 48$^{b.}$), and on the next page, 'Byshope *Fleminge* liethe in an Highe Tumbe in the Northe Isle of the upper Parte of the Chirche in the Walle; and thereby, under flate Stones ly *Oliver Sutton*, and *John Chadworthe*, Bysshope.' Browne Willis adds (ii. 34) on the authority of Cotton MS. *Tiberius* E. 3, that the chantry of *Robert* Fleming, Dean (?nephew to Bp. Fleming), was in Trinity Chapel. This no doubt was the Fleming chantry chapel annexed to the north side of the Angel Choir. I do not know what is the authority to which Venables referred when he said that the Consistory Chapel to the S.W. of the nave is 'said to have been dedicated to the Holy Trinity,' *Murray's Guide to English Cathedrals* (Eastern), 1881, p. 346. It is not in itself impossible that there should be two or more chapels with the same dedication in the same church, for such is the case at Wells, where there were at least three altars of the Holy Cross. Bp. Richard Fleming died 25th January, 1431, and Dean Robert Fleming died 12th August, 1483.

TUNICLES or Dalmatics, worn by Deacon and Subdeacon at high mass. *Black Book*, pp. 375, 383, ' vestimenta leuitica.' *Stat.* ii. p. 394.

VAT. A holy-water bucket, '*situla.*' In the *Lincoln Inventory* of 1536 (p. 21) we find, ' Item a Fatte of

sylver for holy water with a strynkell both ungylte,'
weighing 70½ ozs. '*extrahitur per capitulum.*') We
lose sight of this in 1548; and in 1557 the Marian
Chapter have, for the lost silver bucket, a ' holy water
fatte of lattyn,' *id.* p. 72. In 1566 the return to the
Commissioners says, 'holliwater fattes—j with a
sprinkle, bothe of brasse, remayning' (p. 80). The
strynkell *(aspersorium)* is mentioned in *Novum
Registrum* part 1.* It is to be handed to the Bishop,
after the altars have been sprinkled, that he may
sprinkle the principal officiants. According to the
Black Book, p. 370, a choir boy *(quidam parvus de
choro)* comes in on the south side, after compline, to
sprinkle the choir and the people, after kissing the
Dean's hand. But first the Bishop (or, in his absence,
the Dean or celebrant) sprinkles the choir who come
and stand before his stall or throne *(sedes)*. In the
procession the holy water was carried *a quodam clerico
minore* (p. 383). It was the custom for the Bishop
to send across to the Treasurer (or any other in his
absence) to bless the holy water. In the Bishop's
absence the Dean sent to the Subdean or to any other
canon not a dignitary. But when the Bishop and
Dean were absent none of the confratres might give
orders to another, so the canon on duty blessed it
without any bidding, if the Dean had announced
that he should not be in choir (pp. 283, 390). Holy
water was brought when the Dean anointed a canon
in extremis, p. 295.

---

* "*Aspersorium*" : *Statutes* ii., p. 276.

VERGER. The book of 1527 enters among Whitsuntide payments, 'sex virgariis, cuilibet 3*d*.'
According to the *Black Book*, p. 293, the 'four
servants of the Church' (viz. the 3 carpenters and
the glazier) were to meet the Bishop with their wands
(virgis) at the Minster door and to attend him while
he remained in the Church. They are mentioned
ibid. pp. 353, 389. The first bell-ringer ('sacrista
laicus') was to attend the Treasurer with his staff,
like a bedel, p. 365. The 'bedelli episcopi' were
to walk before the celebrant on double feasts at mass,
and were entertained by the dignitary who took the
lead in the service on doubles and semi-doubles, pp.
376, 378, 380, 389. At the Restoration, Precentor
Featley had a grievance about the right to appoint a
verger. See *Black Book*, ed. 1892, pp. 254-5. As
to the silver verges, see 'Staves.'

VESTRY. The word 'vestibulum' sometimes
meant a porch, sometimes a vestry.* It is used, I
think, in the latter sense in *Novum Registrum* part
I, 5.† The Treasurer (or, as the corrector says, the
Bellringer) is to find mats 'nattas pro choro, capitulo,
et vestibulo,' and the Sacrist is to open the 'ostium
vestibuli' at the first mattin chime, and the first

---

* *Vestibulum* is used as equivalent to the 'sacristia' in the title of the
Westminister Abbey Inventory of 1388, which Dr. Wickham Legg edited in
1890, see p. 19 *n.*, though it is often used of a porch, as where Leland says
in his description of Salisbury (*Itin.* fo. 66—*Collectanea* iii. p. 81) 'the
Vestibulum on the North side of the Body of the Church.'

† *Novum Registrum:* See *Statutes* iii., p. 303, and the marginal note
there.

peal to evensong (or, as the corrector says, at the cope-bell) that the Rulers of the Choir may come and look over their office; and the sick, and those who have been let blood, may say their divine office there ('ibi dicere valeant horas suas ').* This last can hardly have been in the *porch*. The word ' *Vestiarium* ' is found in the Sarum Breviary III. p. 975; also in Alnwick's *Novum Registrum* near the beginning. *Stat.* iii., 275. I rather think it occurs in the St. Paul's Statutes, i. cap. 6, but I cannot at the moment refer to Dr. Sparrow Simpson's edition.† However, the original parallel passage in the *Lincoln Black Book*, p. 273, uses the form ' *Reuestiarium*,' where it says that when the Bishop is about to perform his office, he shall be escorted by the Dean on his right and the next dignitary on his left, from the Revestry to the High Altar or to his throne *('sedem cathedralem')*. There was an altar *in revestiario*, where possibly the holy water was prepared, as I believe was the case if not at Salisbury itself, certainly in many places following Sarum use, ' *in vestibulo*,' (cf. Cavalieri *Opera*, Augsbourg, 1764, t. iv. p. 250^b.) ; and on the vestry altar at Lincoln there stood two large tabernacles with figures in ivory with divers histories and a representation of the Passion (*Inventories*, p. 4). There also stood a silver-gilt foot or socket weighing 30 oz. to hold

---

* *Statutes* iii., p. 355.

† ' *Ostium Vestiarii* ' occurs in an early eighteenth century installation form at Lincoln. See *Statutes* iii., p. 726. ' *Vestiarium* ' is found also in the old Lichfield Customs. *Statutes* ii., pp. 19, 26.

the great processional Crucifix Mary and John,
ornamented with fleurs delices and the Evangelists
engraved as the finials, the head weighing 57 oz.
(*id.* p. 7). The staff *(baculus)* ornamented with
silver measured 'two yards and a half, and one
quarter and a half' (pp. 8, 18). The vestry at
Salisbury, which is an octagon, has on the right hand
of its entrance three large ambries now in use, and
in its western side a recess about 2 ft. square, and 18
inches deep, now hidden by a press. There are several
old recesses in the canons' vestry at Lincoln, but the
wainscot and plaster disguise their original features.
The boys' vestry at Lincoln has a long structural
lavatorium, mentioned in *Black Book*, p. 365, and
an open fire-place and chimney with a stone hood.
I suppose this was used for kindling the charcoal
('carbones,' *ibid.* p. 286) in the censers, for warming
the 'calefactory,' and the water for washing the
altars and for the *pedilavium* on Maundy Thursday,
(p. 292). At Bp. Alnwick's visitation in 1437 one
of the choristers complained that the bell-ringers
'non adducunt carbones viuos tempore congruo.'

WARECTUM, fallow land. *Warectare* to plough up
(properly with a view to laying down as fallow), *Black
Book*, pp. 277-8, and *Nov. Reg.* part 4, apparently
to harrow. When a canon died the incoming prebendary during the year of grace was to have a cow
house *(bovariam)* or other building for his oxen or
cattle ('*averia*' connected with '*avoir*,' chattels or
cattle).

WASHING ALTARS. '*Ablutio Altarium in ecclesia.*' The Treasurer found wine for this Maundy ceremony. At Salisbury the altars were washed in order beginning from the high altar, going out by the north choir door to the altars nearest and so to the retrochoir or Lady Chapel and right round the church still keeping to the right. But at Lincoln, after (the corrector says 'before') the Maundy, the Dean with the principal canon at his side, and the Precentor with the first canon *cantoris*, took their several sides (at least so the marginal note in the draft *Novum Registrum* implies) each going round one side of the Church as they did in censing (*Statutes* iii., p. 303; cf. 284).

WATCHERS. The lay sacrist, the watchman *(vigil)* and the candle-lighter made two scrutinies of the church in winter, to see that no one was lurking there with felonious purpose. The first was directly after curfew: the second search, after midnight mattins. In summer when mattins were said at daybreak the curfew-search was reckoned sufficient, and then the Treasurer provided each of them with seven candles per week, but in winter a double supply. See above, "Searchers' Chamber." The night watchman did not go to bed when the two others retired, but called the hours of the night upon his flute so that the ringers might be ready with the mattin-peal. In the 'computus' or accounts of 1314 and other years W. Hale receives a yearly payment of 6*s.* 8*d.* 'pro custodia ecclesie hora prandii.'

WILLIAM THE CONQUEROR'S CHAPEL.   This name was applied to the most southerly of the three divisions of the east of the Angel choir, or in other words to the extreme east of the Chanter's or South Choir Aisle, where were the Cantilupe and Wymbyssh chantries.

THE WORKS CHANTRY HOUSE.   This stood in East gate, north of the Cathedral and west of the Deanery, and was adjacent to the Treasurer's house. Maddison, *Vicars Choral*, p. 39.   It was originally the Chancellor's residence, but when Ant. Beck cir. 1316 erected the present Chancery the old site was utilized as a college for the chaplains who celebrated for the souls of Benefactors to the Minster Fabrick. The house was pulled down in 1828.   See *Williamson's Guide*, pp. 118-9.   The chapel itself is in the Minster, in the great south transept, next the organ screen.   The stone screen of the Chapel itself has an inscription, " Orate pro benefactoribus istius ecclesie " ; and on either side are little effigies of the four priests of the chantry college, kneeling, with full sleeved surplices and hoods, such as the elderly Anglican clergy of the last generation wore.   In the opinion of the late Mr. J. F. Dimock, *Girald. Cambrensis* vii. p. 217 *n.*) the 'Works Chantry' was founded either by Walter of Coutances (1183) or his successor St. Hugh for the souls of the Benefactors of the Fabric.   The late Precentor Venables has told us that the Works Chantry was founded (for four chaplains) by Henry Duke of Lancaster and Earl of Lincoln, who died in 1360 or 1361. In *Murray's Handbook of English (Eastern) Cathedrals*, 1881, this chapel is marked as "St. Anne's Chapel, re-dedicated to St. Edward," and similarly, in the description at p. 350, the Precentor tells us that the re-dedication title, due to Henry Duke of Lancaster, is *St. Edward the Martyr;* also that arms of England and France, quarterly, appear on the screen in front.

There is reason to think that the Chantry of the Fabrick was also largely indebted to, and deserves to be connected with the name of, John de Welbourn the munificent Treasurer who died in 1381. His obit, in the list of 1527, produces 40s. ' de fabrica beate Marie Lincoln' and pays ' Clerico Fabrice, 6*d*.' In the order of 1531 (*Vicars Choral*, p. 40)—

At 5 a.m. Ro. Vincent, priest of the Chantry of the Fabrick, celebrates Morning Mass at the altar of St. George.

Towards 6 a.m. one of the Chaplains of the Fabrick Chantry, at St. Anne's altar (*ibid.*, p. 41).

Between 8 and 9, I suppose, a third Works Chanter, if he were a Vicar, might celebrate.

At 10 a.m. another Chaplain of the Fabrick cele-brated at the Altar of St. Anne. As I do not find any mention of St. Edward's altar in this list, I am inclined to think that the Lincoln authorities main-tained the honor of St. Anne and did not make themselves parties to the alteration in the title which the Duke intended. Besides the obit of Treasurer ' Welburne ' there are two Lincoln obits in the book of 1527 connected with the Works. 'Obitus Henrici ducis Langcastrie, de fabrica beate Marie, 40*s*. Jnde canonicis residentibus et presentibus toti officio, 26*s*. 8*d*., etc., etc. Clerico fabrice, 6*d*.' And, 'Obitus Johannis Crosby de Fabrica beate Marie, 4*l*. Jnde Canonicis, 18*s*. . . . Clerico subprepositi, 3*d*. . . principali vigili, 3*d*. Sacriste laico, 3*d*. Quatuor virgariis, 12*d*. Clerico Fabrice, 3*d*. Clerico de Re et Ve, 8*d*. Diacono et subdiacono, 4*d*. Janitori portarum, 3*d*. Custodibus tumbe sancti Hugonis, 4*d*. Pulsantibus campanas tribus, 8*d*.' Treasurer Crosby died in 1477, giving a cope of white damask, and a similar cloth for the high altar, embroidered with a representation of the Assumption and St. John Bapt. and St. Katharine on either hand, with linen cloth, canopy, and two smaller cloths of the same suit. There was also a green velvet cope with a morse of blue cloth of gold '*ex dono Dni Crossby, Capellani*,' of whose identity I cannot speak.

In the executors' accounts upon the will of Roger Swynesheed, yeoman, 1499-1501, is a payment of 40*s*. into the hands of 'Dom. Will Gaske custodis Rubie Ciste in Eccl. Cath. Lincoln' ad usum Fabrice eiusdem Cathedralis.' *Gibbons*, p. 198.

Before the times of H. Duke of Lancaster and John Welbourne spiritual privileges and benefits were held out to the Benefactors of the Fabrick of our Lady. We will give in conclusion a summary of the contents of a box in the Chapter Muniment

Room, D. ii. 61. (box 2), so far as it concerns this subject :—

1. Bp. H. Lexinton grants indulgence of 20 days to penitents shrived who shall say three Paters and three Aves for the good of the Church and Land of England, and devoutly attend sermons preached by members of the Chapter of Lincoln. A.D. 1257.

2. Godfrey de Ludham, Abp. of York, grants 20 days to those who attend sermons under direction of the Dean in Lincoln Cathedral Church. Cir. 1258-66.

3. Ri. de Gravesend, Bp., grants 40 days to hearers of sermons in the Minster. 1259.

4. The same, grants like indulgence for sermons by Canons of Lincoln. 1264.

5. Walter de la Wyle, Bp. of Salisbury, grants indulgence of 20 days to attendants on sermons by the Canons of Lincoln, who shall say three Paters and Aves for the souls of *Henry de Lexinton* (*ob.* 8 Aug. 1258), and all the faithful departed. Sept., 1266.

6. Walter Giffard, Bp. of Bath and Wells, grants the like indulgence.

7. W. [? de Breuse], Bp. of Llandaff, grants the like. 1266.

8. Robert de Chause, Bp. of Carlisle, grants 40 days for the like. 1266. (Seal in box.)

9. Henry, Bp. of Galloway, (Candida Casa, *i.e.* Whitehorne), grants 40 days to those who shall hear Canons' sermons at Lincoln, or shall say three Paters and Aves for Henry Bp. of Lincoln, and all

x

Christian souls, or shall do manual alms.* Datum apud Mariscum, 13 Nov., 1266.

10. Roger de Skerwing, Bp. of Norwich, grants 20 days. 1266.

11. Richard [? *Roger* de Molend'], Bp. of Coventry and Lichfield, grants 15 days' indulgence to attendants at sermons preached by Canons of Lincoln, those who shall say 3 Paters and Aves for Bp. Henry, *or shall contribute to the Fabrick.* 1266.

12. Robert Stichell, Bp. of Durham, grants 40 days to hearers of sermons, saying Paters, &c., for Bp. Henry, or doers of manual alms. 12[6]6.

13. Peter, Bp. of Orkneys, grants 40 days. 1274.

14. Robert de Insula, Bp. of Durham, grants 40 days for hearing Canons' sermons. 16 Feb., 1274-5.

15. Archibald, Bp. of Moray, grants the like. (No date, cir. 1253-99.)

16. [Robert de Stuteville] Bp. of Dunkeld, grants 20 days. 1277.

17. William de Geynesburg, Bp. of Worcester, grants 40 days for those who attend Canons' Sermons, and recite Pater and Ave *for the Peace of the King and Queen* (Edw. I. and Eleanor of Castille), and for the faithful living and departed. 1303.

[We have in A. i. 14, fo. 112, a letter from Bp. Oliver Sutton to the Archdeacons, or their officials, ordering special prayers and psalms for K. Edward I., 11 Mar., 1293-4. He had also ordered prayers in

---

* I suppose this means by personally helping in the works, as St. Hugh had done in an earlier generation, when he shouldered his mason's hod.

all parish churches for the Archbishop, after the death of Abp. Peckham, and pending the election of a successor (who was Ro. Winchelsey), in a letter dated 6 Feb., 1292-3. He likewise ordered masses for the King's uncle, W. de Valence, Earl of Pembroke, 30 June, 129 . . ?]*

18. [Richard de Gravesend] Bp. of London, grants 40 days to those who contribute *to the Fabrick of Lincoln and to the High Altar.*

19. ? the same. 1303.

20. [Rob. Wiseheart] Bp. of Glasgow, grants the like. 1304.

21. [John de Halucton] Bp. of Carlisle, grants the like. 1305.

22. [Walter de Geynesburg] Bp. of Worcester, grants the like. 1308.

23. [Walter Reynold] Abp. of Canterbury, grants the like. 1314.

24. . . . . . Bp. of . . . . *anno primo*, 1320. [1319-1320 was the first year of several bishops: Haymo of Rochester, Maurice of Dumblane, J. Wiseheart of Glasgow, Rigaud de Asserio, Winton, and David of Caithness. I cannot say by which of these this indulgence was granted.]

25. [J. Wiseheart] Bp. of Glasgow, grants 40 days to worshippers *at the tomb of John de Dalderby*, Bp., 1321.

---

* The volume in the Chapter Muniment Room at Lincoln marked "A. i. 14" contains a long series of little documents arranged and mounted by the late Prebendary J. F. Wickenden and Canon A. R. Maddison. The portion which occupies leaves 112-152 consists of a file of 178 documents relating to the Archdeaconry of Stowe between the years 1292 and 1300.

26. W. Atwater, Bp. of Lincoln, grants 40 days to persons who will assist in lengthening and widening the Fosse Dyke. Cir. 1515.

On March 24, 1291-2, Oliver Sutton, Bp. of Lincoln, addressed Dean (Ph. Wilughby) and Chapter recommending a certain hospital to the alms of the faithful, in preference to all other charities, *except the Works* of the Minster. Sermons were to be preached in aid of it for three or four Sundays. (A. i. 14, § 2, No. 135, p. 147.) Bishop Oliver Sutton's successor, Bishop John de Dalderby, wrote in 1303 to the Archdeacons of his diocese directing collections to be made in aid of the minster of St. John of Beverley, provided that they do not prejudice the *Works* in progress at St. Mary's, Lincoln. (A. i. 14, § 1, No. 68, p. 68.) In 1302 the official of the Archdeacon of Stow had addressed all rectors, vicars, and chaplains, desiring them to commend to their parishioners the case of the sick outside the Castle of Lincoln (*id.* § 1, No. 93, p. 95).

CHR. W.

St. Peter's Rectory,
Marlborough.
FEAST OF ST. PHILIP & JACOB, 1898.

Index to the Kalendar of Lincoln Use.

L. N. = *Liber Niger* (ed. 1892).

N. R. = *Novum Registrum W. Alnewyke Episcopi* (contained in our Cambridge edition of *Statutes*, fascic. iii., pp. 268-363).

Agathe, V. M., 5 Feb.

Agnetis, V. M., 21 Jan.

Agnetis Octava, 28 Jan., *N. R.*, p. 304, *margin*.

Albani, prothomartyris Anglie, 22 June.

Alphege, archiep. M., 19 Apr.

Ambrosii, Ep. C., 4 Apr.

Andree, Ap. M., 29 Nov., *L. N.*, p. 289.

Andree Translacio, 9 May.

Animarum Commemoracio, 2 Nov.

Anne, matris B. Marie, 26 Jul.

Annunciacio dominica, 25 Mar.

Ascensionis Dies, *L. N.*, p. 293.

Assumpcio B. Marie, 15 Aug.

Augustini, Ep. Doct., 28 Aug.

Augustini, Anglorum Apost., 26 May.

Barnabe, Ap. M., 11 Jun.

Bartholomei, Ap. M., 24 Aug.

Benedicti, Abb. C., 21 Mar.

Benedicti Translacio, 11 Jul.

Bernardi, C., ? 25 Aug.

[Botulphi, C., 17 Jun.]

Brigitte, V., 1 Feb., *L. N.*, p. 365.

Birini, Ep. C., 3 Dec.

Brictij, Ep. C., 13 Nov. Cf. *L. N.*, pp. 280, 388.

Caput Jejunij, *L. N.*, p. 281.

Cecilie, V. M., 22 Nov.

Cedde, Ep. C., 2 Mar.

Circumcisio Domini, 1 Jan.

Clementis, P. M., 23 Nov.
[Concepcio B. Marie, 8 Dec.]
Corporis Christi festum, *L. N.*, p. 249.
Crucis Exaltacio, 14 Sept., *L. N.*, p. 289.
Crucis Invencio, 3 May, *L. N.*, p. 289.
Cuthberti, Ep. C., 20 Mar.
Cuthberti Translacio, 4 Sept.
Commemoracio Fidelium. [This is marked on Monday or Tuesday in Holy
    Week, and again in the 2nd week in Advent in the XVth Century Rolls
    of *Re* and *Ve*. See *Statutes* iii., 814, 823.]

Davidis, Ep. C., 1 Mar.
Dedicacionis Ecclesie B. Marie Lincoln, 3 Oct., *L. N.*, p. 281.
Dionysii, M., 9 Oct.
Dunstani, Archiep. C., 19 May.

Edmundi Cantuar. Archiep., C., 16 Nov.
Edmundi regis, M., 20 Nov.
Edwardi regis, M., 18 Mar.
Edwardi regis, 8 Apr.
Edwardi regis, M., Translacio, 20 Jun.
Edwardi regis, C., Translacio, 13 Oct.
Egidij, abb. C., 1 Sept.
Epiphania Domini, 6 Jan., *L. N.*, pp. 281, 284.
Exaltacio sancte Crucis, 14 Sept., *L. N.*, p. 289.

Fabiani et Sebastiani, MM., 20 Jan.
Fidis, V., 6 Oct.
Frideswide, V., 19 Oct.

Georgij, M., 23 Apr.
[Gilleberti de Semperingham, C., 4 Feb.]
Gregorij pape, 12 Mar.
Gregorij Ordinacio, ? 2 Sept.
Guthlaci, C., 11 Apr.

Hieronymi, Pr. Doct., 30 Sept.
Hippolyti, M., 13 Aug., *L. N.*, p. 289.
Hugonis Episcopi Linc. Deposicio, 17 Nov., *L. N.*, pp. 281, 284, 288.
Hugonis Epi. Translacio, 6 Oct. [1280], *L. N.*, p. 335.
[Hugonis parui. 27 (*al.* 1) Aug.]

Innocencium MM., 28 Dec., *L. N.*, p. 290.
Innocencium Octava, 4 Jan.
Invencio sancte Crucis, 3 May, *L. N.*, p. 289.
Invencio S. Stephani, 3 Aug.

Jacobi, Ap., 1 May.
Jacobi minoris Ap., 25 Jul.
Johannis Evang., 27 Dec., *L. N.*, p. 290.
Johannis Octava, 3 Jan.
Johannis ante portam latinam, 6 May.
Johannis Baptiste Nativitas, 24 Jun., *L. N.*, p. 281.
Johannis Decollacio, 29 Aug.
Johannis de Beverlaco, 7 May.
Johannis et Pauli, *L. N.*, pp. 289–90.
Jude, cum Symone, Apost., 28 Oct.

Katharine, V. M., 25 Nov., *L. N.*, p. 289.
Kenelmi regis, M., 17 Jul.

Laurencij, levite M. 10 Aug.
Leonardi, Abb. C., 6 Nov.
Luce, Evan., 18 Oct.
Lucie, V. M., 13 Dec.

Marci Evan., 25 Apr.
Margarete, V. M., 20 Jul.
Marie Purificacio, 2 Feb., *L. N.*, p. 281.
Marie Annunciacio, 25 Mar., *L. N.*, pp. 281, 288, 293, 377.
Marie Assumpcio, 15 Aug., *L. N.*, pp. 281, 284.
Marie Nativitas, 8 Sept., *L. N.*, pp. 281, 284.
[Marie Concepcio, 8 Dec.]
[Marie Visitacio, 2 Jul.]
Marie Commemoracio hebdomadalis in Sabbato. (*In rotutis de* Re *et* Ve.—
    Vide *Statut.* iii., pp. 805, 812-823.
Marie Magdalene, 22 Jul., *L. N.*, p. 289.
Martini, Ep. C., 11 Nov.
Martini Translacio, 4 Jul.
Matthei Evang. Ap., 21 Sept.
Mathie, Ap., 24 Feb.
Mauricij cum sociis, MM., 22 Sept.
Michaelis Archangeli, 29 Sept.
Michaelis in monte tumba, 16 Oct.

Natalis Domini, 25 Dec., *L. N.*, pp. 281, 284, 290.
Nativitas B. Marie, 8 Sept., *L. N.*, pp. 281, 284.
Nicholai, Ep. C., 6 Dec., *L. N.*, pp. 289, 381.

Octava Natalis Domini, 1 Jan.
Octava S. Stephani, 2 Jan.
Octava S. Johannis, 3 Jan.
Octava SS. Innocencium, 4 Jan.

Octava S. Thome, M., 5 Jan.

Octava Epiphanie, 13 Jan.

Octava S. Agnetis, 28 Jan., *L. N.*, 289, *N. R.*, p. 304, *margin.*

Octava S. Johannis Bapt., 1 Jul., *L. N.*, p. 289, *N. R.*, p. 304.

Octava Apostolorum Petri et Pauli, 6 Jul.

Octava B. Marie (Assumpcionis), 22 Aug.

Octava B. Virginis (Nativitatis), 15 Sept.

Octava Translacionis S. Hugonis, 13 Oct.

Octava S. Martini, 18 Nov., *L. N.*, p. 289, *N. R.*, p. 304.

Octava S. Hugonis (Deposicionis), 24 Nov.

· Octava S. Andree, 7 Dec.

Omnium Sanctorum, 1 Nov., *L. N.*, pp. 281, 284, 288.

O [*Sapiencia*, &c.) Antiphonæ cir. xvi. Decemb., cantandae, *L. N.*, p. 388.

Osithe, V. abbatisse, 7 Oct.

Oswaldi regis, M., 5 Aug.

Palmarum Dominica [in Ramis], *L. N.*, pp. 281, 292.

Pascha, *L. N.*, pp. 281, 284.

Pauli Ap. cum Petro, 29 Jun.

Pauli Conversio, 25 Jan.

Pauli Commemoracio, 30 Jun.

Pelagie, V., 8 Oct., *L. N.*, p. 337.

Pentecostes, *L. N.*, p. 281.

Petri et Pauli Apostolorum, 29 Jun., *L. N.*, p. 281.

Petri ad Vyncula, 1 Aug.

Petri Cathedra [*forsan* antiochena], 22 Feb.

Philippi et Jacobi Apostolorum, 1 May.

Purificacio [B. Marie], 2 Feb.

Ramis Palmarum, Dominica in, *L. N.*, pp. 281, 292.

Reliquiarum Dominica, Dom. proxima post, vii. Jul. ('The 2nd Sunday after
the Feast of St. Peter and St. Paul,' *supra*, p. 270) *L. N.*, p. 281, cf. 255.

Reliquiarum B. Roberti (Grosseteste), 8 Oct., *L. N.*, p. 337.

Reliquiarum Stephani, &c., 3 Aug.

Sanctorum Omnium Festum, 1 Nov., *L. N.*, pp. 281, 284.

Sebastiani, M., 20 Jan.

Silvestri pape C., 31 Dec.

Simonis et Jude Apostolorum, 28 Oct.

Sixti pape, 6 Aug.

Stephani et Sociorum Inventio Reliquiarum, 3 Aug.

Stephani protomartyris, 26 Dec.

Swithini, Ep. C., Translacio, 15 Jul.

Thome, Apostoli M., 21 Dec.

Thome, Archiep. M., 29 Dec.

Thome, M., Translacio, 7 Jul.

Trinitatis, Dies Sancti, *L. N.*, p. 281.

Undecim milium Virginum MM., [Ursule, V.M.], 21 Oct.

Vigilia Pasche (in Sabbato Sancto), *L. N.*, p. 288.

Vigilia S. Johannis Bapt., 23 Jun., *L. N.*, p. 288.

Vigilia Apostolorum P. et P., 28 Jun., *L. N.*, p. 288.

Vigilia Reliquiarum (mense Julio), *L. N.*, p. 288.

Vigilia Assumpcionis, 14 Aug., *L. N.*, p. 288.

Vigilia Nativitatis B. Marie, 7 Sept., *L. N.*, p. 288.

Vigilia Omnium Sanctorum, 31 Oct., *L. N.*, pp. 365, 379.

Vigilia Natalis Domini, 24 Dec., *L. N.*, p. 288.

Vigilia Circumcisionis, 31 Dec., *L. N.*, p. 288.

Vigilia Ascensionis, *L. N.*, p. 288.

Vigilia Pentecostes, *L. N.*, pp. 281, 288, 293, 377.

Vigilia S. Trinitatis, *L. N.*, p. 288.

Vigilia Epiphanie, 5 Jan., *L. N.*, p. 288.

Vigilia Purificacionis, 1 Feb., *L. N.*, p. 288.

Vincencij levite M., 22 Jan.

ad Vincula S. Petri, 1 Aug.

Visitacio B. Marie, 2 Jul.

Wolstani Ep. C., 19 Jan.

Ypoliti, M., 13 Aug., *L. N.*, p. 289.

Finis.